A DESIRE
FOR EQUALITY

Alternatives to Capitalism in the 21st Century

Series Editors: **Lara Monticelli**, Copenhagen Business School and **Torsten Geelan**, University of Copenhagen

---

Debates about the future of capitalism demonstrate the urgent need to envision and enact alternatives that can help tackle the multiple intertwined crises that societies are currently facing. This ground-breaking series advances the international, comparative and interdisciplinary study of capitalism and its alternatives in the 21st Century.

Scan the code below to discover new and forthcoming titles in the series, or visit:

bristoluniversitypress.co.uk/
alternatives-to-capitalism-in-the-21st-century

A DESIRE FOR EQUALITY

Living and Working in Concrete Utopian Communities

Michel Lallement

Translated by Jessica Edwards

Originally published in French by
Éditions du Seuil in 2019 as *Un désir d'égalité:
Vivre et travailler dans des communautés utopiques*

First published in French by Éditions du Seuil as *Un désir d'égalité: Vivre et travailler dans des communautés utopiques* (2019), © Éditions du Seuil 2019

English language edition published in Great Britain in 2026 by

Bristol University Press
University of Bristol
1–9 Old Park Hill
Bristol
BS2 8BB
UK
t: +44 (0)117 374 6645
e: bup-info@bristol.ac.uk

Details of international sales and distribution partners are available at bristoluniversitypress.co.uk

© Bristol University Press 2026

British Library Cataloguing in Publication Data
A catalogue record for this book is available from the British Library

ISBN 978-1-5292-3677-4 hardcover
ISBN 978-1-5292-3678-1 paperback
ISBN 978-1-5292-3679-8 ePub
ISBN 978-1-5292-3680-4 ePdf

The right of Michel Lallement to be identified as author of this work has been asserted by him in accordance with the Copyright, Designs and Patents Act 1988.

All rights reserved: no part of this publication may be reproduced, stored in a retrieval system, or transmitted in any form or by any means, electronic, mechanical, photocopying, recording, or otherwise without the prior permission of Bristol University Press.

Every reasonable effort has been made to obtain permission to reproduce copyrighted material. If, however, anyone knows of an oversight, please contact the publisher.

The statements and opinions contained within this publication are solely those of the author and not of the University of Bristol or Bristol University Press. The University of Bristol and Bristol University Press disclaim responsibility for any injury to persons or property resulting from any material published in this publication.

Bristol University Press works to counter discrimination on grounds of gender, race, disability, age and sexuality.

Cover design: Liam Roberts Design
Front cover image: 'Oak family' by Zualidro

Bristol University Press' authorised representative in the European Union is: Easy Access System Europe, Mustamäe tee 50, 10621 Tallinn, Estonia, Email: gpsr.requests@easproject.com

Contents

List of Figures and Tables		vi
About the Author		vii
Acknowledgements		viii
Note from the Publisher		ix
Introduction: Desire for Equality and Forward Dreams		1
1	A Community Rainbow	13
2	From Walden to Twin Oaks	25
3	The Why and How of Community Involvement	41
4	I, We	62
5	The Rules of the Community Game	79
6	Work: The Shadows of the Market	96
7	Work: Utopia in Practice	113
8	The Flip Sides of Community Work	133
9	Community Destinies	154
Conclusion: Towards a Society of Communities?		167
Notes		174
References		187
Index		194

List of Figures and Tables

Figures

9.1	The number of adult members at Twin Oaks per year (1967–2023)	158
10.1	Number of US communities listed by the Fellowship for Intentional Community	168
10.2	Founding year of 655 US communities listed in *Communities Directory* (2016)	169

Tables

3.1	Four basic forms of composition with the wider world	59
7.1	Average weekly labour quota at Twin Oaks (in hours, by decade)	124
8.1	Division of labour credits by gender and activity at Twin Oaks (April 2016–January 2017)	141
8.2	Distribution of managerial responsibilities at Twin Oaks by gender (1991 and 2016)	143

About the Author

Michel Lallement is Professor of Sociology at the CNAM (Conservatoire national des arts et métiers), Paris, France. His research affiliations are with the Lise-CNRS. He has written numerous articles on work and employment, utopias and the history of sociology. His previous publications include *Le Travail. Une sociologie contemporaine* (Gallimard, 2007), *Le travail de l'utopie. Godin et le Familistère de Guise* (Les Belles Lettres, 2009), *Le travail sous tensions* (Sciences Humaines, 2010), *L'Âge du Faire. Hacking, travail, anarchie* (Seuil, 2015), *Logique de classe. E. Goblot, la bourgeoisie et la distinction sociale* (Les Belles Lettres, 2015), *Makers* (with I. Berrebi-Hoffmann and M.-C. Bureau, Seuil, 2018).

Acknowledgements

This book owes its greatest debt to the women and men who agreed to welcome me into their communities, share their work and their lives, tell me their stories and their hopes, and let me into their archives. I sincerely thank them for the time and trust they gave me. I am particularly grateful to Valerie from Twin Oaks, Gryphon from Acorn, and Phil and Douglas from The Farm, who were my special contacts and guides in their respective communities. This research would not have been possible without the support of the ESCP Europe-Société Générale 'Organisation, Leadership and Society' Chair headed by Claire Dambrin and Alberta Di Giuli. My thanks to them as well. My colleagues at CNAM, especially those in my laboratory, Lise-CNRS, have been invaluable allies at all times, offering me both first-rate material assistance and productive and amicable intellectual exchanges. Special thanks to Isabelle Berrebi-Hoffmann and Marie-Christine Bureau for their reading, criticism, and constructive feedback. I also thank Bruno Auerbach for his reading, advice, and trust, and Jessica Edwards who translated this book with extraordinary interest, proficiency, and professionalism. Thanks, finally, to my family and friends, with a special mention for Célestin who provided invaluable support for this work.

Note from the Publisher

Please note that the introduction in this book is a revised and updated version of the original introduction as published in the French edition of this work, *Un désir d'égalité*.

Introduction: Desire for Equality and Forward Dreams

Faced with the injustice, misfortune, and destruction of the planet wrought by contemporary capitalism, countless women and men, refusing to depend on the goodwill of the world's rich and powerful, have taken a stand for decent living conditions and social recognition worthy of the name. This book is dedicated to them. More precisely, it concerns the builders of 'forward dreams', to borrow a fine phrase from German philosopher Ernst Bloch; that is, the members of those communities in the US that put egalitarian life and work principles into practice. Deliberately leaving aside the dense and often abstract debates on the definitions, nature, and forms of inequality, the primary objective is to understand why and how it has been possible to build and sustain small societies so alien in spirit and practice to the large one that surrounds them. To do so, this book uses the tools of sociology to place these experiments in historical perspective, define the contours of the social space they form, bring to light the logic and meaning of the paths of those who keep them going, and, last but not least, observe what it means in practice to live and work in a utopian community today.

Intentional communities: definition and social space

> My name is Valerie and I live in a tribal village of 100 women, men and kids. We are Twin Oaks, an intentional community and EcoVillage in central Virginia. We have 450 acres of land, and we live together in homes which we built ourselves. We grow our own food and share our meals in a large central dining hall. We make our own art and music, and we have great parties! We're egalitarian and income-sharing. This means that we make our decisions as a group, as opposed to one person deciding for the rest of us. We accomplish this through discussions, written input, etc. All the income we make from our businesses is shared equally among members. We receive housing, food, and money from the community – no one has more or less than anyone else. We also believe in non-violence. We have no TV, as many members want

to live their lives in a culture free of the influences of TV-mass-media (we do have videos though). We are secular and non-religious – we leave the choice of a spiritual path (if any) up to the individual. In general, we strive to live our lives in a culture rich in cooperation and mutual support. Most members work within the community. People can choose whatever jobs they enjoy (except for dish washing, which everyone takes a turn at!).[1]

The description of the little commonwealth in which Valerie lives combines all the features of a utopian narrative. To what fertile mind do we owe such a fiction? To Thomas More, the first of all the poets of the future? Obviously not. There was no television when *Utopia* was published in 1516, and the good place discovered by Raphael Hythlodeus, the explorer whom the English humanist portrays, is located on the edge of nowhere. For the same reasons, we must set aside the Frenchman Étienne Cabet, author of *Voyage en Icarie* (1840), though he advocates absolute equality as practised in Valerie's community. Edward Bellamy, the American journalist who achieved lasting fame with *Looking Backward* (1888), is no doubt a better candidate. Julian West, the hero of Bellamy's uchronia, wakes up in the year 2000 in Boston, a few hundred miles north of Virginia, to find the city awash with innovations each more successful than the last. But Valerie's community is not the fruit of Bellamy's fertile imaginings either. Perhaps, then, we owe this sweet social illusion to the unbridled imagination of a modern-day master dreamer? A remarkable fantasist able to put into words improbable worlds that have broken away from wider society? Not that either. Twin Oaks, Valerie's community, really exists. The utopia is concrete. Since it was founded in 1967, it has stood as 'a socialist island in a sea of capitalism' (Komar, 1983, p 260).

Like Twin Oaks, the collectives discussed in this book define themselves as communities. They are the products of a movement that enlivened the late 1960s and early 1970s in the US. Against a backdrop of protests for pacifism, feminism, universal civil rights, etc., many young people at the time proclaimed their aspiration for communal living. Their forward dreams were in stark contrast to the individualistic lifestyle that dominated a prosperous, self-assured America. To be accurate, the phenomenon can only be characterized as a revival. Indeed, its roots lie deep in US history and its importance and the forms it has taken have evolved considerably over time (Barkun, 1984).

According to historians, one of the founding moments may have been the arrival of Dutch Mennonites in Delaware in June 1663. They were led by Pieter Corneliszoon Plockhoy, a craftsman distrustful of merchants and anxious, in the Christian tradition, to put work at the centre of social life (Bestor, 1970). Plockhoy advocated an egalitarian, democratic society

(Looijesteijn, 2011). Not one to be satisfied with abstract intentions, he obtained permission from the burgomasters and regents of Amsterdam to establish a colony in New Netherland. Having set out his plan in writing for his compatriots (Plockhoy, 1662), he embarked for the Americas in May 1663 with a troop of volunteers. The community, Swanendael, quickly settled on its new property in what is now Lewes, but it lived in peace for just a year. In 1664, the English took possession of the Dutch territory and sacked the fledgling community. Despite the short-lived nature of the experiment, 1663 was a turning point in American history. Since then, the community movement has had its ups and downs, but has never disappeared from the American social landscape.

In 1953, the Fellowship of Intentional Communities (FIC) defined what it considered to constitute an intentional community. It is a group of people united by an intention or, to put it another way, by a common ideal or vision (Fellowship of Intentional Communities, 1959). Whether economic, social, or spiritual in nature, the project always has the ambition of experimenting with new living conditions. The FIC further specified that an intentional community must bring together at least three families or five adults who join forces to form a collective home in shared living spaces. Their action must be guided by principles such as democracy, tolerance, and freedom. Last but certainly not least, these communities are not all closed to the outside world. Some are eager to engage with wider society to promote their values and practices.

As of November 2023, the Foundation for Intentional Community website listed just over 700 intentional communities in North America (US, Canada, and Mexico). Focusing solely on the US, Sky Blue and Betsy Morris (2017) analysed a significant sample (n = 544) of these communities according to their main orientations. Their findings were as follows: 16 per cent were intentional communities based on the principle of income sharing, 25.5 per cent were ecovillages,[2] 39.5 per cent cohousing (private homes with common facilities), 31 per cent shared housing (multiple individuals sharing a dwelling), 7 per cent student co-ops (communal homes mainly but not exclusively for students), 0.4 per cent transition towns (communities focused on environmental protection, permaculture, etc.), 2.5 per cent spiritual and religious communities, 0.5 per cent collectives based on an educational objective, and 14 per cent other cases.

I was able to conduct a multiple correspondence analysis of US intentional communities using the data listed in the 2016 edition of the Communities Directory (n = 930). The results show that at that date, two major oppositions structured the US community landscape. The first (horizontal axis) contrasts communities based primarily on the temporary sharing of common living spaces (cohousing, student houses, etc.) with intentional communities whose members hope for long-term organizational sustainability.[3] The practices and lifestyles associated with each of these poles bear out this opposition. While groups in the first case tend to be urban, outward-looking, connected to communication networks, with varied dietary preferences, etc., in the second case we find forms of rural community with a greater desire for food autonomy, operating by consensus, eating meals together more often, etc. The second opposition differentiates communities with a spiritual orientation from those without.

A renewed analytical interest

Since the early 2000s, social science research into intentional communities has enjoyed renewed interest in Europe, North America, and elsewhere. Studies on the subject have multiplied against a backdrop of economic and political restructuring driven by major upheavals in the capitalist system (such as the 2008 financial crisis), illiberal trends around the world, and a series of technology shocks attributable to the digital revolution. Rarely has the feeling that humanity is at a crossroads been so acute as among our contemporaries, and this has prompted a surge in debates and scenarios about possible futures.[4] One example is Peter Frase's (2016) serious reflection on the possible effects of automation on human labour, which he extrapolated into four sociological fictions (two of them progressive) that might help guide us in the years ahead.

Others have theorized and thematized what Mark Fisher (2021) calls post-capitalist desire. In this galaxy of thought – the heterogeneous nature of which should be highlighted – J.K. Gibson-Graham (2006) intends, for example, to move beyond the capitalocentrism from which the contemporary social sciences suffer. They suggest paying attention to the many existing non-capitalist forms of production, starting with the community economy. Concerned with promoting a good life, the community economy foregrounds values such as health, care, and respect for the environment. It also promotes a form of cooperation based on horizontal organizations that combine direct, egalitarian participation with varied work and shared responsibilities, and the sharing of duties and powers. This kind of thinking was bound to support a return to favour of research on the intentional communities of the past and present, and the potential ones of the future.

In a style peculiar to the social sciences and sociology in particular, the last few years have effectively seen a renewal of fieldwork and analysis devoted to intentional communities. Four main features characterize this research. The first reflects the fact that the theme of concrete utopias – or practical, real, achieved, feasible, or realist utopias, the adjective matters little – has now gained some currency. It happens that intentional communities are almost always associated with this label, which also encompasses other innovations (a massive reduction in working hours, universal basic income, etc.) intended to radically disrupt our ways of living and working (Bregman, 2014). Recognizing the appetite for worlds other than the one promised by the liberal, conservative, and populist forces that took hold on the threshold of the 21st century, a number of researchers have undertaken to offer a new reading of the utopian intellectual tradition, not only to provide keys to understanding the blossoming of communities that can be observed today, but, in return, to question our old interpretations in the light of original and unprecedented practices. This is the case in fields ranging from political theory (Firth, 2012) and the history of economic thought (Kremser, 2020) to philosophical doctrines and sociological paradigms (Griffin and Moylan, 2007).

In this way, research into intentional communities ties in with a more general movement towards thinking about the 'commons' as an alternative to the dominant economic, social, and political regulations.[5] Rather than go into the details of the contributions and controversies on the subject, we can cite the particularly apt definition given by Jacques Rancière (2017, p 50):

> In art as in politics, the common offers itself today as something that is to be constructed with heterogeneous forms and materials, and not as the affirmation of resources belonging to already-constituted units, be they social classes, specialised organisations or defined arts. [...] The invention, here and now, of forms of the common that diverge from the dominant forms remains the heart of emancipatory practices and ideas. And emancipation, now as ever, is a way of living in the world of the enemy in the ambiguous position of someone who fights the dominant order but is also capable of building separate places in it where he or she escapes its law.

The second characteristic of the research conducted in recent years on intentional communities is the assumption that the return to favour of utopia is inextricably bound up with the willingness of many women and men to move beyond abstract hopes to build their own future and that of their descendants. More than ever, these adventurers of everyday life want to put their values into practice here and now, starting with the rejection of inequality and discrimination, respect for nature, and non-violence. To theorize such determination, Lucy Sargisson (2017) proposes using the concept of 'transgressive utopianism' (Baccolini and Tower Sargent, 2021). This approach is concerned to describe community experiments that inextricably blend idealism and pragmatism. Taking seriously such forms of restructuring the world is an original way of giving credence to the capacity in each of us to create commons in the body of societies dominated by market and state regulations. In the US, sociologist Erik

Olin Wright has also proposed to closely link utopia and action. In *Envisioning Real Utopias* (2010), Wright considers that many initiatives (municipal participatory budgeting, Wikipedia, self-managed workers' cooperatives, unconditional basic income, etc.) are experiments, now recognized as viable alternatives, that give everyone an emancipatory power to act.

The third characteristic of current research on intentional communities is that it acknowledges the ambition for macrosocial transformation that these alternative collectives embody. Wright (2010) defines three models of social transformation: ruptural (revolutionary socialism, communism), symbiotic (social democracy, progressive adaptations), and interstitial (anarchism, the construction of counter-models of society). Concrete utopias, to which intentional communities pertain, come under the last category. In line with a model of dissemination which Charles Fourier was one of the first to theorize with his Phalanstères, it is by gradually gaining ground throughout society that, according to Wright, intentional communities could shake up the dominant order. This type of concern and analysis also directly echoes those which gave rise to prefigurative politics. In using this label, I refer to studies whose common feature is to examine in detail strategies and configurations that aim to put an end to domination of all kinds (those represented by contemporary capitalism first and foremost), to restore old forms of regulation that avoid exploitation and alienation and, finally, to invent new models of collective life through experimentation.[6]

The final characteristic of current studies on intentional communities is that they expand the horizons of investigation beyond the Western world. We have much to learn from what has been built and what is being played out elsewhere than in Europe and North America. Lucy Sargisson and Lyman Tower Sargent (2004) set the tone a few years ago in exploring the world of intentional communities in New Zealand. Yaacov Oved (2013) further broadened the spectrum by analysing the globalization of intentional communities. This work is a useful complement to the monographs devoted to small alternative societies such as the internationally renowned Auroville in India (Clarence-Smith, 2023) and lesser-known South-East Asian societies that promote, in practice, personal autonomy, political egalitarianism, and social solidarity (Gibson and Sillander, 2011). Clearly, there are still many lessons to be learned from these little-known communitarian worlds.

A sociology of concrete utopias

Though conducted in the US, the study documented in this book is fully in the spirit of this new sociology of intentional communities. The underpinning research focused primarily on egalitarian communities, groups that immediately attracted attention when they were founded in the late 1960s and early 1970s. Many of them claimed utopia as their foundational social project. Twin Oaks is no exception. 'Obviously Twin Oaks isn't Paradise', wrote one of the community's pioneers. 'For one thing, I'm no Angel, and if you were here, you wouldn't be one, either. Ordinary mortals can't create Paradise. We can, however, strive for Utopia. Never mind we haven't quite got there yet. We're working on it' (Kinkade, 1994, p 308). At Twin Oaks, some members like to say that they don't live in the land of utopia, but that from where they are they can at least make out its shores.

While this may seem like an engaging catchphrase, it is not self-evident. Indeed, utopias regularly meet with suspicion spread by discourses of various origins which, through malice or ignorance, tend to equate all fictions about the no place/good place[7] with a foreshadowing of worlds crushed by control, domination, and despair. To conduct a serious examination of utopias, we must get past such a charge and its ill-concealed ideological overtones. From this point of view, Miguel Abensour's critical philosophy is key. In setting the actions of the 'master dreamers' against a historical background, Abensour (2014, p 310) observes the emergence of a new utopian spirit after 1848 that authorizes 'open and experimental' utopias. Unlike the neo-utopians – epigones who dissolve the corrosive narratives of their mentors into an intramundane substrate – 'the new utopian spirit fights integration into the dominant culture in order to preserve the heterogeneity of the unitary theory of social revolution, as found in Marx' (Abensour, 2014, p 311). It is not enough, then, to 'get rid of the scars of capitalist society' (Abensour, 2014, p 317); one must become a migrant so as to experiment elsewhere with new ways of thinking, acting, and feeling.

Despite his distrust of the social sciences, which are too imbued with scientistic leanings for his taste, Abensour thus sketches out a research programme that offers the opportunity to forge an original alliance between political philosophy and the sociology of work and lifestyles. From this perspective, the purpose of this book is to take seriously the will of those actors of social change who resign themselves neither to the realism to which the prevailing discourses urge them to adhere, nor to the impotence to which those who officially side with the dominated nonetheless sometimes condemn them. My aim, in other words, is to contribute to establishing a sociology of 'concrete utopias'.[8]

Rather than sketching an improbable summary of what is in fact a very disparate literature, in this book I want to dig deeper in a direction that I embarked on some years ago now (Lallement, 2009; 2015). Building on previous insights, I propose to call *concrete utopias* of all configurations communities that combine the following four characteristics: they are *real* experiments that crystallize into empirically observable practices; they are *collective* experiments that require common, coordinated action; they are *situated* experiments that take shape on the margins of established social environments, possibly with the aim of pollinating their surroundings; they are *moral* experiments which, in the name of 'living well together', carry with them axiological demands that are at odds with the dominant values in the rest of society.

This definition has three implications. The first is that, because these are experiments, effective lifespan is not a discriminating factor for sorting real concrete utopias from fake. The reasons for the transience, as well as the durability, of these social experiments are worth examining carefully. Any real utopian practice, even the most ephemeral, deserves consideration in order to enrich new forward dreams. The historical analysis of traces, in the sense proposed by Bloch (1930), must be an integral part of any sociology programme dedicated to concrete utopias. In a short article on how to write history, Arlette Farge (2004, p 319) observed that researchers would do well not to 'settle for the linearities and conventional meaning of a past assumed to have unfolded logically' and to carefully examine those past events, even the most improbable and ephemeral, which indicate that the future remains open. In proposing to look at how utopian communities came into being and have evolved over the last half-century, and in taking seriously the many forms of social bricolage they have devised to make equality a daily imperative, this book means to draw its fundamental inspiration from such a spirit.

The second implication is methodological. The poetries of the future, as they are embodied in the flesh of the world, lend themselves to investigation just like any other social phenomenon. Observation, interviews, statistical objectification, documentary analysis, archival research, and so on are all techniques worth employing to sociologically investigate such a case. In other words, empirical research is a prerequisite for understanding concrete utopias, as it is for any other area of the social sciences.

The third implication is that work is an important, not to say vital subject in the analysis of concrete utopias. Two arguments support this principle. The first is de facto. All abstract utopias, from Thomas More's to André Gorz's, grant a major, though often paradoxically overlooked, role to the question of work. Moreover, the vast majority of communities that have managed to survive, in the US at least, are collectives that place work at the centre of their social life. By giving themselves the means to produce the resources required for their own projects, they do not just meet needs and protect themselves from the risks of reliance on the outside; they also invent other ways of working, cooperating, giving meaning to productive activity, and so on. The second argument is analytical: making utopia is, by definition, a Promethean act. Bloch (1954, 1955, 1959, p 560) was convinced of this, concluding the third volume of his *Principle of Hope* with these words:

> The root of history, however is the laboring, creative human, engaged in reshaping and overcoming given conditions. Once he has grasped himself and that which is his, without alienation and based in real democracy, so there will arise in the world something that shines into everyone's childhood, but where no one has yet been: homeland (*Heimat*).

The work in question from this perspective is more than simply an activity. It is a social practice that is entirely geared towards shaping matter, symbols, the self, the collective, and the world. For that reason, this book grants it central importance.

Investigating community practices, identities, and destinies

In the US, there is no shortage of publications on intentional communities. Many books offer historical pictures of the various waves and experiments that have occurred since the 19th century. When the method used amounts to a historical roundup, the reader usually gains an informative overview. But such an approach has its downsides. The description of each experience is often cursory, incomplete, and imprecise. There is therefore much to be gained from reading the many detailed monographs on past and present communities, and travel diaries such as those of Richard Fairfield (1972), Robert Houriet (1973), Erik Reece (2016), and even Peter Jenkins (1979),[9] which recount the community-focused peregrinations of their authors day by day. The methodological choice applied in this book is different again. I have drawn not only on the abundant literature mentioned above, but also on the many writings and accounts published in the form of books, articles, mimeographed documents, films, and so on by the actors of the intentional communities themselves. The magazines *The Modern Utopian* and *Communities*, together with the yearbooks published by the Fellowship for Intentional Community, were prime sources of information and data. With the permission and active support of Valerie, Twin Oaks' outreach officer, I gained access to the community's archives. These are held at the University of Virginia in Charlottesville where I was able to consult them freely and work on all the documents they contained (letters, minutes of meetings, posters, leaflets, press cuttings, photos, etc.).[10] Thanks to Isabelle Berrebi-Hoffmann's information and goodwill, I was also able to consult the Skinner archives at Harvard University. More precisely, I examined the complete correspondence between Burrhus Skinner and Twin Oaks between 1976 and 1979.[11]

I also had the opportunity to do seven weeks of participant observation in American intentional communities: three weeks at Twin Oaks in Virginia (May–June 2016), two weeks at Acorn, a small anarchist community about 20 kilometres from Twin Oaks (June 2017), one week at The Farm in Tennessee (October 2018), and a final week for a conference at Twin Oaks attended by members of intentional communities from across the US (September 2017). As part of my first stay at Twin Oaks, I spent several half days visiting and working in intentional communities located near Twin Oaks and Acorn. And I was lucky enough to be able to attend the 50th anniversary of Twin Oaks in June 2017. Besides current members, the event attracted many former members who came to celebrate the community's half-century of existence. Note, finally, that in writing this book I have anonymized first names and surnames where appropriate. When individuals gave me their consent to be cited with their first name or when they expressed an idea in a public source (archives, Internet, traditional media, etc.) that I mention, I did not render them anonymous.

Even if this book is by no means limited to presenting and analysing the egalitarian practices promoted at Twin Oaks, this collective serves as my main field of investigation. The aim is to show how it is currently organized, but also the transformations that it has undergone from its inception to the present day. Given the lack of sources for certain periods, I could not envisage doing a proper historian's job of charting and describing the evolution of Twin Oaks year after year. I therefore chose to systematically focus on three significant periods in its history so far. The first is the period of its founding (1967 to the mid-1970s). Ample information is available on this initial phase thanks to the community newsletters published at the time (*The Leaves of Twin Oaks*) and two books by Kat Kinkade (1973; 1994), one of the co-founders of Twin Oaks. Meanwhile, the archives held at the University of Virginia provide a particularly detailed picture of life at Twin Oaks almost 20 years later. They mainly cover the period from the mid-1980s to the first half of the 1990s. My participant observations allowed me to support the discussion of the third phase, namely the mid- to late 2010s. Since then, a major event has transformed the life of Twin Oaks. It was a fire on March 20, 2024. Over 200 acres burned through the night. Several buildings were destroyed, including the hammocks workshop, with damage totalling more than a million dollars.

This book is composed of nine chapters.[12] The first contextualizes the community revival that began in the US in the late 1960s and outlines the highly diverse community landscape that subsequently took shape. Three ideal types (societal, anarchist, identity-based) are, at times, highlighted. Chapter 2 traces a genealogical thread. The proposed path begins with the emblematic figure of Henry David Thoreau and his seminal book, *Walden*. The following stage is charted by the work of psychologist and utopian B.F. Skinner, the author of *Walden Two*, which sheds light on the conditions that led to the birth of Twin Oaks in 1967. Chapter 3 helps to understand who chooses to become a communard and for what reasons. At Twin Oaks, as elsewhere, withdrawing into a community is mainly the preserve of the young, white, and middle class. This chapter also examines the various strategies that intentional communities use to retain their members long term. Chapter 4 looks at everyday life at Twin Oaks and Acorn through a Goffmanian lens. The focus at this stage is investigating the ways in which a community identity is built and deciphering the multiple codes and logics that structure ordinary social interactions. In this section I also show that there are divisions that structure representations and practices. Gender, parental status, and age are major factors.

Chapter 5 challenges the myth of freely organized, dispute-free communities. By focusing on the many rules that shape communal life, it concludes that communities are above all spaces of compromise between members. The next three chapters focus on work, a regulated and conflict-ridden practice *par excellence*. The first (Chapter 6) describes the organization of commercial community work, its principles, and its empirical variations. The second (Chapter 7) presents the utopian origins of the work arrangements adopted at Twin Oaks and tests their implications in areas outside market control. The third (Chapter 8) looks at the flip sides of community work. This means, firstly, the dark side of productive activities, which are not always as pleasant as utopian rhetoric might suggest, but also the set of resources (housing, food, education, leisure, etc.) to which one is entitled by working while respecting a minimum of collective standards. The final chapter provides data on the fortunes of communards who have chosen to return to the outside world, identifies the motivations that led them to make the move, and concludes that the community experience was, in the vast majority of cases, not simply a frivolous interlude in the course of an individual's life. The conclusion describes the evolution of the social space of US intentional communities. Over the past 50 years, it has changed a lot. Many micro-societies have perished, but others have been born. The range of organizational forms has also expanded. Finally, the communities are organized into networks and are increasingly open about their proselytizing.

All in all, there is every indication that utopian communities, far from being the archaic remnant of a bygone past to which some have tried to reduce them, have become ferments of the future. Among the directions that are open to us in charting the course of our future, they point out the original path of a society based on the principles of freedom and equality. That is why it is worth taking seriously all those who, for almost half a century now, have been bringing their forward dreams to life.

1

A Community Rainbow

1966 was a pivotal year in contemporary US history. In March, the construction of the World Trade Center finally began. More importantly, the country had not long been at war: 390,000 young soldiers were far from home fighting the Vietnamese People's Army and the Viet Cong. The country was paying dearly for its engagement: military spending had soared, blowing a hole in the federal budget. 1966 was also a year of social unrest. In January, public transport strikes brought New York to a standstill. In July and August, race riots further upset the established order. The civil rights movement suddenly gained in strength and visibility. In October, Bobby Seale and Huey Newton launched the Black Panther Party for Self-Defense. The following month, Cleveland became the first big city to elect a black leader. At the same time, future Republican president Ronald Reagan was elected governor of California. Finally, 1966 was the year when, with the hippie influence growing, American citizens became aware of another cause taking shape alongside the civil rights movement: that of intentional communities.

It was in June, to be precise, according to Ronald Creagh (1983), that the movement of young adults seeking an alternative lifestyle began to gain momentum and visibility. The founding event was organized in Freeland, Maryland, by the School of Living and the New York Anarchist Federation. Still in existence in 2023, the School of Living is a community whose founder, Ralph Borsodi (1888–1977), promoted an educational programme based on the principles of independence, justice, and freedom. In *A Decentralist Manifesto*, Borsodi (1958) offered a brief summary of his core convictions. The current system had reached its limits. It was time to reinvent a 'good society'. Because they ensure economic prosperity and political autonomy, small communities were the ideal vehicle for change. Despite the normativity of his discourse, Borsodi rightly foresaw what would happen a few years later. At the turn of the 1970s in the US, local utopias were indeed in vogue.

The conditions of ferment

When the community boom took off in the second half of the 20th century, some of the protagonists felt that they were inventing *ex nihilo* a counterculture to the dominant ways of life in post-war North America. In reality, the innovation was not nearly as radical as it might first seem. The revival was part of a long history, which Rosabeth Moss Kanter (1972) proposed to summarize by distinguishing three ideal types of community (religious, politico-economic, and psychosocial) whose empirical variations succeeded one another over time. These three models have several points in common: a rejection of the established social order, the conviction that people are perfectible and that it is possible to change things here and now, and a focus on nature as an ideal site of experimentation. Qualitative changes over the decades nonetheless call for a distinction to be made between each of the three configurations.

Religious groups were the first to set the tone. Their history dates back to the country's beginnings. The Reformation spurred the departure of many Puritans from Europe, fuelling a migration of which the communities of the 1960s and 1970s, and indeed those of today, inherited the legacy. The various Protestant sects that found refuge on the other side of the Atlantic had in common their refusal to merge into a wider society that they viewed as the domain of all sins. Polluted by a vast array of moral impurities, the world as it was going was an obstacle between people and God. To overcome this major difficulty, they looked to the teachings of the Bible and tried to put into practice the principles of enclosure (the community did not welcome just anyone), harmony, and cooperation. The communism of early Christianity served as a template to give meaning to these requirements and justify a ban on private property. All the experiments that can be assessed in the light of this model were driven by the same quest: one for a new unity between people and their creator.

A second ideal type is required to characterize the politico-economic communities that emerged on American soil in the 19th century. Often inspired by socialist and communist doctrines imported from Europe (Owenism, Cabetism, and Fourierism), these groups saw society as the realm of inequality. Industrialization and urbanization, reputed to be sources of poverty, overcrowding, disease, and many other ills, were deemed the main roots of the problem. These politico-religious communities aimed to create counterpoints by inventing small socialist and communist societies from scratch. A rejection of competition and exploitation on the one hand, and the development of new models of work organization and education on the other, were two of the main options pursued to that end (Lallement, 2021). Despite a lot of trial and error, a multiplicity of practices that were not always mutually compatible, and some bitter failures, these experiments have not been erased from the collective memory. In the contemporary community movement, in any case, the memory of these pioneers is ever present.

More than half a century after the 'politico-economic' wave had subsided, the late 1960s kicked off a new community boom. R.M. Kanter dubbed 'psychosocial' the collectives that fostered and sustained it. According to the American sociologist, the refusal that justified the community craze from the 1960s onwards corresponded to a rejection of a society considered sick. Alienation, loneliness, injustice – typical expressions of a nonetheless prosperous world – were new scourges that the promoters of emerging communities intended to combat by offering those who wished to do so the chance to put their freedom into action, express their creativity, and find paths to their personal growth. Unprecedented in the 20th century, this wave of community-building benefited from a structural reorganization of American society on multiple fronts (demography, economy, culture, morals, politics, etc.).

To be more precise on this point, we must first note that in many respects, the community movement whose embryonic revival can be discerned as of the mid-1960s had elective affinities with the 'new social movements' that were flying the flags of racial equality, women's rights, and pacifism at the time. There was also a marked convergence with those who contested the damage done by industry, urban development, and any other kind of organized destruction of the natural world. For Keith Melville (1972), in any case, the link was obvious. The older generation had given up, he observed in *Communes in the Counter Culture*; class struggle was no longer on the agenda. Co-opted into the system by an income redistribution policy that afforded them a decent lifestyle, the working classes no longer had much incentive to upset the capitalist world that fed them. The young, especially those not yet caught up in working life, were taking over the reins of protest. The economic prosperity of the period saw them relatively untroubled by material concerns, unlike their elders who had not forgotten the effects of the 1929 crash and the Second World War. In a context free from material worries, the community movement was shaping a new repertoire of collective action that had replaced economic concerns with cultural demands (the search for an alternative way of life, a quest for spirituality, etc.).

It is understandable, then, that students should be in the vanguard of protest. This was all the easier given that in the two decades following the Second World War, the campus population tripled. There were 1.7 million students in 1946. As a result of the baby boom, the number of students skyrocketed: 3.8 million in 1960, 6.5 million in 1965, and 8 million in 1970. Armed with more cultural capital than their elders, and blessed with more favourable living conditions, the generation that arrived at university in the 1960s hoped after their studies to occupy positions that were at least as comfortable and well-paid as their parents'. The tragedy was that, for demographic reasons, the labour market could not meet everyone's expectations. This relative frustration fuelled resentment and fostered protest.

While it does not cover all the explanatory reasons for youth protest in the 1960s, such an existential contradiction undoubtedly contributed to the mood of the times. Aware that they risked a drop in status, the young generation proved particularly sensitive to the problems of poverty, injustice, discrimination, and political manipulation, all phenomena against which the rebellion was organized. The hippie movement illustrates the radical counterpoint promoted by a young population opposed to the lifestyle of a 'plastic society'. The term 'hippie' appeared around 1965 (Stevens, 1987):

> Thus, in the mid-1960s, the San Francisco Chronicle coined the pejorative epithet 'hippy' (derived from 'hip'). *Time* magazine placed the epicentre of the movement in the Haight-Ashbury district of San Francisco; the *Chronicle* soon announced in big headlines that next summer, a hundred thousand 'hippies' would be invading their new Mecca; The very next day, the mayor of the city made it known that any hippy would be treated as a *persona non grata*. A year later, in 1968, the death of the movement was officially declared. (Creagh, 1983, pp 211–212)[1]

The community revival of the 1960s and 1970s

Although certainly too impressionistic, the panorama painted above helps to understand how decisive the new spirit of protest that characterized the post-war growth years may have proved for the community revival that occurred in the same period. To avoid conflating them, however, it would be worth looking at precisely when the first intentional communities were formed. Such an undertaking is in fact impossible. No hard and fast starting point can be identified for the community movement of the 1960s because of the kinship with groups whose roots stretch much further back. As the executive director of the Fellowship for Intentional Community recalled in 2017, the term intentional community was coined in the 1940s.[2] Equivalent at the time to 'cooperative community', it was used to refer to groups who shared a rejection of war, racial segregation, and classism, and who valued environmental conservationism. The engineer Arthur Morgan, author of *The Small Community. Foundation of Democratic Life* (1942), was one of its main theorists. Timothy Miller (1990), for his part, stressed that many groups were already trying out community life before the 1960s, either to promote radical political activism, to make material autonomy a concrete ideal, or to advance the cause of sexual freedom.[3]

The fact remains that in the second half of the 1960s, a new page was turned. Hence, a second question: what was the scale of the community movement that was taking shape across the US? Unfortunately, this question is equally difficult to answer with any confidence. There are no truly reliable estimates. A survey published on 17 December 1970 in the *New York Times* estimated that at that point, 2,000 communities were established in 34 states. In an interview with the *San Francisco Chronicle* on 17 February of the same year, Benjamin Zablocki, then assistant professor of sociology at the University of California, Berkeley, provided a more generous estimate (Houriet, 1973). In his view, there were some 3,000 communities across the country, with a third of them located in rural areas. The National Institute of Health gave a similar assessment (Otto, 2010).[4] And although it is not clear how it was arrived at, in 1969 *Newsweek* put forward the figure of 10,000 hippies in over 500 communities.

All these assessments have been taken up by various specialists of intentional communities, but without their credibility ever being tested. In a half-personal, half-scholarly essay, the poet and teacher Judson Jerome painted an even bigger picture. He asserted that in the early 1970s, about 750,000 people (0.3 to 0.4 per cent of the US population) could claim to have had an alternative living experience in the tens of thousands of communities that existed at the time. Estimating that the phenomenon had involved at least half a million young people, Hugh Gardner (1978) concluded that while no one could provide reliable data, he was certain that the country was witnessing community engagement on a scale never before seen in US history.

To avoid floundering in total imprecision, we can look to *Communities*, a North American magazine devoted to intentional communities that first appeared in December 1972,[5] for some useful indications. In its first instalment, the magazine featured nine concrete utopias. After 1972, *Communities* regularly published special issues devoted to an inventory of American communities.[6] The format changed in 1990. Since then, the Fellowship for Intentional Community has published a special directory (*Communities Directory*) at varying intervals in association with other partners (including School of Living, Federation of Egalitarian Communities, Twin Oaks, Sandhill Farm, and Shannon Farm), which includes geographical maps and synoptic tables on the multiple characteristics of each community listed.[7] Feature articles complete the package.

A review of all these documents is not enough to establish the real evolution of the number of intentional communities, many of them having existed under the radar. It does confirm, however, that the phenomenon did not die out after the communal explosion publicized by the media in the late 1960s and early 1970s – on the contrary. It also gives an indication of how effective and visible the network of intentional communities has become, with the internet facilitating contact between and the counting of the many groups in the US and around the world. In 1974, *Communities* listed 254 intentional communities in the US.[8] By 2016, that figure had risen more than three and a half times.

A galaxy and its planets

At the turn of the 1960s to 1970s, several broad trends characterized and contrasted intentional communities. The first had its roots in a multitude of religious traditions. A 1970 survey by the Liberated Church in America (Berkeley) counted over 400 communities deploying a wide array of beliefs. This composite picture included Mennonite families who founded the Reba Place association in Evanston, Illinois, underground houses set up by priests and nuns who had broken with the Catholic Church, traditionalist Hasidic communities formed by young Jews in San Francisco and Boston, advocates of complex theology and folk masses (the Ecumenical Institute in Chicago), and fundamentalists such as those of the Jesus Movement.

Not all communard collectives were driven by such religious ideals. Anxious to chip away at a world whose prevailing options aggrieved them, many collectives attempted to put into practice values traditionally associated with the left wing of the American political spectrum, from liberals to radicals. The Movement for a New Society (Philadelphia), for instance, founded in the early 1970s, sought to invent a new model of social organization with a commitment to the principle of non-violence. Its members promoted what some of them called 'decentralized socialism' or 'community anarchism'. Determined to act then and there, they set up 20 or so houses in West Philadelphia to realize this political forward dream, each with a specific focus (feminism, children, religion, neighbours' organizations, and so on). In a significant modulation of the community ideal, finances remained an individual matter. Consequently, the cost of community residence was kept to a minimum so that members could avoid having to work full time and be able to engage in activism for social change.

Less overtly politicized than the latter, but just as concerned with working in practical ways to transform a society deemed iniquitous and corrupt, several communities openly advocated a return to 'natural' practices (refusal of soap, veganism, distrust of established medicine) (Move, Philadelphia). Nudism was frequently practised in groups that, in the name of nature, health, and sensuality, called for more permissiveness. Others were involved in social welfare, such as Vocations for Social Change, which worked for a better match between job vacancies and labour supply, and Synanon (California), a community specializing in the care and rehabilitation of drug addicts.

Those who hoped to revolutionize society through communitarian means also had a particular interest in gender relations. They especially challenged the norm of monogamous marriage. Founded in 1971, the small community of Kerista (San Francisco) invented a new 'polyfidelity' model. The basic sexual unit was not a heterosexual couple bound by marriage but a BFIC (Best Friend Identity Cluster), a small group that shared a room and whose members took turns sleeping with each other. The idea was to extend the boundaries of marriage to include more than two people in the same basic unit (Constantine and Constantine, 1973). While some others also took up the practice, the number of experiments of this kind was fairly limited. Herbert Otto (2010) estimated that barely two dozen families in the US tested the alternative model of multilateral marriage featured in Robert Rimmer's short story *Proposition 31*, published in 1968. That said, other experiments intended to counter the traditional marriage model were kept under wraps for fear of reprisals.

Similarly, gays and lesbians and feminists took advantage of the community craze to advance their causes. WomanShare, a lesbian community founded in Oregon in 1974, declared itself 'women's country'; 23 acres of land where men could only exceptionally set foot. To support the group, the members (there were never more than five) did tasks traditionally seen as men's work, such as repairing cars and handling chainsaws. According to Miller (1999), at the end of the 20th century, there were still dozens of American communities whose identity was chiefly structured by gender and gender relations.

Three basic forms of community

Whether we try to understand communities through their orientations or through the works that inspired them, they are no more resistant than any other social phenomenon to the two common temptations which consist, on the one hand, in perceiving only an infinite variety of singular realities and, on the other, in encapsulating the plurality of cases in a single model. Sociology has taught us to avoid these two extreme positions in order to take seriously 'family resemblances' – that is, in Ludwig Wittgenstein's (1921) sense of the term, the common traits linking people who are related and yet irremediably singular. Communities are no exception. To put it another way, they are like a rainbow: they can be arranged in a wide gradation of shades while also being grouped into colour families. Producing typologies, and with them ideal types,[9] is an effective way to meet the paradoxical sociological requirement of segmenting complex material without dividing it *ad infinitum*.

Through the rudimentary statistical analysis of a sample of 98 communities whose main characteristics were published in *Communities* in 1978, I was able to bring to light three basic forms of community. A first (horizontal) axis, resulting from the correspondence analysis I carried out, contrasts the small rural communities with their urban alter egos (all of which are larger). A second (vertical) axis separates open communities from inward-looking groups.[10] It is also clear that the form of regulation of romantic and/or sexual relationships was a differentiating factor in the space of American intentional communities in the second half of the 1970s.

Based on such statistical analysis, it is reasonable to suggest that three forms of intentional community coexisted more than a decade after the hippie wave swept through the US. The first is characteristic of the groups intent on going back to nature. These more than others swore by the principle of small is beautiful, which is consistent with the left-libertarian governance options that they favoured. The relatively closed nature of the community and sexual freedom complete the picture which, because they place great value on individual free will, can be described as *anarchist*. The second type, which is more urban, essentially encompasses communities which share the characteristics of being governed by a charismatic figure and of building their cohesion on the basis of similarity. In the sample used here, the roots of these communities lie in the choices and sexual orientations of their members. *Identity-based* community seems the most appropriate term to refer to such a group. Finally, a third set groups together large communities that are open to the outside world and based on a principle of social regulation (of romantic or sexual relationships in particular). Insofar as these communities, given their large number of members, the way they are governed, etc., can be likened to small societies, they can be called *societal* communities.

The foundations and coherence of each of the community types distinguished above merit further analysis in order, among other things, to understand how the different types manage to accommodate a principle of equality. That is one of the main objectives of the following chapters, based on my fieldwork at Twin Oaks (a societal community) and Acorn (an anarchist community). For methodological reasons, I forewent any direct observation of an identity-based community. Many of those that come close to this ideal type are organized on a spiritualist basis and use a charismatic type of government. To live there, even for the duration of a participant observation, I would have had to demonstrate a minimum of empathy with their prevailing values and practices. I was, however, able to stay briefly at The Farm, which started out with identity-based characteristics before morphing into a societal community. Its history is worth knowing for at least two reasons. First, it reveals what the social dynamics specific to identity-based groups could be like, and still can be. Second, it demonstrates through experience that no community is condemned to stick to the organizational mould in which it initially chose to cast itself.

A community under charismatic domination

The history of The Farm is inextricably linked to that of Stephen Gaskin (1935–2014), a former marine who taught in the linguistics department at

San Francisco Public University. In the late 1960s, every Monday night, several hundred students came to listen to him and discuss spirituality and religion. As one of them tells it, Gaskin:

> was really good at public speaking, crystallizing the issues of the time and channeling the energy of the group. [...] It looked like he had the 'answer', when really what he had was the energy of the group. He was a psychedelic father figure who basically said, 'Come be a part of this new family where you'll be understood and accepted and you'll be given the opportunity to grow spiritually'. (cited in Stevenson, 2014b, p 3)[11]

It was not a token invitation. Before long, Gaskin suggested that the students leave the classroom behind and go on the road with him. Sixty school buses set off in a great caravan of peace and love (Gaskin, 1972). Under the leadership of its guru, the caravan travelled across the US, stopping in nearly 40 cities. In 1971, Tennessee was chosen as the last Eden. There, 600 people settled on a 1,700-acre piece of land and founded The Farm. The project was clear:

> [W]e wanted to have a way to make our living, because we were a Church and wanted to live a spiritual life. If you really want to be spiritual, you don't want to have to sell your soul for eight hours a day in order to have sixteen hours in which to eat and sleep and get it back together again. You'd like it that your work should be seamless with your life and that what you do for a living doesn't deny everything else that you believe in. (Gaskin, 1974, p 4)

Gaskin – who was a little older than the average of those who followed him, most of whom were around 20 – remained more than ever the undisputed leader of this rural, hippie monastery. Before a candidate could join the group, they had to speak personally with Stephen and acknowledge him as their spiritual father. His hold was strong. Every Sunday for the first ten years, Gaskin gathered together all the members of the community. They began with an hour of Eastern-style meditation. Then, like a father superior, he addressed the assembled congregation and performed weddings. He was, however, largely indifferent to practical matters. Yet a minimum of organization was required to have a hope of surviving. Owing to the sheer number of Farmers, the community soon took on a faintly bureaucratic cast. Gaskin appointed straw bosses who were responsible for working groups of four or five people specializing in various fields (construction, farm work, food production, care, budgeting, etc.). The straw bosses had a large degree of independence in decision-making and the day-to-day organization of work. They met at least once a week to coordinate their activities. While Gaskin served as The Farm's spiritual leader, the straw bosses – there were 12 of them when the system was introduced in 1972 – formed its executive government.

Excluding two types of external profit-making activities (construction and publishing), cultivation was the main collective resource. The community lived mainly on the produce they grew on their land (tomatoes, peas, potatoes, cucumbers, melons, apples, wheat, and so on). The members were vegetarian and drank no alcohol. Inspired by the Bible, the lifestyle was frugal and based on the principle of sharing all goods and income. 'If you live on the Farm', reads an illustrated booklet written by Gaskin (1974) and some other members, 'you give the Farm everything, because The Farm is going to take care of your needs'. As in many other communities, the work was time-consuming. To give the gruelling practice meaning, the official rhetoric suggested treating it like yoga. To work was to meditate on the move …

No matter how people dealt with it, work was a crucial driving force. Thanks to their work, the community not only produced enough food to feed itself, but also built a full-blown village, which in 1974, in addition to a number of makeshift dwellings, consisted of ten houses, a six-unit apartment building, a central building equipped with meeting rooms and a kitchen, a print shop, baths, a laundry, mills, a repair shop, a school, and several buildings still under construction. The families, finally, were composed of couples or singles with children. Gaskin strongly encouraged the communards to marry and not divorce. In 1974, 320 married people and 180 single people lived on The Farm (Jenkins, 1979).[12] Multilateral marriage existed but remained marginal. The community's basic units were groups of 15 to 30 people who lived together in a collective living space, with members sharing domestic tasks. Overall, however, The Farm upheld a traditional division of social roles. The men all worked outdoors. Women, while not all involved, were exclusively responsible for childcare, cooking, and laundry (Pfaffenberger, 1982).

Despite everyone having their basic necessities met, some time out to relax (The Farm had a rock band; the community broadcasted its own radio) and open sexual relations (sex being seen as a sacred practice), the early 1980s brought disillusionment. The members had more trouble putting up with the poverty that they had vowed to live in as the community's financial situation deteriorated. Meanwhile, the utopian hope had faded. The Farm now looked less like an ashram and more like a collection of families concerned primarily with raising their children. They were unwilling to keep living in poverty and found themselves competing for access to scarce resources. Tired of such vicissitudes, many communards threw in the towel (Traugot, 1994).[13]

The Farm's societal transformation

The difficulties having mounted over the years, in 1983 the community undertook a reform, the Changeover, to rectify the situation. As one resident who had lived at The Farm since 1980 told me, "We were sick of taking care of people who did nothing. We were living on top of each other, as best we could. It couldn't go on like that."[14] To put it another way, the decisions made at the Changeover were a response to what Max Weber called the routinization (*Veralltäglichung*) of charisma. As a quality attributed to a person whom others are willing to obey because they consider him or her extraordinary, charisma is bound to fade fairly quickly. Any charisma 'is on the road from a turbulently emotional life that knows no economic rationality to a slow death by suffocation under the weight of material interests: every hour of its existence brings it nearer to its end' (Weber, 1978, p 1120).[15] At The Farm, a break with the original way of operating was, if not certain, highly probable.

The Changeover deeply undermined the roots of the identity-based model and laid the foundations for a societal transformation (Stevenson, 2014a). First, Gaskin was side-lined. "He was a good spiritual leader but a very bad manager. We are grateful to him for organizing the community in its early days. But we had to evolve."[16] In conflict with his wife and their son, Gaskin was forced to distance himself from the collective that he had long guided on the path of spirituality. The 1983 reform was also, and above all, organizational. "The Farm wanted to change the world," as D. Stevenson likes to say, "but the world also changed The Farm".[17] The first decision was to put an end to the previous communist system and leave it up to each member to earn their own income. As a consequence, many of those whose role was to serve others in the community (teachers, health care workers, shop managers, etc.) became unemployed. The other effect of giving up the principle of solidarity was to hasten the departure of many communards and exacerbate an exodus that had begun earlier. There were 1,400 people living at The Farm in 1980. By 1983, there were only 800. The population dropped to 400 in 1986 and 225 in 1994. In 2018, The Farm was home to 200 people, including about 30 children, forming 60-odd families, for a total of 84 houses which each could house one or two domestic units.

Yet the Changeover did not do away with resource sharing entirely. The land remained common property and some collective services were still provided to everyone: road and path maintenance, maintenance of the water system, the payment of taxes, and access to communal areas. In 2018, adult members each paid the very modest sum of $100[18] per month for this. These dues were used to fund a common budget, but they also determined who could have a say in The Farm's various committees – 'You pay, you vote' (Stevenson, 2014b, p 24).

The 1983 reform was also an opportunity to formalize the management structures of The Farm in compliance with its legal status. This was codified in Section 501(d) of the Internal Revenue Service, which treated The Farm, like most other intentional communities, as a monastery. To facilitate the Changeover and usher in a new organizational model, the collective took stock of its finances and tried to figure out how it would pay off the $600,000 in debt that had accumulated over the years (the equivalent of $1.3 million including interest owed to the bank). The conditions for becoming a member were also thoroughly reviewed. Gone was the guru's spiritual endorsement as a ticket in, gone too was the vow of poverty which committed each person to turn over all their possessions to the community as a whole.[19] To become a Farmer, you now needed to have two thirds of the community vote in your favour, undertake never to behave violently (and therefore not own a weapon), and so on. More generally, applicants had to accept that they were stakeholders in an organization with clearly identifiable outlines and rules.

A concern for democracy reinforced the societal framework that took shape with these reforms. Each autumn, all members were invited to vote on the budget which the finance committee had drafted beforehand. More generally, the community operated through the coordinated action of several specialized committees. In addition, community events (meals, ceremonies, parties, markets, sports events, concerts, leisure activities, etc.) fostered a sociability that varied in intensity according to each person's desires and predispositions. The Farm effectively came to function like a village or a small society of acquaintances which, based on shared values, has decided to pool resources and manage them with as little bureaucracy as possible, while offering each person the opportunity to take part in community activities to the extent that suited them.

Professional activities also provide an opportunity on a daily basis to develop close social ties. The Farm is an economic hub that combines electronics manufacturing, permaculture, organic food production, book publishing, handicrafts, events, training courses, and more. Admittedly, not all the communards work in the small Geiger meter factory, the Village Media Services, or the Book Publishing Company that are still located on the common land. Many of them now run their own businesses, with private residences serving as both headquarters and workplaces. The Farm also has educational facilities, including its own primary school. In the tradition that made its reputation early on, it is also specialized in training midwives. With the consent and under the supervision of the public authorities, the community's College of Traditional Midwifery offers a 36-month degree programme. Clearly, then, as a societal community, The Farm's relationship with its surroundings is no longer anything like the one that characterized its founding period; the community now knows how to live – to borrow a Weberian turn of phrase – both in its world and of this world.

2

From Walden to Twin Oaks

New Harmony: before being associated with the names of Robert Owen and William Maclure, who bought it in 1824 for $150,000, this small town in Indiana was the second seat of the community founded by self-proclaimed Pietist prophet George Rapp. In addition to the shared brick houses, a granary, a mill, and so on, all the Rappites had access to a garden. A symbol of paradise on earth, this piece of nature was particularly appreciated. The communards could wander as they pleased through a labyrinth of greenery comprising flowering shrubs, vines, and trees (Arndt, 1997). A place conducive to meditation, the garden signified what the communal utopia owes to nature – that fantasized world of all possible rebirths. In reality, the Harmonist garden bore all the hallmarks of civilization: formal beds in straight rows, cultivation of exotic and non-native plants (such as lemon trees), and the use of agricultural tools and techniques (such as a greenhouse on rollers).

As the specific case of the Rappist garden suggests, there is some irony in confusing nature with a pre-industrial Eden, a wilderness supposedly free from social turpitude. Yet in the 19th century and again in the 1960s and 1970s, it was in these terms that many communards justified their rejection of the urban world and desire to return to the land. William Cronon (1995), a leading contemporary scholar of environmental history, has shown how much this association between nature and the purity of new beginnings owes to changing collective representations. Having first been invested with religious values mixed with an exaltation of individualism, in the 19th century the wilderness became a 'sacred icon'. For Americans, 'The mythic frontier individualist was almost always masculine in gender: here, in the wilderness, a man could be a real man, the rugged individual he was meant to be before civilization sapped his energy and threatened his masculinity' (Cronon, 1995, p 78).

Henry David Thoreau perfectly symbolizes this enchanted relationship with the environment, even if in some of his writings he conveyed a less dreamlike representation of nature than in *Walden, or Life in the Woods*, his best-known work. It is with Thoreau that I will begin the following reflection, which links together the questions of nature, of organization, and of work in the light of utopian demands. The reason for such a choice is that, through the medium of American psychologist B.F. Skinner and his 1948 utopian novel *Walden Two*, Twin Oaks, the Virginian community at the centre of the present work, indirectly inherits ambitions expressed by Thoreau. To be exact, Twin Oaks was initially an attempt to apply the blueprint devised by Skinner in a 'natural' space of the kind dear to Thoreau. The title Kathleen Kinkade (one of the founders of Twin Oaks) chose when she published the first review of the community's experience leaves no doubt as to the intellectual origin of the project: *A Walden Two Experiment. The First Five Years of Twin Oaks Community*.

Thoreau's ecocentrism

In the US, the wilderness has long been a source of collective representations whose common thread is to make the natural world serve as an escape from social dysfunctions. Henry David Thoreau (1817–1862) embodies this anti-conformist, ecocentric ideal, which sees a retreat from the social world as the means to realize a set of ideals – freedom first and foremost. Thoreau was born in Concord, not far from Boston. The son of a modest storekeeper and pencil maker, he was a rather solitary child. He went to Harvard University at the age of 16 and graduated four years later. After a short stint as a schoolteacher, he distanced himself from the world. He turned to books and became friendly with the philosopher and poet Ralph Waldo Emerson, one of the leading figures of transcendentalism and author of *Nature* (1836). After the tragic death of his brother, Thoreau chose to go into seclusion to ease his torment. For two years, two months, and two days, he lived in a cabin in the middle of the woods near Walden Pond (Massachusetts) on land owned by Emerson. Thoreau gave multiple reasons to explain his choice. To all appearances, however, a rejection of the urban lifestyle was his primary motivation.

Thoreau began his new life on 4 July 1845, the anniversary of American independence. He built himself a small pine cabin measuring 10 feet by 15 feet, for a total cost of about $28. The cabin was just over a mile from Concord, so Thoreau could continue to meet and spend time with friends and acquaintances on a daily basis. While he was not, therefore, in total isolation, the choice was nonetheless one of retreat. For 26 months, Thoreau lived in harmony with nature. He walked for several hours a day, bathed in the pond, played the flute, carefully studied his surrounding environment, and wrote. He adopted a vegetarian diet. He grew wheat, beans, corn, and potatoes and made his own bread. He gave up cigarettes and alcohol, but also tea and coffee. Thoreau's asceticism was not out of keeping with his country's puritanical values, particularly as he also extolled sexual abstinence and productive effort.

Walden, or Life in the Woods, published in 1854, describes Thoreau's life during this woodland retreat. Its literary style does nothing to disguise the author's philosophical views. Like his friend and mentor Emerson, Thoreau defends a perfectionism that ranks the values of freedom and autonomy foremost among moral requirements. *Walden* conveys this stance through a systematic critique of modern urban life. As the book unfolds, Thoreau (1854, p 54) denounces, in no particular order, luxury, fashion, over-consumption, haste, waste, the race for progress, the accumulation of money and material goods, the useless quest for detail, newspaper gossip, the absurdity of 'spending […] the best part of one's life earning money in order to enjoy a questionable liberty during the least valuable part of it' – in short, all the failings of the 'chopping sea' that is civilized life.

The brief Skinner sensation

Nowadays *Walden* is the most widely read and quoted of all Thoreau's works. Although the first edition met with only moderate success upon its release, the book has become a classic. *Walden* specialists and commentators have often drawn parallels between this work and those which in turn, sometimes long afterwards, have extolled the virtues of nature, America's wide open spaces, long journeys, a rejection of urban frenzy, and the freedom to roam. In this game, Jack Kerouac and Jim Harrison often lead the pack. Among the many other heirs, the case of B.F. Skinner (1904–1990) deserves special attention. The author of *Walden Two* accomplished a literary act that might seem unexpected coming from a psychologist and academic who had lent his name to works and intellectual choices with a clear behaviourist focus.[1] Yet in fact, as a student, Skinner chose to earn his first degree in English literature. After an unsuccessful attempt to write a novel, he turned to psychology.

But the professor did not give up writing, notably to express his concern for the state of the world. That is how *Walden Two* should be read, as a response to the issues of a period haunted by the deadly effects of the Second World War. Democracies had been sorely challenged by totalitarian forces. They had paid a high price for it. This observation fuelled Skinner's political disillusionment. He no longer believed in the capacity of the elite, or of most people for that matter, to voluntarily embark on a favourable course. To escape the trap in which modern democracies had caught us, it was necessary, in Skinner's view, to devise a way of modifying people's behaviour. To this end, his ambition for *Walden Two* was sweeping: the idea was nothing less than to design an alternative model of organization which, by influencing individuals' environment, would structure their ways of being and doing in the most diverse areas of social life (the assigning of status, the economy, education, gender relations, health, leisure, and so on).

Through the voice of Frazier, the hero of his book, Skinner explains that Walden Two, the name of the community featured in the novel, was chosen:

> in honour of Thoreau's experiment, which was in many ways like our own. It was an experiment in living, and it sprang from a similar doctrine of our relation to the state. Several ambiguities in the name amused us. Thoreau's was not only the first of the Waldens, it was an experiment with *one* life, and social questions were neglected. Our problem was to build a Walden for Two. (Skinner, 1948, pp 208–209)

Skinner further innovated by moderating the naturalist argument in favour of a behaviourist doctrine intended to clarify the best way to build community. *Walden Two*, a utopian story *par excellence*, is full of descriptions, arguments, and proposals all geared to this end.

Work and social organization in *Walden Two*

A 'world without heroes' kept together with the aid of many rules and rituals that inform daily life, Walden Two is fundamentally a work community. The first basic principle is the following:

> Labor-credits are a sort of money. But they're not coins or bills – just entries in a ledger. All goods and services are free […]. Each of us pays for what he uses with twelve-hundred labor-credits each year – say, four credits for each workday. We change the value according to the needs of the community. (Skinner, 1948, p 45)

When Burris (one of the novel's main protagonists) visits Walden Two, the equivalence in force is one labour credit for one hour of work. In other words, each member is required to work an average of four hours per day. Following the principle that Edward Bellamy (1888) suggested in *Looking Backward*, the value assigned to different kinds of work may vary. Unpleasant jobs, such as cleaning sewers, are worth more credit than others. To reach the daily quota, a sewage worker has to put in just over two hours a day. The more gratifying jobs, on the other hand, have coefficients of 0.7 or 0.8 (which means a working day of five to six hours for those who choose it). Ornamental gardening is another case again, with a very low value (0.1). In short, everything is done to avoid boring, uncreative, and poorly paid work as much as possible.

Work is, moreover, an obligation at Walden Two, including for children and visitors. Workers do not receive a wage in return for their daily services. The wealth produced goes back to the community. On the other hand, members have free access to all the resources (housing, food, clothing, and so on) that they have helped to produce or acquire. The sharing of property is all the easier to put into practice given that the community chooses to consume little. A radical departure from the practices and lifestyles that were beginning to take hold in post-war industrial societies, this option resonates with the many critiques of the 1960s – and of today – calling for an end to consumerism.

If the lifestyle choice of Walden Two's members is perfectly clear, they still needed to set up a government that could ensure their existence and continuity. Skinner did not have harsh enough words for democracy, a 'pious fraud' that operates on a conception of human beings devoid of any valid scientific basis. Free suffrage, asserts the leader of the community, is 'free fiddlesticks' (Skinner, 1948, p 183). It is therefore no surprise that in Walden Two, the only government there is did not emerge from a ballot box. It is a board of planners, usually composed of three women and three men.

The managers, meanwhile, are:

> specialists in charge of the divisions and services of Walden Two. There are Managers of Food, Health, Play, Arts, Dentistry, Dairy, various industries, Supply, Labor, Nursery School, Advanced Education, and dozens of others. They requisition labor according to their needs, and their job is the managerial function which survives after they've assigned as much as possible to others. They're the hardest workers among us. (Skinner, 1948, p 48)

Managers are no more elected than planners. They are appointed on the basis of their skills and their willingness to work for the welfare of the community. Two other categories of members exist alongside the managers and planners: workers, the linchpins of the entire productive organization, and scientists, who conduct experiments in a range of fields (plant and animal breeding, the management of infant behaviour, education, the use of raw materials, and so on).

Bringing *Walden Two* to life

When community utopias came back into fashion in the mid-1960s in the US, the behaviourist psychologist B.F. Skinner was by no means an unknown. Because he was primarily interested in continuing his academic research, he did not capitalize on his success to try and put the model he had devised in *Walden Two* into practice himself. Others took on the task. Things kicked off in 1966 with a summer conference (the Waldenwoods Conference) funded by a large foundation that wanted to help set up a network of Skinnerians. Eighty-three adults and four children met near Hartland, Michigan, from 28 to 31 August 1966.[2] Skinner was not among them, though he sent a written message of support. During the conference, participants were asked to work on the practical details of building communities inspired by *Walden Two*. Seven workshops were organized. They covered topics such as recruiting members, choosing a location, organizing community collectives, finances, and so on. Despite a common reference to *Walden Two* and, at first, a fairly clear goal, an irreparable split soon emerged. Reports of the meeting[3] reveal that there were two tendencies represented by two different groups.

The first consisted of staunch behaviourists who could not imagine turning Skinner's paper utopia into reality without remaining faithful to the scientific credo of their intellectual guide. A handful of community experiments would be conducted in this spirit. The second group, while not unaware of Skinnerian psychology, attached much less importance to it. They were above all in a hurry to act. This was the case for a small collective that founded Walden Three in the early 1970s. In 1971, the group reviewed its situation:

> Walden Three at present is comprised of eight individuals residing in a large house in Providence. We are based principally on behavioral, cultural, and environmental design as presented by B.F. Skinner in *Walden Two*. We have been influenced by other writers in the behavioral and environmental sciences, such as Ruth Benedict, Ashley Montague, and Bucky Fuller. Although small at present, we would like to expand to a community of five hundred to a thousand members on a rural location with facilities for light industry, such as foundry, woodworking, metals fabrication, farming, etc.[4]

Did the community manage to survive? There is no indication that it did. In fact, one has to cross the border to find sustainably active Walden communities in two neighbouring countries. The first of these, Dandelion, settled in Ontario, Canada. When it was founded in 1974, it had five members. Nine years later, the group had grown to 16 people living on 50 acres of land. The community specialized in handicrafts. They made rope hammocks and recycled tin cans into candle holders, lamps, and planters. Skinnerian behaviourism was the group's official ideology. Its principles were transposed into a code of behaviour with 140 articles dealing with the most varied aspects of daily life. Dandelion folded in the 1990s.

Los Horcones, the second community that managed to keep the Skinnerian ideal alive, still exists in the early 2020s. Founded in 1973 by young Mexicans who settled on the outskirts of Hermosillo, in north-western Mexico, Los Horcones grew over the years, thanks largely to the arrival of children born to the founding couples. In 1980, the community moved to the Sonora desert. Living well out of town on 250 acres of land they bought cheaply, the members of Los Horcones were able to develop new activities such as permaculture, raising animals, and cheese- and bread-making. They also learned to build. The community erected many functional buildings to serve everyday needs (meals, education, laundry, and so on) and provided private living spaces for everyone. It now rents out bedrooms and meeting rooms in a remarkably pleasant setting where the vegetation has managed to eclipse the aridity of the immediate surroundings.

The Walden House experiment

Although the experiments mentioned above shared the virtue of attempting to quickly establish Walden Twos in flesh and stone, they did not attract B.F. Skinner's attention in equal measure. Twin Oaks can claim a special mention in this respect, as the psychologist had extensive contact with the community for almost two years. Before going into the details of this singular relationship, it should be noted that the history, or rather the prehistory, of Twin Oaks began a few months before the Waldenwoods Conference in the summer of 1966.[5]

Bill was one of the first protagonists of the venture. A former theology student at the University of Chicago, he was early among the pioneers trying to bring *Walden Two* to life. Bill was particularly keen to put into practice Skinner's post-Freudian precepts, Bellamy's model of labour credits, and the recommendations of group marriage theorists. He partnered with a friend to buy a big old building in Washington DC that could accommodate a dozen people, which they named Walden House. As the newsletter issued in December 1965 put it, it was 'a place for impatient Walden Two enthusiasts. It is the scene of necessarily limited but determined action toward the founding of a society like the one Dr. Skinner described.'[6]

The founding duo scrambled to attract other people. George and Kathleen (Kat, a divorced mother) were among the first to join the two founders. When Richard Fairfield (1972) visited Walden House in the spring of 1966, he found he could almost count the members and boarders on the fingers of one hand. Everyone paid the same amount per week for rent and food. The two boarders, who were not members, were exempt from household chores. On the other hand, they had no say in decisions affecting the fledgling community. They also had to be prepared to leave on short notice if a new member wanted their room.

By the spring of 1966, although still a resident of Walden House, Bill was no longer a member of the community. A dispute had quickly arisen between him and the rest of the group – Kat (the only woman) in particular. Kat, who at 35 was also the oldest, categorically rejected the idea of group marriage and the prospect of sharing her bed with a different partner every night. Although Kat described the fate of this joint venture as a failure, the split did not damage the group, which survived by virtue of the jobs they all held outside the community. A new chapter in Twin Oaks' prehistory was written in the summer of that year when George and Kat, newly married, attended the Waldenwoods Conference. Also at the conference were two students from Atlanta who ran *Walden Pool* (a newsletter advocating the creation of a Walden Two community) and a young businessman from Virginia. Together, they decided to join forces to make the Skinnerian utopia a reality.

It took several months of discussion to reach a basic consensus on the project. The young people deliberated, for instance, over who should be welcome in their future community. Would homosexuals be admitted? Were mental health criteria necessary? Should recruitment be based on moral, political, or religious standards? And what about people with financial problems?[7] After three more associates joined the core founders, the collective took advantage of a $30,000 contribution from one of its members to take the plunge. The group visited a dozen properties and finally set their hearts on a 123-acre tobacco farm in Virginia. The owner, who was getting too old to run the farm, had decided to sell up. With his help and sound advice from the local representative of the Department of Agriculture, the small group quickly began to plant and grow their own food (corn, celery, potatoes, carrots, salsify, cabbage, beans, etc.), even before they officially took possession of the farm on 16 June 1967.

Twin Oaks: foundation and early achievements

The opening lines of the first Twin Oaks newsletter describes the arrival of the founders, who were all convinced at that stage that their community would be a concrete application of the principles set out by Skinner:

> On June 13 the newly purchased school bus left Washington for Atlanta. It was empty when it left, having had all of its seats removed. It had been painted blue-green and white, in order to comply with a law that prohibits privately owned buses from resembling school buses. On June 16 the bus arrived on the farm, loaded with furniture, appliances, printing presses, household and personal miscellaneous, plus a bee hive, a skunk cage with a skunk inside, and two motorcycles. Skillful packing, plus a small trailer behind one of the cars, did the trick. Those of us who had not gone to Atlanta hurried out to the farm to meet the Atlanta group. The farm was dark when we arrived. The house was locked, the electricity disconnected, which meant no running water as well as no light. The exhausted group located their bedrolls from the midst of their belongings and camped out under the apple trees. And the community began.[8]

There were eight of them embarking on the adventure: Connie and Rudy, George and Kathleen, Susan, Scott, Joseph, and Bud. Despite the intense excitement of getting started, the first problem wasn't long in coming. Bud, who had advanced the money, walked out after clashing with the rest of the group because they refused to elect him as a planner. He would never get to experience the life that his friends were about to invent from scratch. Most of them — and this would also be true of those who joined them later — were students who had given up their studies. Hailing from middle class families, they were driven by a fierce desire to break with the world they had grown up in. They were converts to the values of the counterculture and refused to contemplate a life structured by a standard job in a traditional company. To assert this alternative lifestyle project, should they name the community in explicit reference to *Walden Two*, the model that inspired the core founders? The debates on the subject were heated. Sixteen proposals were soon brought to the table. To avoid attracting curious hordes and ward off systematic comparison with the eponymous book, the eight founders preferred to opt for a more neutral name. Following a suggestion from a neighbour who came to pay a courtesy call, the name chosen was 'Twin Oaks', a nod to the double-trunked tree that stood in pride of place on the property. It was a wise choice, since the vast majority of the young people who would join the community over the months to come had never read Skinner and did not claim to follow him. They did, however, share a common desire for equality.

In June 1967, the small group of founders got organized to make their piece of land fit to live on. To start with, it had a small farmstead, a woodshed, a henhouse, a smokehouse, and some barns. Two months later, the community was ten members strong. They were making rope hammocks, growing tobacco, woodworking, raising pigs, a chicken, and a cow, publishing a newsletter, and welcoming visitors. In some ways, the apprentice farmers were like pigs in clover. Yet living conditions were rudimentary in the first few weeks. They washed at an outdoor tap on the other side on the road that bordered the property. When the weather permitted, many communards slept outside. Otherwise, they took refuge in a barn where they lay on straw mattresses. But even there, they could not escape the mosquitoes, the leaks, or the cold.

The first year at Twin Oaks was also spent feeling their way towards rules for communal living in an atmosphere that was never free of interpersonal tension. Characters and moods did not automatically match. In addition to personality clashes, insufficient involvement always bred suspicion and conflict. In September 1967, the group asked Quincy, who worked too slowly for the others' liking, to leave the community. Sandy, meanwhile, who often got up at noon, didn't much care for the spirit of the place. Drawn more to the hippie world — especially the promise of psychedelic trips — she was the first of the founding group to pack up and go. In November, she announced that she was leaving for Haight-Ashbury in San Francisco. Despite these defections, the group hung on. Soon enough, the organizational backbone that would enduringly sustain Twin Oaks had been put in place. Having discovered the boring and unpleasant nature of compulsory meetings and the inefficiency of consensual decision-making, the communards adopted a model taken straight from *Walden Two*.[9] Three planners were elected in July 1967. They were entrusted with many important tasks, starting with community development. The planners appointed managers to ensure that the many different areas of activity and life at Twin Oaks – hammock making, community health, vegetable gardening, welcoming visitors, and so on – ran smoothly. Finally, an original system of work distribution, also inspired by *Walden Two*, was set up to organize the six hours of work that each person owed the community every day of the week.

The struggle for economic independence

In the months following the founders' arrival, Twin Oaks grew more comfortable. Meals were cooked on gas, the bath water was hot, the fridges were filled with food and the basement shelves were stocked with jars of home-made jam. Music livened up the common rooms and workshops. The community had a telephone, machines for laundry and dishwashing, and two tractors to make the farm work easier.[10] A new building (Harmony) was also constructed in just three months. The Oakers were able to move in in December 1967. Their building skills were more keenly tested when, a while later, they decided to build a dome – a fashionable structure in community circles at the time. The idea was to expand the facilities for the conferences that Twin Oaks wanted to hold on a regular basis. Having found plans in specialist publications, the Oakers made a first unsuccessful attempt to construct the building using wooden posts that they normally reserved for curing tobacco. They then used metal tubes to build the skeleton of the structure. The resulting frame was covered with a polyethylene material. The structure measured '32 feet in diameter, 16 feet high. Originally we meant to make it bigger than that, but a simple arithmetical error forced us to cut the struts shorter than we intended. Moral: When you build a dome, check your multiplication.'[11] Originally intended for conference dinners and storing agricultural equipment (including tractors), the dome, which leaked in heavy rain, ended up housing only a handful of picnic tables and was occasionally used as a refuge for communards wanting a nap.

But amateurism was not the greatest difficulty. The real problem lay elsewhere: despite calls for subscriptions and relentless work (supplemented by the work of visitors who were also required to do their bit), income was scarce in the first few years. Tobacco did not bring in much money. Despite a rustic and frugal lifestyle, in April 1968 the budget was in deficit. Consequently, half of the members had to take outside jobs to fund the common treasury.[12] It would be a year before they could give up their jobs and return to work in the community, particularly making hammocks.[13] At Twin Oaks, 1968 was marked less by the turmoil of outside revolts than by internal tensions, the birth of the community's first baby, and the many arrivals and departures, including that of one of the founders who could no longer stand the poverty he was living in. Fortunately, there were encouraging signs the following year: the community was able to buy ten cows and make a tentative start at raising cattle, and the hammocks began to sell.

By mid-1970, despite taking over a small store near the community, Twin Oaks was once again dependent on the income provided by its outside workers in Richmond. Each member would make the effort for two months at a stretch, then another communard would take over. When Houriet visited Twin Oaks in August, outside workers were providing an annual income of $32,000, that is, half the community's cash flow. In 1972, there were still eight members working outside. To avoid the daily commute, which was both financially and physically costly, four of them lived in the city where they worked during the week. The community gave them $50 to cover food and accommodation costs.[14] By 1972, Twin Oaks was already five years old and had 40 members. Only two of the eight founders still lived there. Yet the material situation had improved considerably. The little farmhouse next to the twin oaks, which had housed the first group of communards at the beginning, had been refurbished. It now had a kitchen, three common rooms, and a bathroom. The community also had other operational buildings. One housed a mechanic shop, a woodworking shop, a printing shop, a hammock workshop, some bedrooms, and a storage area for shared clothes. A second building offered yet more bedrooms, a handful of which were reserved for visitors. In the common room, a large library took pride of place. Outside, extensive gardens were carefully planted and maintained.

Skinner and Twin Oaks: from recognition to divorce

By the early 1970s, when the living conditions at Twin Oaks were finally on a firmer footing, Skinner was at the height of his fame. The psychologist, who had made no secret of his intention to see a true Walden Two community established in the very heart of American capitalism, was aware of Twin Oaks' existence. For several years, he maintained regular contact with the community through several of its members. The first to benefit from the prestigious academic's patronage was Kat Kinkade. Skinner wrote the preface to her 1972 book, *A Walden Two Experiment*. Of the six pages he penned, the psychologist devoted only one, the last, to the Oakers. Twin Oaks, he wrote, was certainly not an exact reflection of *Walden Two*, but the community undeniably owed a lot to many of its constituent principles. There was every indication that Twin Oaks was moving in the right direction.

The community was ready, for example, to raise children according to behaviourist precepts. Better still, the 'world in miniature' that was Twin Oaks invented solutions every day to problems that the rest of the world also faced: food, education, health, culture, and so on. For Skinner, then, Twin Oaks was more than just a local experiment. It was a laboratory for social change in its own right.

A few years later, another link was forged with the community. The opportunity came in August 1976 when the author of *Walden Two* visited Twin Oaks for the very first time. Using the event as a pretext, David Ruth, an Oaker, decided to write a short article intended for publication in *The Leaves of Twin Oaks*.[15] The paper acknowledged the community's initial closeness to the perspectives developed by Skinner but also noted that, since 1972 at least, many 'neophytes' professed total independence from the spirit of *Walden Two*. A test carried out among the current members indicated that the array of beliefs was indeed quite wide, ranging from Marxism to liberalism via Kropotkin-style anarchism. Nonetheless, Ruth continued, Skinner was not indifferent to what was happening at Twin Oaks. He had shown an interest, enthusiasm even, to the point of loaning $2,000 to the community. Which is why, said Ruth, the 14 people who had left the community in the previous six months out of disillusionment may have been a little too quick to throw in the towel. Skinner himself realized that the right approach was not to blindly apply principles taken from the outside. He would say, more precisely, 'that experimentation would lead people to discover the laws that governed their behavior, and that ultimately a utopia would be built which would operate according to the laws so discovered'.[16]

On 2 November 1976, Skinner responded to the article that Ruth had just written before its publication. Everything was perfect. 'I have only one request. If possible delete the point about my loan. I prefer to have that anonymous.'[17] In the subsequent correspondence, Skinner went into more detail about what he had seen and heard during his visit and what he knew more generally about the community. Twin Oaks could be one of the greatest experiments of the 20th century if its members were willing to innovate even further, especially in education. However, Skinner lamented, 'I had the impression that your people were perfectly content with normal familial practices.'[18] Other topics – organizing a conference, preparing a special issue of a sociology journal, exchanging articles and information, making appointments, information about recent events and daily life at Twin Oaks, views on the influence of the kibbutz model on intentional communities – were peppered throughout the regular correspondence between several community members and Skinner.

In 1978, the main business that brought the protagonists together was the preparation of a documentary in which Skinner wanted to involve Twin Oaks. More specifically, it was an episode of the American television programme Nova entitled 'A World of Difference. B.F. Skinner and the Good

Life'. Broadcast in early 1979, the programme presented B.F. Skinner, his life, ideas, experiments, and inventions.[19] The majority of the documentary (36 minutes of the 53-minute run time) was devoted to Twin Oaks. Skinner was filmed on his second visit to the community, which then had 85 members. Viewers learned about the central principles adopted at Twin Oaks in terms of work, economics, education, and community decision-making for living the 'good life'. Never short of references to *Walden Two* or to the psychological principles dear to Skinner, the Oakers were featured in the hammock workshop, the courtyard, and the children's area. Several discussions allowed Skinner to ask the communards questions and to clarify his own views. At the end of the film, the professor reiterated his judgement. Twin Oaks was an extremely stimulating experiment, close in his eyes to *Walden Two*. But in practice, it was still far from reproducing all the options of the paper utopia that had served as its model.

Through this documentary, Twin Oaks unquestionably served as a foil to Skinner. Moreover, he was delighted about it. For him, the most successful part of the programme was the part about the community.[20] The Oakers, who watched the documentary together, also seemed satisfied.[21] They were all the more so given that Skinner gifted them the audio-visual equipment used for the shoot. Even if the psychologist saw room for improvement in the way things were done at Twin Oaks, especially on the education front, he confirmed in his letters that he had no doubt that the Virginia community was more advanced than any other with regard to his behaviourist criteria.

Despite such encouragement from Skinner, in the late 1970s, the Oakers, as we have seen, were by no means all won over to Skinnerian arguments. Kat Kinkade, who did not appear in the 1979 documentary film (she was living in Boston at the time), had noted the extent of the gap early on. In her books, she acknowledged the debt Twin Oaks owed to *Walden Two*. The community was largely inspired by Skinnerian precepts in the beginning. But this influence was subsequently watered down. Rather than taking the long-term gamble that it is possible, through the levers of Skinnerian behaviourism, to build a society in which each person voluntarily and willingly undertakes what they have to do, the community preferred to shore up its organization with at least some structures and rules. For Nexus, a former Oaker, the problem was there from the start.[22] Looking back at the frustrated relationship between Twin Oaks and B.F. Skinner, he reasoned that fulfilling the principles of *Walden Two* was, by definition, an unachievable task. Perhaps, Nexus concluded, we should have placed ourselves under the socialist patronage of E. Bellamy rather than giving in to the scientist siren calls of behaviourist psychology.

The divorce was not solely attributable to the communards. As the years went by, Skinner distanced himself from the community movement. In the mid-1980s, he observed that the collectives initially inspired by *Walden Two* had failed to withstand the hippie wave. In 'News From Nowhere, 1984', Skinner's assessment of the countercultural trend was all the more critical because he did not identify with the libertarian anarchy promoted by young people who wanted to overthrow the established order, rid themselves of economic contingencies, and replace the religion of their families with spiritual mysticism (Skinner, 1987).[23]

Twin Oaks, an American kibbutz?

While B.F. Skinner's influence on the principles and organization of Twin Oaks gradually diminished in the late 1970s and early 1980s, another reference gained ground: the Israeli kibbutzim. The comparison is not incongruous. Founded with a similar utopian aspiration, the aim of the first kibbutzim was to bring the principles of equality and justice to life:

> The kibbutz, originally, is a community where all resources are administered in common. Adult members live in private quarters, while children are usually accommodated in children's houses. Meals are prepared and eaten communally. The members have regular meetings to discuss community matters, to vote on issues requiring decisions, and to elect managers for the various areas of activity. All these features led to the kibbutz of the first decades being described as a communal utopia. (Ben-Rafael, 2018, p 139)

The members of Twin Oaks knew what they were doing when they named one of their buildings – the one for children – after the first kibbutz, Degania, founded in Israel in 1909. Despite this proximity, it was not until the 1970s that the kibbutzim movement attracted any real interest from American communards.

One of the first to broker a link between the US and Israel was Vince Zager, a Twin Oaks member and one of the editors of *Communities*, who visited many kibbutzim in 1975. In Israel, M. Bentov, himself a *kibbutznik*, was developing contacts around the world to publicize his country's experiments and facilitate exchanges between communities. In 1976, he founded the International Communes Desk, which published a small newsletter. In the same year, he invited Kat Kinkade – then a member of the East Wind community – to stay in Israel. Subsequent to her visits, the American communard made the following observation:

> When we founded Twin Oaks in 1967, we already had some notion of the kibbutz, and knew that there was a certain ideological similarity between us. I myself had read the book of Melford Spiro about the kibbutz, and the achievements of these people excited and impressed

me. For years, I thought of writing to them, particularly in order to raise practical questions ... But we never did this, because we thought that the kibbutz would be too busy to bother about us. They, too, knew very little about us. (cited in Oved, 2013, p 284)[24]

Upon her return from Israel, Kinkade put her experience to good use. She first wrote a series of articles on kibbutzim in *Communities*. Eager to offer lessons for North American communities, she was full of praise for the organization she had just discovered, whether in terms of housing, work, or family relations. Together with others, Kinkade founded the Federation of Egalitarian Communities (FEC) in 1978 in reference to and with the help of the Federation of Israeli Kibbutzim. That same year, Twin Oaks hosted a delegation from the Young Zionist Movement. When Allen Butcher (1987) reviewed the FEC's history and foundations after almost a decade of existence, he concluded that before the kibbutzim movement's liberal and individualistic inflection, it had been decisive for the foundation and development of American egalitarian communities. Many of their members had studied the Israeli communities, with a particular focus on their architectural and educational aspects. Several of them had even lived in kibbutzim.

Are the similarity of the founding principles and the exchanges that emerged in the mid-1970s reason enough to support the idea sometimes put forward that, in breaking at least partially with *Walden Two*, Twin Oaks became an American kibbutz? In fact, apart from a few exceptions, past and present Oakers make no reference to kibbutzim in defining their community. Brian, who arrived at Twin Oaks in 2002 after living on Kibbutz Ketura (in the Arava region of Israel) from 1989 to 2001, wrote a short piece to point out the incongruity of equating Twin Oaks with a kibbutz that didn't know it.[25] There are certainly common features between the two types of collective, such as the egalitarian ideology, income sharing, and democratic decision-making processes. But there are also many differences. In Ketura, everyone eats in their own home, all money earned is pooled without exception, the number of days holiday is limited, the functional counterparts of the planners have less influence in decision-making, and so on. Even if, to complete the demonstration, note should be taken of the privatization and differentiation of practices from one kibbutz to another after the crisis of the 1980s, this observation alone is enough to cast doubt on the idea that, having failed to bring *Walden Two* to life, Twin Oaks took on all the trappings of an Israeli community.

What is left of the Walden tradition today?

The myth of the great outdoors and the glorification of radical individualism still figure prominently in the American social imaginary. This is probably one of the reasons why H.D. Thoreau's name has not been forgotten by his compatriots. Though his 'eccentric paradoxes' (Granger, 1994) may be puzzling to some, there is no denying that the practices and ideas of the leader of the 'Walden Pond Society' have never left people indifferent. From the outset, for instance, *Walden* has interested those seeking to lend legitimacy to the environmentalist arguments that have gained increasing currency over the years. So what about *Walden Two*, one of the key references for the world of North American intentional communities in the late 1960s and early 1970s? It is safe to say that Skinner's *Walden Two* has not stood the test of time as well as Thoreau's *Walden*. The Harvard professor's personality and contested theories have doubtless played a part in that. Noam Chomsky (1973), for one, has methodically pointed out the contradictions in Skinner's writings and assertions.[26]

In 1999, *Communities* magazine published a special issue entitled 'Walden Two communities: Where are they now?' The issue's editors went some way to restoring the image of *Walden Two*'s creator. Specifically, they noted that if Skinner's writings were successful in the US, they were also influential in Canada, Mexico, and Ireland. Yet it could hardly be called a tidal wave. Only a small handful of communities could, at some point in their history, lay claim to a behaviourist heritage. Most had now disappeared or abandoned any reference to *Walden Two*. Kat Kinkade, a contributor to this special issue of *Communities*, admitted having had a real epiphany when she read Skinner's book, to the point of even falling in love with Frazier, the community's leader. 'I recognized him as the man I had always wanted. There he was, mentally brilliant and emotionally warm, given his life to something worth doing and succeeding in bringing about a community where I wanted to live. I wanted him for my life partner.' (Kinkade, 1999, p 49). As the months and years passed, the emotional shock wore off. In the end, time got the better of the initial enthusiasm for *Walden Two*.

In her article in *Communities*, Kinkade also enumerated many areas of disagreement with Skinner. She did not hold back in pointing out his errors of judgement. The professor was too radical in his approach to the education of young children, he underestimated the importance of the women's movement and had not foreseen the sexual revolution, he was far too optimistic in believing that four hours of work a day would be enough to sustain a community, and he was totally ignorant of economic matters, and so on. And yet, wrote Kinkade, without *Walden Two*, Twin Oaks would not have existed. It owed many practices to Frazier. The most decisive influence of the behaviourist utopia was no doubt the principle of equality, to which the Harvard professor had managed to give a concrete social form. 'For me and for Twin Oaks, the vision of *Walden Two* has died, but when it was alive, it did good things! Thank you, Skinner, for writing the book that inspired us. Bless you, *Walden Two*, and rest in peace' (Kinkade, 1999, p 52).

3

The Why and How
of Community Involvement

Dear Mr Skinner,

I really don't know how to start this letter except, perhaps to say, I just finished reading *Walden Two*. I'm sure you are a terribly busy man, so I'll make this as brief as possible. I'm tired of commercialism, sexism, and all the other facets of this society which seem to be causing its ruin. I'm tired of 'nine to five', and the need to use alcohol, nicotine and caffeine to relieve the pressures of a life that seems so fruitless, compared to the life depicted in your novel. I'm a willing worker, but there must be more to my life than just a pay check. I most sincerely feel that I'd love to live in a planned community, and I've given this great consideration. However, I know of no planned communities, and this is where I hope you can help me. I would not trouble you if I knew of any other way to obtain this information. Could you possibly send me the names and locations of some planned communities with whom I could correspond? Thank you so much.[1]

This letter, to which Skinner replied with advice to contact Twin Oaks, gives a fairly good illustration of the existential malaise felt by many of the young people who decided to change lifestyles and settle in intentional communities from the mid-1960s onwards.

Seeking refuge in a self-contained world that is nonetheless embedded in the society from which one is fleeing is no trivial choice. Those who make such a decision share a desire to distance themselves from what they variously call 'the straight world', 'the real world', 'the outside world', 'the big world' or 'mainstream society'. In the following pages, my first aim is to explain more precisely such a desire to withdraw, to find out who feels it, and to account for the choice to live in community. My second objective is to highlight the various organizational strategies that the sustainability of such a commitment depends on. For this chapter and those that follow, Twin Oaks, and to a lesser extent Acorn, will serve as my main fields of investigation.

White, middle class, and educated

Who chooses community life? A survey conducted at Twin Oaks in the late 1960s yielded two findings: the average age of the 40 members was 23.5 years old, and the communards generally had two years of university education. The more focused group portrait that Kat Kinkade paints in *A Walden Two Experiment* (1972) provides some additional but, sadly, rather scattered and discreet indications. Of the 12 members mentioned (seven men and five women), more than half had attended university, one was the son of a clergyman, and two had lived on a farm. A handful of them used drugs and two had behavioural problems.

From her observations at the turn of the 1970s to 1980s, Ingrid Komar (1983, pp 69–70) compiled a fairly comprehensive list of profiles of the candidates for membership whom she stayed with at Twin Oaks:

> many visiting students and teachers, gays (for whom special outreach efforts were made), a divorced secretary, nurses, psychologists, a middle-aged woman street poet, a retired bookkeeper who was a fruitarian, activists from Boston, a young working-class Italian-American from the Bronx, folks from Atlanta, Georgia, Iowa, and California, a Polish-born set designer who was raised on a Midwestern family farm, a Quaker, a feminist journalist, a retired engineer turned mystic, physically disadvantaged people, a female computer programmer, an ex-WAC, and a young man just discharged from the Navy who had served on a nuclear submarine. A good many of these visitors became members.

While the average age of the Oakers was around 20 in the late 1960s, Komar adds, by the early 1980s it had risen to around 30.

My observations and discussions support the preceding information. At both Twin Oaks and Acorn, the vast majority of those I spoke to described their parents' status with reference to occupations typically associated with the middle class: managers, shopkeepers, military personnel, teachers, translators, journalists, computer specialists, and the like. Informal conversations also confirmed that, much more so than in the 1970s, the communards had finished high school and gone to college. The range of occupations that some had worked in before moving to Twin Oaks or Acorn included many service activities, particularly care work: health care, therapy of all kinds, teaching, social work, the non-profit sector, the book trade, etc. Environment-related jobs and, in a slightly different vein, IT jobs had also been popular with members of both communities.

Finally, few members of either community do not have white skin. Without being able to differentiate between everyone's ethnic origins, I can only draw one certainty on this point from spending time with the members of Twin Oaks and Acorn: during my two visits, I counted three black people in the first community and only one in the second. In *Is It Utopia Yet?*, Kat Kinkade (1994) addressed this problem of massive over-representation of white people. She endorsed the hypothesis put forward by the only black person living at Twin Oaks in the early 1990s: the community's prevailing practices and norms (occasional nudity, sloppy dress, unkempt and sometimes unclean housing, small families, etc.) are at odds with those valued by most black people, which hardly entices them to try community life. In the early 2000s, the community considered the issue again.[2] It reached the conclusion that it is difficult for people of colour to conform to the dominant culture at Twin Oaks, which translates for example into an obligation to avoid loud, vehement talk, not to express extreme emotions, and to favour vegetarian or vegan food. Well aware of the problem, the collective resolved to take action to fix it ... yet without knowing what concrete measures to adopt.

The imperative to attract and select new members

Although the above findings indicate that certain social conditions may predispose people to retreat from mainstream society, integrating into a community is never automatic. Moreover, it is not enough to want to be a communard to become one straight away. The vast majority of collectives based on an intentional model decide whether or not they want to accept new people. The Oakers debated early on how members would be admitted. Should the door always be open to whoever wants to join, or should there be a selection and, if so, based on what criteria? In the pioneering period, Kinkade (1973) admits, any candidate was accepted. It was enough to pay $200 as an entrance fee. And even then, the founding group waived this rule for the first four new recruits because they didn't have the money. Over the years, with the community's growing success, the vetting became more selective. Specifying certain norms and preferences – the prohibition of drug use, the tendency towards a scientific and pragmatic approach to human behaviour, the value placed on the quality of everyday interactions, the choice to share all resources, and so on – was in itself sometimes enough to dissuade applicants whose minds were not yet made up.

But the self-selection of potential candidates did not suffice; the community had to be able to select actively. In the early 1970s, after a candidate had spent two weeks in the community, each member of Twin Oaks completed a short questionnaire with two blocks of questions, the first to find out their degree of affinity with the applicant, the second to assess the conditions in which they could join. In this way, a score could be derived for each applicant. Below a certain score, the application was rejected outright. This was the case for five people in the few years that the questionnaire was used systematically. Quite quickly, however, the system posed a problem for those who considered it impossible to get to know someone in just two weeks and who, at the same time, maintained that living in a community could shift the attitudes of people who were willing to make a radical change in their way of life.

Since this pioneering period, other systems – internships, residencies, exchanges, visits, and more – have been tested and are now commonly used at Twin Oaks, Acorn, and elsewhere, to attract new members and increase the collective work force. At Twin Oaks, the visit is now a prerequisite before applying for membership. The system is particularly well-oiled and structured. To become a visitor, interested persons have to write a letter of introduction, on which basis the community decides whether or not to welcome them. As of the mid-2010s, visits last three weeks. They are scheduled from February to November, which means that there are about ten periods per year during which visitors (there are six on average in each session) take part, equally or thereabouts, in the many events and activities that shape the daily life of the community. They get help finding their feet from the Community Visitor Program (CVP), a small group consisting of at least two full members. The CVP's mission is to offer newcomers guidance and direction, answer their questions, and help them solve any problems, material or otherwise. Finally, since 2008, information and orientation meetings – Viz Oreos in local parlance – have been integrated into the visitors' schedule to provide them with information on such crucial topics as the organization of work and the Twin Oaks education programme, community government, the values and forms of commitment it upholds, and so on.

In the late 1980s, a short visitors' guide described the community's attitude towards those it hosted in the hope of recruiting them:

> In some ways, Twin Oaks is like a small rural town, where strangers are seen as interesting, but not easily accepted as friends, or invited to join activities. It takes time to get to know someone. On the other hand, since every visitor is a potential member, it is crucial that we get to know them, so we try to make them feel as comfortable and accepted as possible, and we try to open ourselves enough to let them get to know us. But with over 500 visitors per year it is easy to burn out on reaching out to new people.[3]

These few words sum up the paradoxical nature of the visits. They are essential to ensure the community's sustainability. But it is not always easy for members to spend their daily lives with newcomers whom they don't have time to get used to. In 1987, to overcome this problem, a rule of conduct (which no longer existed in 2016) stipulated that visitors should arrive at meals ten minutes late. That way, members did not face the awkward situation of having lunch at a table mostly occupied by visitors whom they do not necessarily want to get to know. Conversely, to avoid being isolated, visitors had to ask permission to join one of the groups of members that had already formed for the duration of the meal.

Visitor at Twin Oaks

22 April 2016, 1.43 pm. I get off the train from Washington at Charlottesville station. The weather is perfect for my first day as a visitor at Twin Oaks. After an hour's wait, a minibus arrives in the car park. At the wheel, Brynn, a young woman with cropped grey hair and a long green linen dress, drives around the small town picking up the new arrivals and the few Oakers who had decided to take a turn outside the community. Once the whole group is finally present, it takes us about 40 minutes to reach Twin Oaks. There, I get acquainted with the other visitors. The most voluble among us is Ruth: 28 years old, short hair, glasses, a tattoo on her thigh. A native of Baltimore, she is currently an art student. 25-year-old Troy has just graduated with a degree in agricultural engineering. Born in San Francisco, he was a member of a student co-op in Davis, California. Peter, in his mid-forties, serves – along with myself – as senior visitor. This rugged fellow with a cowboy hat permanently perched atop his salt-and-pepper hair is also from San Francisco. An arborist by trade, he is married and has lived in many communities in the US and around the world. Jake, 23, attracts attention for his style of dress. He is the only one wearing a work shirt (with the Amoco logo), smart trousers, and sturdy shoes. He quickly tells us that he comes from an Amish community an hour's drive from here. After leaving school at the age of 14, he specialized in construction and distanced himself a little from his community. Abey, lastly, is as young as Jake. This frail-looking young woman from Maryland had started environmental studies at university but soon dropped out. Since then, she has been on the road, occasionally going back to stay with her parents, both of whom are geographers in a government agency, then leaving again, her activist beliefs (for animal rights in particular) stronger than ever.

After the introductions, Seane, a man in his sixties with a boyish physique, long white hair held back in a coloured headband, a torn, mismatched shirt, and glasses on a leash, takes the group of newcomers in hand. He leads us to the small wooden house, Aurora, which serves as a visitors' residence. After giving some practical instructions, Seane leaves us to look around the house: a small common room with a wood-burning stove, six spartan bedrooms, and two bathrooms. The new group that we form meets the next morning to set the rules for living together. Clearly, all the visitors have a basic grounding in anarchist culture. We start by agreeing on how to discuss things and make decisions: a moderator will lead the discussions, we will use hand signals to complement the verbal exchanges (for example, to show agreement with the speaker, we simply raise a hand, place it horizontally and wiggle our fingers), and we will use fist to five[4] to reach a consensus as quickly as possible. Once the communication methods have been agreed on, we discuss noise, cleaning, heating, nudity, bathrooms, toilets, and so on. The rules we adopt are then posted on the wall.

The next day Seane gives us a grand tour of Oaker territory. It takes three hours. The area that Twin Oaks occupies has almost tripled since the first land was acquired. In 2016, the community has 350 acres. The property forms a vague rectangle into which a wedge of the neighbouring land intrudes to the south-west. To the north, a road and a river (the South Anna River) separate the community from the outside world; to the south, a tarmac road alone does the job. The main entrance is on the north side. Two small parallel paths lead off the road. The first runs alongside the community's large gardens, passes the milking buildings to its left and arrives at a car park. The second and most used path skirts the gardens to the west and leads to another parking area adjacent to the historic heart of Twin Oaks: the central courtyard. There, four buildings enclose a broad expanse of impeccably maintained lawn. The area is brightened up with colourful flowerbeds and fruit trees hung with an array of hammocks.

Seane, our guide for the day, tells us the name and function of each of the buildings that line the central courtyard. Llano, a little white farmhouse that the first Oakers lived in when they arrived on their land, stands next to the twin oak tree that inspired the community's name. The building houses a kitchen, offices, and some other functional rooms. Facing Llano is Ta Chai, where part of the ground floor is also reserved for administrative offices. But Ta Chai is mostly frequented by those who come to work in the hammock weaving shop. The adjacent room (named TCLR, for Ta Chai Living Room) is used for parties and other occasional events (sports classes, meditation workshops, and so on). The first floor is made up of bedrooms. Oneida, a third large two-storey building, also wooden, has no offices or workshops. A collection of bedrooms, common rooms, and bookshelves that spill out into the corridors, it is inhabited by women only.[5] Moreover, after 6 pm, men are not allowed to enter. The last important building is Harmony. As well as more bedrooms and more bookshelves, this collective living space is partly given over to a laundry room and a woodwork shop. In a corner of the courtyard, a small hut called the Compost Café serves as a meeting place for the smokers.

Once the presentation of this historic centre of the community is over, we leave the central courtyard by a small path that separates the carpentry workshop from a dozen or so clotheslines where shirts and underwear are hung out to dry. "Don't forget to write your name on a piece of paper with the things you hang up," Seane explains as we walk past. "Otherwise, anyone can come along and help themselves." After this warning, the old communard leads us along a path about 100 metres long lined with barns that have several functions, but which seem to be used primarily to pile up miscellaneous materials. Below, towards the west, we glimpse a pond with its beach and sauna. A few minutes later, we reach a small square dominated by Modern Times, a residential building and repair shop for motor vehicles. Aurora, the visitors' house, is just a few dozen metres away, a little further east. We quickly continue our circuit southwards. We are now walking through undergrowth that we will remain in until the end of our tour. From where we are, it takes about 15 minutes of brisk walking to reach the southern end of the property.

Before we head there, Seane leads us to the small tofu factory, a building of about 300 square metres located right next to Zhankoye – ZK in local parlance[6] – the real heart of the community. This enormous building is fitted with two kitchens – a large one for preparing communal meals and a small one for individual use – and common rooms including two dining rooms. ZK is where all the Oakers meet for lunch and dinner. It is also where all the written information necessary for the community to run smoothly is displayed. Two types of noticeboard are mainly used. The first operates with standard sheets of white paper where members and visitors provide detailed information, give their opinion on a problem, and so on. The second uses small three-by-five-inch cards (the 3×5s) on which people write short notices (to announce an event, request a service, announce someone's upcoming arrival at Twin Oaks, etc.) that do not call for comments. The system is like a group email *avant la lettre*. The cards are slid into horizontal rails fixed at head height on large wooden boards attached to the walls. Each of the ten rows can hold about 20 cards. New messages are always posted on the left. They then automatically slide to the right as new information is added to the noticeboard. Such a device makes it easy to get a panopticon view of current news and to figure out when it was posted.

On leaving ZK, we take the central path through the woods of the property. After a few dozen metres, we see Morning Star on our right. Like Oneida or Harmony, it is a small living group (SLG), that is, a communal living space with around 15 bedrooms, a kitchen, and common rooms. A few metres from Morning Star, a large two-storey wooden building that we walk through at a brisk pace, stands Degania, Twin Oaks' school. We visit the other SLGs, all at least 100 metres apart, which mark out the territory of Twin Oaks. Like the previous ones, they are all named after famous communities.

The south of the property is named Emerald City in reference to the Wizard of Oz.[7] When we get there, the noise of the machines makes it clear that this is a workplace. The ropes and wood for the hammocks and chairs woven at Twin Oaks are made here, in two workshops adjacent to a huge warehouse where the products are stored, ready for the community to send around the world. A sawmill and a greenhouse complete the scene of this small piece of industrial land buried in the woods. "So that's Twin Oaks," Seane concludes at the end of the tour. "This is where you will live and work with us for the next three weeks. And maybe longer after that …" At the end of our stay, only two of us go on to apply for membership: Troy and Jake.

For those who want to take the plunge, there are precise rules that we soon learn. Visitors who would like to become Oakers should make it known a few days before the end of their stay by posting a letter in the ZK dining hall to all members of the community. The latter are then free to speak with the candidates. Next, each candidate attends a formal interview with the Community Member Team (CMT), a committee of six members who ask them about their lives, their background, their motivations, and their plans. Nearly 90 questions are asked during what is, effectively, an entrance exam.[8] After the CMT has given its opinion, all the members meet to decide whether to accept the candidate's application (formally, no percentage of votes is required for a positive response), to request a second visit, or to reject the request to join. Although important, the meetings to discuss membership applications attract only half the community at best.[9] In 2016, Sunia, a woman in her early twenties, told our group of visitors that she had been accepted with the consent of barely a third of the members. On the day, 25 people voted yes, with one person objecting on the grounds that she had been seen with her phone clamped to her ear. It is rare, Sunia added, for a candidate to be rejected. Finally, when a request to join is accepted, the candidate must spend at least one month away from Twin Oaks before returning. This rule is designed to give the new recruit time to consider their decision. At the end of this short period of absence, if the future communard confirms their commitment, they are placed on a waiting list, which varies in length depending on the period and the rooms available. Once they move in to the community, the new Oaker has a provisional membership status for six months. At the end of this long probationary period, if the community does not object, they may become full members.

Anarchist Acorn

6 June 2017. A little over a year after my stay at Twin Oaks, here I am again at Charlotteville Station, but this time on a visit to Acorn. 10.30 am: a car drives up and parks next to the small building that houses the ticket offices and the waiting room. It is my driver, a boy of about 20 with shoulder-length hair. I am the only passenger. Without further ado, we set off for 80 kilometres of fast roads, green landscapes, and snatches of conversation. Once we arrive at Acorn, the young man who drove me shows me the bathroom and the building where I can hope to find a bed to sleep in. Then

he disappears without a word. I won't talk to him again until the end of my stay. Fortunately, I already know the place a little, having spent a day there when I was a visitor at Twin Oaks. Like Twin Oaks, Acorn is a rural community, with part of its land given over to forest and part devoted to agriculture. The total area is about 72 acres.

Acorn is close to Twin Oaks in two respects. First, geographically – the two communities are only ten kilometres apart. Their histories are also intertwined, as Acorn's birth certificate, published in the Twin Oaks newsletter of January 1993, makes clear:

> We are moving forward with our new community. We have people: several Twin Oakers, several people from Twin Oaks' waiting list, people we met during September's communities conference, and others who have heard of Acorn by word of mouth. We have money: Twin Oaks is lending Acorn up to $250,000 to buy land, materials for the first big building, and miscellaneous other stuff we'll need. Some members may have saving to lend as well. We have available work: Twin Oaks will provide some work, and most Acorn members have marketable skills and/or job experience.[10]

Ira – a black woman born in 1948 and the only founding member still living at Acorn – confirms these details in the many discussions I have with her during my stay there. "About ten of us started the project. At first, the idea was to call the community 'The Blue Heron'. Then we settled on Acorn. It's an allusion. Acorn is the seed of the oak."[11] The early stages of the community were not unlike those of Twin Oaks.[12] During the first days of occupancy, the water from the pump was brown and undrinkable. They had to go to Twin Oaks to fill buckets with the precious liquid. Upon closer inspection, the newcomers discovered that the entire wastewater disposal system needed to be replaced.[13] Furthermore, the main building was very poorly insulated, which made heating a serious problem. But thanks to the members' experience and the Oakers' support, the community made rapid progress settling in. A functional building with 20 bedrooms and numerous common areas was soon ready for use. The garden supplied an abundance of fruit and vegetables. When a young woman died by suicide in her bedroom, the group's morale plummeted.[14] It picked up again thanks to the heavy consumption of potatoes, corn, melons, and raspberries. Singing, poker games, and time set aside to get to know each other better quickly improved the group's cohesion. Morale was also maintained through efficient work. The Acorners made 250 hammocks a month, contributed to tofu production at Twin Oaks, supplemented the collective kitty with some work outside the community, raised chickens, cultivated their fields and gardens, and so on. By the winter of 1993, less than a year after moving in, the Acorn population had already doubled in size to 21 communards, with almost perfect gender parity.

When the community opens its doors to me in June 2017 – not, strictly speaking, as a visitor but as a volunteer willing to offer time and energy – the number of members has barely risen. This is the first major difference with Twin Oaks, where the population is four times larger than at Acorn. On the day I arrive, I immediately notice a second difference. The organization is much less structured. This means, for example, that no tours are planned to welcome visiting sympathizers. So on the day of my arrival, I have to fend for myself. I spend the afternoon introducing myself to people and trying to find a place to sleep. This will be in 'the rack', a small white house with six wooden bunks like those found on boats. With my bed secured, I set off to explore. Since 1993, the community's main gathering point has been Heartwood, a large two-storey house. There, a large ground floor opens onto two kitchens of unequal size, followed in succession by a dining room, five bedrooms, and a bathroom. The kitchen area is – more so than at Twin Oaks – the realm of felt pens and tape. As I will soon realize when tidying up or preparing a meal, labelling things is a simple, albeit demanding, way of avoiding misunderstandings about who owns an object, where to put it or look for it, or what a food is. The first floor of Heartwood has more bedrooms and a common room crammed with benches, books, computers, board games, and other paraphernalia. In front of the house is a wooden deck that makes an ideal observation point. Standing, or even sitting in the rope chair where people like to come and swing, you barely need to turn your head to take in the grassy area between Heartwood and the car park, the many community gardens and, to the left, the majestic Seeds Business Office.

This colourful building is entirely dedicated to the seed business that Acorn specializes in. Here, the precious seeds are stored in a dedicated space kept consistently cool, the packets are prepared, and young plants are packed in batches to meet orders from all over the world. Inside, the commercial offices are adjacent to the workshops. On the first floor, a common room leads to several single bedrooms. It takes no more than a few minutes to walk from the Seeds Business Office to a small white colonial-style building, the farmhouse. This was the first to be built on the property. A few communards still live there.[15] A forest path separates this dwelling from a pond where, like H.D. Thoreau and the Oakers, the Acorners like to swim. The property takes on a different aspect when the visitor retraces their steps and goes around the back of the seed building. On the day of my arrival, I discover a blue two-storey building, freshly built and as yet unfinished. It is intended to house offices, bedrooms, and a music studio. The house is next to an above-ground swimming pool, a campfire area, a smokers' hut, and the 'rack' where I will spend my nights with four others. A little further on, an old barn, uninhabited and partly dilapidated, serves as a permanent storage shed.

Several dozen metres away, at the end of a large grassy area, a large covered stage has been set up. There the communards put on shows and concerts, watch films together on a big screen, challenge each other to video game tournaments, and so on.

It takes me barely another 15 minutes to finish the tour of the property. Once I enter the undergrowth on the edge of which Heartwood was built, I successively come across a caravan occupied by a young woman, washing lines, piles of firewood and, much further on, six treehouses (built in 2009) and some faded tents. These makeshift abodes are also inhabited. A few hundred metres away, the community keeps a dozen pigs, as many goats, and chickens that I don't manage to count with any accuracy. In the days following my arrival, I quickly understand that the difference in size between Acorn and Twin Oaks has multiple implications. Not only is the community I have just moved into able to dispense with the bureaucratic rules of its older counterpart in favour of a much less formal, more flexible anarchist organization, but the everyday interactions are also very different. Here, contact is more frequent and intense. To my great pleasure, this really reduces the distrust of visitors. During my stay, the procedure for becoming a member was similar to the one at Twin Oaks. At Acorn, after a three-week visit prior to making an official application, the candidate had to go away for ten days while the community decided on the matter. If the answer was yes, they became a provisional member for one year. In 2018, the rules changed. Now, after a visit that can last up to six months, depending on the candidate's goodwill, each Acorner gives their opinion. Three choices are available: 'excited', 'accept' or 'have reservations'. To be accepted, at least half of the votes must be 'excited', bearing in mind that a 'have reservations' automatically cancels out an 'excited'.

Candidates for community withdrawal

Research on concrete utopias, whether conducted in France or in the US, sometimes fails to satisfy those who want to know why, at some point in their lives, young people choose to withdraw into community. As I suggested earlier, historical context, social background, and relative frustration are useful in shedding light on the nature and meaning of such choices. But do these parameters always prove heuristic when tested against material of sufficient granularity to move beyond the general diagnoses that all too often litter the specialist literature on communities? To answer this question, I analysed the content of 289 letters of application to Twin Oaks written between 1981 and 1993.[16] In most of the documents, the applicants give an account – usually extremely positive – of the three weeks they spent in the community, explain what enthused them, and talk about the values they share with Twin Oaks and the activities they would like to engage in if they are accepted. Finally, they explain what they will be doing during the obligatory break before they return to Twin Oaks.

Although the letters are not equally effective at answering the questions that most concern the community (who are the applicants? Why do they want to come and live at Twin Oaks?), there is much to be gleaned from them. The first set of information concerns the candidates' profiles: 47 per cent of the letters were written by women and 53 per cent by men. Their average age, regardless of gender, is about 32.5.[17] Most of the candidates were born and raised in the US. There are nonetheless some foreigners: nine Canadians, nine West Germans, two people born in the UK, two French, and one Swiss. Most of the US citizens come from the northeast of the country (65 per cent of those who indicated their geographical origins), including Illinois, Massachusetts, New York City, New Jersey, Maryland, and Washington DC, with Virginia paradoxically remaining a very small source of applicants for Oaker status (3 per cent). To the west, California alone provides 14 per cent of applicants. The overwhelming majority of the prospective communards were born and lived in urban areas. Another notable fact is that of the 289 letters, only one mentions that its author is black.

The other information contained in this epistolary sample confirms certain classic hypotheses and calls for others. First, it is apparent that Twin Oaks is still dominated by the middle classes. As one might therefore assume, just as in the early 1970s and the mid-2010s, the vast majority of the communard applicants are university educated, much more so than the average American of their generations. The figures obtained from the letters cannot be taken as accurate, but they do provide indications that are worth considering. Of the 80 letter writers who mention the subject, 55 per cent studied social sciences (anthropology, psychology, education, history, social work, women's studies, etc.), 20.5 per cent studied philosophy, literature, or art, 13 per cent opted for science subjects (mathematics, environmental studies) and only 3 per cent studied law or economics. In the letters that specify the degree courses taken, almost one in five mentions having dropped out of the programme.

What about the occupations of the applicants at the time they applied to Twin Oaks? Not everyone in the sample provides precise information on the subject, but the number of those who do (about a quarter) gives some idea of the distribution of social profiles: 40 per cent are specialized in human services (social work, health professions, teaching, etc.), 25 per cent work for companies (as computer specialists, consultants, managers, sales representatives, etc.), 13 per cent are students, a little over 10 per cent state that they have had a series of odd jobs without qualifications (waiter, semi-skilled worker, driver, delivery person, salesperson, etc.), and just under 10 per cent are artists. The few remaining people report trade experience as carpenters, electricians, or in the food trade.

Presenting arguments, justifying them

Whether the applicants are young or not so young, the motivations given in the application letters are similar. Several typical arguments come up regularly. The first is based on a critique of urban life as being too stressful and oppressive. In the candidates' eyes, the rural environment has all the opposite advantages: beauty, tranquillity, harmony, respect for fauna and flora, a natural pace of life, a direct relationship with the land ... all these advantages which H.D. Thoreau would certainly not have denied are mentioned in one letter after another. 'I can't say enough how lucky you all are to live here. The beauty of the land is something that it is easy to take for granted, but it is something that affects me daily and distinguishes my time, my feelings in a consistent way', writes Charlotte. 'That is one of the biggest reasons I would want to come here to live and I think I could be happy here (far away from the things of man).'[18]

Work, too, is systematically discussed to justify the desire to become an Oaker. No candidate condemns work. On the contrary, they all believe that working is important; that is why they long to be rid of the way work is organized in the outside world. The air of the capitalist world is so tainted that there is little use changing jobs or employment when these prove unpleasant. 'I'm looking for a more honest and open atmosphere', writes Cathy.[19] Twin Oaks is the ideal place. The interesting nature of the work is another asset:

> Regardless of my sex or skills I could conceivably 'work' at things that I really enjoy: gardening, cooking, bread baking, maybe forestry, woodshop or the saw mill some day. People here are supportive and try hard to cooperate to make things work. It's refreshing over what mainstream society offers – competition and a get-ahead mentality.[20]

The possibility of matching fundamental values (equality, rejection of racism and sexism, feminism, the sharing economy, respect for the environment) with everyday practices is the third argument put forward in many applications. The quality of interpersonal relations (the chance to form many friendships, respect for each person's singularity, and so on) completes the rhetorical arsenal used in many documents. Significantly, nearly one in five letters use the word 'home' or, slightly less frequently, 'family' to describe Twin Oaks and its atmosphere.

Despite this apparent optimism, a close reading of the letters reveals that many applications are submitted against a backdrop of disappointment and disillusionment. As in the early 1970s, many prospective communards profess to be engaged in activities that involve an untenable contradiction. Often coloured with a strong vocational tone, their projects (caring, educating, helping, facilitating, supporting) had quickly run up against demands to control, sort, count, and so on that were incompatible with their ethics and their appetite for autonomy, versatility, and creativity. 'I really enjoyed the work in the hospital, spesialy [sic] with old people', wrote a candidate for Twin Oaks in 1983, 'but always I had the feeling not to have enough freedom. Every mornings I had to go to the same working place and I totaly [sic] disliked the hierarchy.'[21]

Time, however, has done more than just entrench the old critiques. As a result of the economic crisis, the community model is also becoming a response to the social damage wrought by liberalism. In the application letters of the early 1990s, the theme of economic security appeared. 'I can do a variety of work, and work I enjoy, such as organic farming (my most recent job, which I loved) and still be financially secure. Financial security isn't easy to come by at minimum wage.'[22] When I talk to Damian, one of the young communards I live with in the rack at Acorn, he explains that he finished high school but did not want to go to university. "I had to do something. So I started looking at communities to try and find a job and a place to live. That's how I ended up here. And I don't think I'm the only one."[23] As a community trainee, Damian does not know what the future holds for him. At a time when Donald Trump is pushing for social spending cuts, the young man at least has room and board.

Detaching from the wider world

Jonathan, a cartoonist specialized in depicting everyday life at Twin Oaks, showed the world as the Oakers see it on paper.[24] At the bottom of the picture is a close-up of Twin Oaks with its buildings and land. The South Anna River appears just above, meandering from left to right. As in the classic utopias of Thomas More and William Morris, it separates the community from the rest of the world. Cross the river and one immediately sets foot on outside territory. Right next to the river, Jonathan placed Acorn and the small town of Louisa side by side, with Charlottesville not far away. On the left, an arrow points towards Richmond, on the right towards Ganas, a famous intentional community in New York. A little further up, after crossing the Blue Ridge Mountains, two other communities (East Wind and Sand Hill) have taken up residence. To convey a sense of distance, the young illustrator first mentions Mexico, California, and Oregon. Next come the Pacific Ocean and Hawaii. Lastly, on the horizon, China, Japan, and the former USSR hover near the clouds.

This drawing alone speaks volumes about how communards view the world, at Twin Oaks and elsewhere. Such a 'di-vision' (Bourdieu, 1980) maps the social space in a binary way: the community versus outside society. In his study on culture among the working classes, Richard Hoggart (1958) pointed out that to strengthen their identity and cohesion, most social groups split the world in two. In the English working classes, the 'them' that is opposed to 'us' is 'a composite dramatic figure, the chief character in modern urban forms of the rural peasant-big house relationships' (Hoggart, 1958, p 53). For the American communards in Virginia, this 'them' is chiefly symbolized by city people. Engaged in an absurd race for productivity and consumption, the urban population is fettered by individualism, competition, warmongering, waste, and superficiality. The communards contrast this model with a lifestyle that differs in every respect. In this way, they construct a collective identity – an image of an 'us' that tends to obscure internal differences and tensions. The construction and maintenance of such a two-tier representation depends on a process of detachment and attachment without which, as R.M. Kanter (1972) has shown, communities cannot hope to mobilize their members over the long term.

First, detachment. In the array of representations that the communards at Twin Oaks share in order to make sense of their commitments and their collective identity, urban capitalism plays a central role. It acts as a foil in the same way as Satan did in the imaginary of the Puritan sectarians of yesteryear. On the odd occasion when Ingrid Komar, ex-Oaker and author of *Living the Dream* (1983), left Twin Oaks for the nearest small town, she wondered 'how people could live happily in those little row houses confined by their neatly drawn property lines. I was sure the children playing listlessly with their pathetic, plastic toys on squared-off plots of lawn must be bored and lonely' (p. 131). The Oakers adopt and share such a representation all the more readily given that when they first enter the community, they are already largely predisposed to rejecting mainstream values. The application letters I presented earlier are full of phrases denouncing the absurdity and harmfulness of the straight world. One example among many others of such a repudiation: 'Society, the hustle, bustle of everyday life, plus major parts of our population living individually, not connecting, not communicating, not caring, just more isolation.'[25]

At both Twin Oaks and Acorn, many choices and practices of greater or lesser consequence maintain the communards' detachment from mainstream society on a daily basis. The first of these has historically been to cut themselves off from television – a medium that pumps out so much of what are felt to be highly questionable images and discourses. Neither Twin Oaks nor Acorn has subscriptions to any TV channels. Yet as can be seen at Twin Oaks, the arrival of the internet has disrupted the way all intentional communities relate to the media universe. The special issue of *Communities* magazine ('Technology: Friend or Foe?', 2014) dedicated to communication technologies shows that, when it comes to assessing developments in this area, opinions differ. Provided that people do not get addicted, some see the internet as a prime resource for disseminating information about intentional communities and topics usually ignored by mainstream TV and radio, for fighting injustice and discrimination, for keeping in touch with distant friends, and so on. Others, however, resist, either by denouncing the pernicious effects of intensive computer use on interpersonal relationships and on the environment, or by striving for a life free of any dependence on fossil fuels and consumerism.

A second way that communards mark their rejection of mainstream society is to divest themselves of attributes that blatantly symbolize its values. For instance, no communard, at Twin Oaks, Acorn, or elsewhere, wears expensive clothing or jewellery, although it is possible to own them. No one wears make-up, except at festive events or, discreetly, by wearing coloured nail varnish to assert an identity free of the gender binary. No one owns a gun in either of the two Virginia communities. Moreover, any episode of physical violence ends with the offender's almost immediate eviction. Throughout its history, Twin Oaks has constantly condemned the use of nuclear weapons, sexism, ruthless ambition, and the typically mainstream domination of those who, because they talk too much, crush others under the weight of their certainties:

> Not leaving enough air space to allow the quiet, hesitant types to speak is a worse offense than loading up one's plate with seconds at the steam table before everyone has had time to get a first helping. Forget the recipes for popularity in the TV commercials. No one at Twin Oaks will reject you if your deodorant fails, or even if some of your digestive processes become audible. On the other hand, if you have an incurable habit of interrupting people – do not bother to apply for membership. (Komar, 1983, p 59)

Detachment requires more than a capacity to be moved by the dysfunctions and perversities of mainstream society. It also calls for a minimum of reflexivity and an ability to align one's behaviour with norms other than those that shape the outside world.

Attaching, sharing

To create a community 'us', breaking ties is not enough. Work also must be done to attach the members of the group that needs cementing. Sharing all goods and resources is a practice commonly used in egalitarian communities to bind individuals to the collective. At both Twin Oaks and Acorn, everything belongs to everyone, with the sole exception of a few personal items which, to escape the rule, must be stored in their owners' rooms. This norm of sharing, I was often told in justification, is fair (it guarantees equality for all) and long-standing (supposedly the legacy of the Protestant sects of old). In an article in the 2000 *Communities Directory*, Valerie puts things a little differently. The policy of income sharing, she begins by explaining, dates back to the time of 'tribal life'.[26] Monks and nuns did it, as did some 19th-century communities (Oneida, for example). The basic principle is simple: whatever the source, the goods and income produced by members go to the community. In exchange, the community provides them with food, clothing, shelter, transportation, and so on.

In the rhetoric that Valerie deploys, two sets of arguments are used to justify the socialization of resources. First, sharing does not only satisfy an axiological requirement. It is a rational choice. Sharing everything is an effective form of insurance against life's risks (illness, unemployment, loss of property, etc.). Second, by collectivizing skills as well as land, housing, vehicles, and so on, a community enables everyone to benefit on another level, namely work efficiency:

> One member is a talented programmer (easily monetized skill set) but terrible cook, another is a talented cook and handy person (less easily monetized skill set). The programmer can spend more time programming without worrying about keeping fed and keeping their domestic machinery functioning, the cook and handy person can spend time cooking and fixing things around the house without worrying about earning money.[27]

Another effective strategy for building a homogenous 'us' is to celebrate the way of life that all members of the community share. Nature plays a key role in this regard. At both Acorn and Twin Oaks, communion with the environment is the rule. As in most of the rural communities founded in the 1970s and since, they use wood for heating and dry toilets. Smoking is limited to restricted spaces. Nakedness is accepted as a 'natural' expression of closeness to the environment. Conventional and scheduled time is rejected in favour of freedom of action and enjoying the moment. A 'healthy' diet is promoted, based as far as possible on home-made foodstuffs and local agricultural produce. Furthermore, at Twin Oaks, the woods and land owned by the community are the object of special care, indeed devotion. This devotion takes many concrete forms, such as the close and long-standing attention paid to the variety of trees (nearly 20 different species) that make up the forest ecosystem, the concern not to sacrifice the natural heritage to meet external demands, the limitation of motorized traffic within the community, the collective celebration of natural events (emergence of new growth in spring), and the shared satisfaction of biting into freshly harvested fruit or vegetables from the garden.

Engagement through values is a final way of nurturing and sustaining the community flame. The better collectives are at regularly reasserting what their identity is and should be, the greater the chance that the 'us' will gain in strength and homogeneity. When asked, the communards have little difficulty in saying what causes they promote or intend to promote. On the internet, the Twin Oaks website indicates that many of its members are advocates of peace, ecology, anti-racism, and feminism.[28] This kind of presentation does not only serve to build an image for the outside world, it also acts a lever to shape individual commitments and increase the internal coherence of the collective. In this spirit, Twin Oaks decided in 2016 to dedicate each month of the year to a value it holds dear. Regularly, the PTM (Process Team), which oversees the operation, puts up a large poster in the ZK dining hall. The format is always the same. Below the generic title (Visiting our vision), two columns are drawn in felt pen. The first collects answers to the question: 'How do we put this value into practice?' The second is reserved for suggestions ('How can we live this value?'). It is up to each individual to propose answers that suit them but also commit them in terms of their future behaviour.

'Composing' with the wider world

Bringing to light these detachment practices and attachment strategies is not enough to fully illuminate community practices and modes of socialization. In addition to these two aspects is a third, which R.M. Kanter did not include in her analytical framework: composition,[29] or, in other words, the forms of compromise between communities and the outside world. To understand the meaning and scope of such a claim, the sociology of Christian institutions of Ernst Troeltsch (1865–1923) is particularly useful. Following in the footsteps of his colleague and friend Max Weber, Troeltsch (1912) defined the Church as an institution that has a monopoly on the means of grace. The latter is dispensed to the communicants by ordained officials who employ a set of rites for that purpose. Finally, the action of the Church depends on the recognition of the secular authorities. It is therefore conservative: it is in the Church's interests to opt for compromise and to accept the secular social order as much as it can. A sect, meanwhile, is a voluntary association of people who share the same ethical-religious ideal and who manifest it through similar behaviour. Within the sect, grace is not subject to organizational mediation and is not regarded as the exclusive property of the association.[30] When considered from the perspective of social ethics, the sect presents itself in two possible forms: either as a revolutionary institution that wishes to radically and explicitly reform the existing social order, or, on the contrary, as a passive group that finds in small communities the ideal means of practising a religious ideal purged of worldly interests.

Reasoning by equivalence, it is easy to draw some insights from the above reflections for an analysis of intentional communities. More precisely, we must wager that the tension between the city of God and the human world that structures religious institutions is formally equivalent to the opposition between the social utopia that serves as a beacon for community practices and the mainstream society from which the members of intentional communities wish to distance themselves. Yet the comparison can be subtly refined in two ways. First, by taking account of the observation that intentional communities and straight society are necessarily linked by compromises, as are sects and the profane world. Given this irreducible composition, instead of a clear-cut distinction between the passive and the revolutionary, it may be preferable to take a graduated perspective. More precisely, rather than trying to label a grouping with a general term, there is every reason to wager that within the same group, some registers of activity are more passive or revolutionary than others. This is, in other words, a useful means of describing the types of composition that communities favour. Second, unlike what Troeltsch suggests, compositions with the world are not necessarily concessions; they can contribute to its subversion just as they can help to reinforce the dominant order. For this reason, I prefer to replace the passive/revolutionary pair with passive/active.

Therefore, to model the basic forms of composition with the wider world, I adopt the terms passive composition and active composition. Passive composition designates configurations comparable to the registers of practices which, according to Troeltsch, characterize passive sects, such as an inclination to withdraw, a desire for independence, little contact with the outside world, and a negative view of the necessary relationship with mainstream society. In contrast, active composition describes configurations that have a positive collective drive in the relations that the communards establish with their environment. A second distinction is worth using to complete the analysis. It contrasts situations of societal domination (in interactions between the community and the wider world, the latter imposes its norms) with situations of community opposition where, through various means, society is directly or indirectly contested. By combining these two dimensions, we arrive at four possible cases (see Table 3.1).

Table 3.1: Four basic forms of composition with the wider world

	Passive composition	**Active composition**
Societal domination	**Constraint** Examples: specialized care, tax paying	**Involvement** Examples: trips to town, sale of products made at Twin Oaks
Community opposition	**Withdrawal** Examples: organization of work, links with family	**Protest** Examples: civic engagement, political demonstrations

The first case that can be identified is constraint (passive composition + societal domination), a situation that reflects the difficulty, if not impossibility, for utopian communities of extricating themselves from straight society. This is true of the obligation to pay taxes, from which no intentional community can legally escape. The absence or limitation of specific skills in a given register of practices may also force communards to submit to external constraints. This is the case in terms of healthcare, for example. At Twin Oaks, minor illnesses are easily treated on site using pharmaceuticals that are freely available to everyone. Furthermore, several members are nurses and provide care when needed. It is impossible, however, to expect to be self-sufficient in the event of serious accidents, serious health problems, or treatments (such as dental care) that require specific skills. In this case, there is no option but to cover the costs of consulting health specialists from outside the community.

In the panoply of forms of composition with the wider world, withdrawal (passive composition + community opposition) is the closest to Troeltsch's passive sect. Here, societal influences and burdens, while never nil, are particularly limited. This can be illustrated by Twin Oaks' current capacity to provide work for its members. To be more precise, job loss and reduced income due to the transition to retirement are two risks that do not require external support. The system of work organization is such that the notion of unemployment does not exist within the community: there is always scope to provide all members with occupations worth labour credits. Moreover, although the number of working hours owed to the collective decreases over the years once Oakers pass the age of 50, older workers continue to have access to exactly the same resources as younger workers. Under the 2017 rule (one hour less of work per week each year after the age of 50), one would have to wait until the canonical age of 92 to be able to stop working entirely and still benefit from the resources available to all.

Involvement (active composition + societal domination), the third form of composition, is the closest to what we usually call a compromise of principle. In this case, the community is prepared to actively engage with a world whose values it condemns and play by the latter's rules. Such a choice is not disinterested, of course. The archives show, for example, that Twin Oaks has long been investing some of its savings to earn interest. Moreover, those in charge of finances are quick to change their strategy if more lucrative options become available.[31] Although it is partly a matter of necessity, the choice to develop commercial activities, and thus to participate in market competition, also belongs in this register. In other words, the market is one of the spaces of compromise for which the communards accept the rules of the game, even if they are defined from outside. As early as the 1970s, many communities opened restaurants and garages or started small-scale craft production. Few of these enterprises proved profitable (Jerome,

1974). Some groups, however, have managed to profit from their activities and to combine commercial compromise, economic development, and the promotion of alternative trade.

Protest, the fourth and final form of composition with the wider world (active composition + community opposition) is closely related to Troeltsch's revolutionary sect. The aim is to actively take part in changing the outside world. In 2002, a budget of 500 hours was allocated at Twin Oaks to those who wanted to lend a hand to Food not Bombs, a non-profit organization that serves free meals to the homeless, lobbies local authorities to improve the lot of those living in poverty, campaigns for environmentally friendly policies, and more. In 2011 and 2012, the Oakers participated in the 'Occupy' movement. Around the same time, several were members of Not on Our Fault Line, a local anti-nuclear activist group that sprang into action after the earthquake on 23 August 2011 in Virginia reignited fears about the effects of an earthquake on the nuclear reactor in North Anna, Virginia.[32] At the demonstration held in Charlottesville on 12 August 2017 to protest the removal of a statue of Robert E. Lee, Oakers were also present. They also went to Washington in July 2022 to protest against the rollback of abortion rights. So, from the outset, politics and civic engagement more generally have pushed the communards to abandon their reserve and refuse the withdrawal that they advocate in other areas of social life. By crossing the boundary between 'them' and 'us' in this way, they occasionally become revolutionaries, in the sense that Troeltsch uses to characterize those sects which, refusing passivity, take action to shake up the 'big world' around them.

4

I, We

Shedding light on the pathway that leads from straight society to its margins and recognizing the existence of variables that predispose certain people to follow that route is necessary to account for the community phenomenon. But it is not sufficient. To more thoroughly understand and explain this social reality, we must also get a sense of what constitutes the fabric of daily life in community. To do so, let us start to let go of the simplistic representation that sees small utopian worlds as groups that bury individuals under such a layer of constraints and conformity that they are unable to manifest their free will in any shape or form. Except in extreme cases (religious sects in the everyday sense of the term), this is not what actually happens. There is always some leeway for individuals to negotiate their identity as communards by managing the gap between the image they wish to give of themselves and the expectations that the collective has of them.

This interpretive framework has been extensively developed by interactionist sociologists, first and foremost Erving Goffman, from whom this chapter borrows several fundamental notions. Drawing also on the perspectives developed by Claude Dubar (2000), the chapter aims to bring to light the singular way of associating the 'I' and the 'we' within intentional communities or, to put it another way, to describe social practices of far greater fluidity than one might spontaneously imagine. Two registers of analysis will be explored to this end. The first, typically Goffmanian, is that of the staging of self; the second is that of the internal networks of sociability – or communities within the community – to which different people are more or less firmly attached.

Building a community front: ways of speaking

In the theatrical model that he uses to make the interactions that shape the course of our daily lives intelligible, Goffman (1959) uses the notion of 'social front' to describe the set of attributes (clothing, sex, age, skin colour, manner of speaking, and so on) that an individual carries with them, which characterize them in the eyes of others and serve as props for staging themselves. Goffman further notes that elements of a given front (the suit used by a lawyer to receive a client in his office) can also be used in other circumstances (to go to the theatre with his wife, for example), so that the different elements of sign-equipment (decor, manner, appearance) are rarely used in a single context. In *The Presentation of Self in Everyday Life*, Goffman suggests that individuals know how to play on the dramatic intensity and depth of their actions, the point being not only to express what they would like fundamentally to communicate with others but also to prove the extent to which their behaviours partake of a shared ideal, which they reinforce by giving it concrete expression. 'The world, in truth', concludes Goffman, 'is a wedding' (1959, p 36).

In intentional communities, both the presentation of self and everyday interactions can be read in the terms that Goffman proposed. Even if similar components are used on some of the social stages of straight society, the assemblages of sign-equipment that the communards use allow us to speak of a 'community front' to characterize the main attributes that they display. The way of speaking is one of them, and not the least important. At both Twin Oaks and Acorn, it is striking how varied the accents are, so much so that it is sometimes hard for people with the most pronounced accents to make themselves understood. This diversity in the music of speech is explained above all by the plurality of geographical origins. Kat Kinkade noted this in the early days of Twin Oaks. In 1967, the community welcomed women and men from Georgia, Michigan, Connecticut, South Carolina, Tennessee, California, and elsewhere. Everyone had their own expressions and grammar. The community magic was such that a relatively standardized mode of communication soon began to take shape. For example, 'might be able to' soon disappeared from the Oakers' preferred language register in favour of 'might could'.[1] Acquiring a specific vocabulary and way of speaking gradually became one of the conditions of full community integration. In 1993, the Twin Oaks newsletter invited its readers to practice speaking Twin Oaksese. That meant using:

> more Twin Oaks specific words like: 'Backreq,' 'overquota,' 'belize,' 'conference site,' 'snarky,' 'serene,' and 'not OK.' Add the 'ula' ending to everyone's name. Anytime there are two people together, ask them if they are having a meeting. Another good trick is to learn to sprinkle lots of acronyms into your speech: The CPs are in TCLR. The CVP got LCs at ZK for helping the CB do BTU for PCSs. Doing OPP for the FEC at MT was OK. My SLG is the STP. Also don't forget to pepper your speech with words like 'far out,' 'groovy,' 'peace,' 'love' and 'wow!' So try and learn to use these concepts for your everyday

conversations. People will think you've lived at TO all your life, and so will you!²

In 2016, the Twin Oaks visitors guide provided some other basic pointers: CP = community planners; Honcho = leader of a working group; Hx = hammocks; TMT = Tofu Management Team; Viz = visitors; lexing (for labour exchange) = working for another local community; Oreo = visitor orientation session; ZK (ZhanKoye) = central building dedicated to collective meals and meetings; Req (for labour requisition) = the way in which work is distributed; primary = person who takes care of a child at Twin Oaks; meta = member of the educational team. The archives at the University of Virginia contain a document that lists 211 terms and acronyms used at Twin Oaks.³ The vast majority have a community-specific meaning. Semantics are undoubtedly conducive to the creation of a collective identity.

Ways of presenting oneself

Some of the vocabulary specific to the community is picked up fairly quickly in the course of everyday exchanges. It is also part of the basic knowledge that the Twin Oaks visitor programme is supposed to pass on to newcomers. As part of this training, some time is set aside for the trainees to get to know the members of the community and, in the process, to learn the basic rules of self-presentation. One April evening is the Visitor Social, an event that brings together about 20 Oakers in addition to the six visitors who arrived the day before. We meet on the deck of an old barn. Cody, one of the team in charge of the visitors' programme, is facilitating. He explains the rules of the first game. Everyone takes turns saying 'If you knew me more, you would know that ...', then completing the sentence as they please, for instance by describing a character trait, a favourite activity, or a fragment of their personal history. Once the appeal of the first game has worn off, each participant is given the floor to introduce themselves more formally.

At Twin Oaks, Cody explains, two pieces of information must be provided: your first name and the pronoun that others should use to refer to you. For example: "My name is Valerie, call me 'she'". For the pronoun, three options are possible, corresponding to three gender identities that everyone wants to see recognized by others: he (masculine), she (feminine), and co (a third gender that corresponds to neither of the others). Co is also used as a functional equivalent of him and her.⁴ From the root 'co' is derived cos (plural) and coself. Such a component is crucial to the construction of the community front. As in other communities (such as transgender, queer, and student communities) that use pronouns with similar functions (they, xe, ze ...), Twin Oaks recognizes androgyny as a gender identity in its own right.

Indeed, in both spoken and written form, co is in everyday usage to refer to a person who wants their 'socialized self', or their 'virtual social identity' (the image they present to others), to correspond as closely as possible to their 'human self', or their 'actual social identity' ('assimilating oneself with a third gender').[5] Co(s) also serves as a generic pronoun to encompass all gender identities.

The strategy of self-presentation is based, then, on a denomination that others are asked to use to identify and interact with the self. The first behavioural code adopted at Twin Oaks already indicated the founding group's philosophy on the matter. 'We don't use titles. All members are equal in the sense that all are entitled to the same privileges, advantages and respect.'[6] Another rule of self-presentation still in place today is to use only a first name, often short and rarely hyphenated, as a form of identification. The surname is never used, either during verbal interactions or in written documents produced by the community.[7] Abandoning the surname, that mark of social belonging, is a strategy for breaking with the outside world. But it also establishes integration into a neo-domestic space united by a common symbolic reference: the name of the community to which one belongs. At gatherings between intentional communities, when people introduce themselves, two attributes are systematically used: their first name and the name of their community. This also applies in community media, such as *Communities* magazine, where the same presentation strategy is used to stage the communards.

The second characteristic of the first name as a useful resource for building a community front is that it may, if the new communard so desires, be different from the one given to them at birth. Changing one's first name is an even more radical way of marking a break with one's previous life. 'Twin Oaks membership is a break from the past. We come here committed to changes and expecting them. A new name is just the beginning.'[8] Various methods are used to come up with a new name. Some, indeed the majority, choose a pleasant-sounding name or one that seems particularly meaningful to them. When it is not an implicit reference to a personal story, an allusion to the natural world is the most common option. This is the case, for instance, with Apple, Bean, Cloud, Fox, Koala, Moon, Rainbow, River, Sky, Summer, Tiger, Tomato, Tree, and Woody. Others tinker with their original names, for example retaining only part of them (with such a process, Angelina becomes Jelly, Virginia turns into Gini, and so on) or, on the contrary, embellishing them (Brude becomes Brudefish, for example). Others choose androgynous names that blur gender boundaries. Rye or Three might find favour with women, for instance, and Carrol or Siri with men. Others subvert the order of ordinary administrative language by turning their surname into a first name, modifying it if necessary to sound more informal (Schepps becomes Schep or Scheppy). It is not uncommon for visitors who are already acculturated to community environments to introduce themselves with a name of their own invention.

The change of name meets a third requirement characteristic of the identity attributes of community fronts: uniqueness. It is unthinkable for two members of the same community to be called by the same name. One reason for such a rule is practical: because individuals cannot be differentiated by their surname, unique first names are needed to facilitate daily interactions.[9] But such an option also reflects the desire to form bonds through the addition of individualities who are not to be confused with one another. There is no question, then, of crushing individual differences in order to merge subjectivities into an undifferentiated whole. The construction of identity by and through the uniqueness of first names is a major argument of the community front. There is in fact only one exception to this requirement, and it concerns visitors. All visitors are referred to by their original first name with the addition, on all written documents where their identity appears, of a V (for visitor) to help identify them.

Choice of appearance and blurring of gender boundaries

A third defining attribute of the community front is dress and physical appearance. Goffman (1959, p 36) pointed out that in the US, 'the most important piece of sign-equipment associated with social class consists of the status symbols through which material wealth is expressed'. Goffman (1959, p 40) used the notion of 'negative idealization' when he observed, with regard to this norm, that some of the poorest groups intentionally accentuate some of their material difficulties (for example, by presenting their children to welfare investigators in shabby clothes) in order to stay in the welfare department's good graces. In a similar vein, we might speak of 'reverse idealization' to characterize strategies of self-assertion that deliberately run counter to those prevalent in the middle and upper classes, as is the case in intentional communities. In this respect, appearance is an ideal element to play upon.

The overwhelming majority of communards wear outfits that suggest modest means if not destitution: basic T-shirts, cheap shirts, dresses, shorts, jeans and canvas trousers – sometimes ripped in several places – used pullovers and parkas, and nondescript shoes. Weather permitting, it is not uncommon to see communards walking around barefoot and bare-chested. With a few exceptions, bodies tend to be slim or muscular, proof that the food is not overly high in calories and, above all, that they all engage in regular physical exertion (agricultural work, industrial production, and so on). Nor do their bodies bear any trace of the adulterations usually attributable in the outside world such as make-up, hair gel, eau de toilette, and the like. For men and even more so for women, shaving and hair removal is kept to a minimum. All the signs indicate that a unanimous choice has been made, one in favour of the 'natural', physical effort, and temperance.

Yet appearance is not just a matter of restraint or privation. Dyeing hair, growing it long (for men), and tattooing parts of the body are common practices that reflect both the ability to break free from straight norms of self-presentation and to assert a singular identity. A long skirt, always made of cheap fabric, and painted fingernails serve as markers for young, often slender men who want to display their queer identity, though they may not mobilize such attributes every day. But the skirt is not just that. It is also a collective means to undermine conventional dress codes, including for those who do not identify as queer. At Twin Oaks, 'our culture does not limit this style choice to female-bodied members, and [...] we'd prefer all members be able to be comfortably attired instead of having to adhere to an arbitrarily-imposed fashion norm' (Renwick, 2014, pp 24–25).

For women, the play on appearances is just as decisive. Communard women at Twin Oaks have been wearing overalls – usually associated with male attire – since the community was founded. Today, more than ever, they continue to assert alternative ways of presenting themselves. In a series of photos taken at the 2016 Women's Gathering at Twin Oaks,[10] more than 30 women of all ages, variously dressed or undressed, took turns posing with a large whiteboard on which they had written how they were 'smashing patriarchy'. The theme of physical appearance featured in one in five slogans. In almost every case, the statement reflected the same demand: to give free rein to the 'natural' and thereby free oneself from the canons of femininity imposed by the mainstream world. 'I smash patriarchy by refusing to buy into the beauty industry', wrote one woman; 'by not buying into "feminine products" & listening to natural wisdom', 'by letting my natural facial hair grow', 'by supporting & empowering women to trust their bodies in childbirth', and 'by taking off my shirt in safe places', others added.

Interactions and rules of conduct

Is the production of an adequate social front enough to create community? Certainly not, if we consider that 'to *be* a given kind of person [...] is not merely to possess the required attributes, but also to sustain the standards of conduct and appearance that one's social grouping attaches thereto' (Goffman, 1959, p 75). Such a requirement immediately makes sense considering that the communards' main problem is managing to live and work on good terms in a limited space where, unlike in the wider world, the overwhelming majority of members constantly rub shoulders. Recognizing the importance of this challenge, Twin Oaks states on its website that 'Although we are a community, we are aware of the necessity for solitude and intimacy.

Members have private rooms, and we also have a retreat cabin, a sweat hut and many living rooms available for individual use.'[11] But being able, at times, to withdraw from communal space is not the only condition for making living together in a community environment viable. It also, and perhaps more importantly, requires knowledge of the codes that govern everyday interactions, as well as those used in the more exceptional performances that the community stages to celebrate itself.

Whether in community or elsewhere, all interaction can be understood as a ritual, that is, a reasoned, symbolically-charged individual activity oriented towards an object for which the action has value (Goffman, 1967). The object in question is none other than others, for whom Goffman believes that the person manages an image of him- or herself (his or her 'face') that has all the trappings of the sacred. This interpretive framework is particularly heuristic in the case of communities. At both Twin Oaks and Acorn, interaction rituals must heed a major imperative: each person must be able to be in constant contact with others without necessarily bothering them with signs of civility which, if repetitive and ostentatious, could be detrimental to the quality and smooth execution of actions and interactions. Such a requirement is not unknown in the family circle and in professional or social environments in the outside world: family members do not embrace every time they pass each other while going about their everyday business in the home, no more than colleagues shake hands and ask after each other's health at every interaction during the working day. In communities, however, the problem is heightened by the increased likelihood of frequently crossing paths and, especially, the greater number of people with whom the self can interact. What can be done, in these circumstances, to avoid the two opposite pitfalls of absolute indifference to others on the one hand, and a constant onslaught of civility on the other?

At Twin Oaks, the answer is formalized by two principles that structure the most banal of daily interactions. The first principle is 'make eye contact'. To eliminate the cost of repeated displays of urbanity, eye contact is required prior to any interaction. When two people pass each other, then, they can deliberately ignore each other, look at each other more or less furtively, or smile at each other in recognition and complicity. When one person purposely avoids the other's eye, the signal is clear: there is minimal willingness to communicate. This 'avoidance ritual' should not be understood as a sign of disdain or ignorance. Apart from the psychological savings that the absence of eye contact allows, a principle of equality is being put into practice here. Nothing should oblige a peer to submit to the encroachment imposed by a presentational ritual.[12]

The second principle is 'ask to ask'. In order to move further into another person's territory and enter into more or less lasting contact, a formal agreement is required. The best way to avoid unwanted intrusion is to ask the potential interaction partner if it is possible to ask a question. This reflex is fairly quick to acquire, just as a non-American quickly learns to ask any person with whom he or she interacts in the outside world (a customs officer, a shopkeeper, a passer-by) how they are and to wait for their reply before finally getting to the substance of the communication.

A host of other rituals are used to regulate ordinary interactions. Many of them could be described with rules that amount to unwritten norms of community 'manners'. At mealtimes, for example, it is inappropriate to jump the queue to the buffet where everyone comes to serve themselves. It is equally unseemly to take a second helping of food when others have not yet had their first. At Twin Oaks, it is also improper to sit at a table without having been invited by the people already sitting there (the only exception to this rule is a large table in ZK dedicated to this purpose). There is, however, no obligation to talk to your neighbours. It goes without saying that everyone has to take their used plate, glass (often a jar, in fact, which serves as a glass), and dirty cutlery out to the baskets provided. If someone should fail to respect these basic principles, they would quickly be called to order by any member who had witnessed the moral lapse.

Many more rules – too many to list – shape the actions and interactions of daily life. One of the most unusual for a non-communard involves clearly separating what is common property and what is a personal possession. Twin Oaks and Acorn, like many other anarchist spaces, are equipped with two kitchens. The first, lavishly equipped with utensils, is dedicated exclusively to the preparation of communal meals; the second is available for anyone who wants to make a snack or a more solid meal whenever they want. This second space is a kind of extension of the self's territories, but shared; a half-common, half-collective sphere. Personal items (cups, flasks, teapots, packets of coffee, and so on) may be stored there, but the owner must label them with their name to ensure that they are the only ones to use them. Similarly, two fridges (one communal, the other for private use) serve to organize the territories of possession.

The time of rituals

Taking temporal rhythms into account provides useful and complementary insight into the many rituals that inform community life. At Twin Oaks, mealtimes (which begin at noon and 6 pm Monday to Saturday, and at 10 am and 6 pm on Sundays) are periods whose social quality is not the same as that of the ordinary occupations that shape the rest of the day. The time of dispersal is followed by a time of regrouping, before everyone goes about their business again. In these moments of minor communion, the community comes together in Twin Oaks' central building. The week also has an original cadence. Unlike in the outside world, it starts on Friday, the first day of the weekly timetable drawn up by the small team of managers in charge of distributing the work to be done over seven days on an individual basis. Sunday is therefore an ordinary day, or almost: the morning is free of any productive work obligations and a brunch is offered from ten o'clock onwards (instead of the traditional midday meal).

There are also many key dates throughout the year that break the ordinary course of everyday life. Every 14 February, instead of Valentine's Day, Twin Oaks celebrates Validation Day. The custom began in the 1980s when a communard called Cristy moved to Twin Oaks from East Wind and brought the idea with him (Renwick-Porter, 2000, pp 38–39). The aim is to avoid cheap romanticism with commercial overtones. In the first two weeks of February, handmade cards, one for each member, are available to the whole community. The communards are invited to write a 'validation' – a warm message recognizing the recipient's importance to them, or the value of their work for the community, for instance – in each card. Traditionally, children hand out the cards at a special Validation Day dinner. Today, new technologies having made their mark, the messages are exchanged over the internet.

Although less spectacular, the ordinary rituals of straight society are intentionally undermined on other occasions. Halloween is one example. At Twin Oaks, as elsewhere, dressing up for Halloween is *de rigueur*. A particularly popular trend is to disguise oneself as another member for the evening, putting on distinctive items they usually wear and mimicking their behaviour. During the day, the children take part in the community's customary social subversion by reversing the rules of play in outside society: rather than begging for sweets, they hand out sweets to adults.

Communities within the community

All the practices and rituals mentioned above contribute directly to social cohesion. Despite this, but also despite the image they sometimes like to give of themselves, intentional communities are not homogeneous blocks. Several fault lines run through them, defining overlapping territories with ever-changing borders. Certain divisions persist between those with classic communard profiles (white, middle class) and minorities (non-white, working class); to this day, the problem of unequal representation among these different groups has not been resolved, and nor have the concrete implications of these divisions in daily life.[13] The question still stands. And it is likely to go unanswered for a long time, at least as long as the emancipation that intentional communities propose is based on an ideal of poverty, which holds little appeal for those who have experienced financial hardship and deprivation throughout their childhood and adolescence. "It's not by making people camp in the woods in the rain that you're going to attract black people," one participant, herself black, remarked wryly at one of the sessions of the Twin Oaks communities conference in September 2017.

Other segmentations maintain the heterogeneity of communard collectives. At Twin Oaks, the existence of a multiple small living groups (SLGs), each reserved for about 15 people who share the same building with bedrooms, bathrooms, common areas, and so on, effectively breaks up the collective into a set of sub-communities.[14] Although they have no authority to depart from the general principles that structure Twin Oaks, each SLG may adopt its own rules and customs. Some have a collective dinner once a week, for instance; others hold meetings to deal with day-to-day matters. The profile of the inhabitants may also differ between SLGs. Tupelo, for instance, which is particularly well equipped for communal cooking, is popular with families; Kawea attracts young people who like some nightlife; and Oneida is mainly for women.

Besides the SLGs, Twin Oaks is also structured by peer groups. Children, for example, form a small community of their own. The way they are integrated and educated has varied over time. While the youngest generation was present in the community's earliest days and a child manager role[15] was soon created, their behaviour was so disruptive that the Oakers decided shortly afterwards, in 1969 to be exact, to no longer accept them. The communards went back on their decision three years later on the strength of a demanding principle: children are not the property of their parents but of the community. To give the principle substance, it was decided that as soon as breastfeeding was over, each newborn child would go to live with the other Twin Oaks children in Degania, a building that the community built for them in 1972 ('Twin Oaks & Little Folks', 1974). Until they reached school age, the children lived there permanently, in the care of adults. Later, living arrangements and forms of schooling fluctuated from one period to another. In the late 2010s, children lived with their parents. Divided into age groups, they nonetheless formed a little community of their own and were still given tailor-made lessons in Degania by those communards who were willing and competent.

Senior citizens form another community for which age is the identifying and motivating factor. The fact is the communards have aged. In 2017, there were 22 members in their twenties, 31 in their thirties, 12 in their forties, 11 in their fifties, nine in their sixties, and four over 70.[16] Those who opted for community in the 1970s and have stayed for the duration are now grey-haired. Twin Oaks rejects any form of ageism that would stigmatize and isolate them. For them, however, it nonetheless became necessary to build adapted living spaces (with air conditioning, easy access for people with reduced mobility, and so on) and to reduce the working hours of the older members. Similarly, to ensure that the collective workforce is not weakened by an ever-increasing average age, Twin Oaks no longer accepts new members over 50. Such measures clearly mark out a new sub-community that coexists with the sub-communities of children and of adults in the living environment.

Feminism and women-only groups

Gender plays as important a role as age. Since 1967, it has constantly structured interactions and forms of integration within the community. In the first months of communal living at Twin Oaks, relations between the sexes still clearly bore the stamp of the wider world. Gender relations were largely beholden to the most common representations in mainstream society. Despite the rhetoric of breaking with dominant practices and the stated desire to do away with traditional roles, tasks were unequally distributed. In the community's early years, flirtations were also governed by traditional conceptions of the masculine and feminine ideal, romantic interactions conformed to the rituals inculcated in the family and at school ... Twin Oaks was not, by any means, a paradise of gender equality. 'Living here [Twin Oaks] has, for many of us, stifled or made us pessimistic about our original utopian dream ... we believe in equality, yet we are unable to face the staggering implications of total and real social equality'.[17] At Twin Oaks as elsewhere, then, sexism was also sustained by a form of acquiescence that considerably dulled the desire for gender equality in the early years.

Practices began to change with the arrival in 1969 and 1970 of women with some experience of the women's liberation movement. These younger, more radical women challenged their elders. They drew their attention to the patterns of domination that shape gender relations, including in intentional communities, and wanted to hold meetings about empowering women for collective action. The years 1972 to 1979 brought unprecedented change to Twin Oaks in this regard (Passehl, 2004). First, women took on traditionally male-dominated work roles. In the television programme 'A World of Difference: B.F. Skinner and the Good Life' broadcast in 1979, which includes a long sequence on Twin Oaks, a young woman is featured from the 25th minute. She is seen wearing overalls, her hands covered in grease, fixing an engine in the Modern Times workshop, then sharing her mechanical knowledge with another young woman.

But what resistance had to be overcome to get to that point! In the fall issue of *Communities* that same year, Margaret, one of two lesbians then living at Twin Oaks, wrote of the misgivings expressed when the decision was made to introduce affirmative action for people working in non-traditional jobs (Oaks, 1980). For some, this constituted a fundamental contradiction of the principle of equality. When there is a vacancy in construction and building work, is it not a form of inequity to rule out qualified men in favour of a woman who is willing to learn but has little experience, simply because she is a woman? At Twin Oaks, Margaret explained, their way of resolving this problem was 'to focus on the non-sexist ideal while not losing sight of the ultimate goal of equality. So the construction crew will continue to apprentice women until the crew is balanced. The same is true in child care where half the "metas" (child care workers) are men' (Oaks, 1980, p 45).

To further advance gender equality and women's rights, the female Oakers set up reading groups to discuss and deepen their knowledge of feminist literature. In 1978, they started to organize dinners and dances where they could get together. The community's vocabulary, meanwhile, received special attention. Certain terms were revised to avoid a masculinist bias. 'Person' replaced 'man' in words such as 'workpersonship', for instance. Men's initial reactions to these initiatives were varied. Some immediately took the young women's demands seriously, while others wore skirts to poke fun at what they felt were overly radical egalitarian claims. But the women didn't let that stop them.

They also organized into support and activity groups. The idea that relationships between women could be stronger than those between two people of the opposite sex had gained ground (MacLeod and Bedard, 1975; 'Women in Community', 1974). In 1979, still at Twin Oaks, Margaret met weekly with a handful of fellow female Oakers (four to seven according to circumstances). Together, they talked about their daily lives, discussed politics, thought about ways of empowering women in the community, read and circulated feminist and lesbian newspapers, played music and broadcast it in various work and living spaces, and so on. They also organized women's events (such as films and slide shows), to which all were invited, regardless of age or gender.

In response, men decided to create men's gatherings, where they could play volleyball or poker together, discuss their lives in particular and the world in general, give each other moral support, and invent a different male culture from that of mainstream society. Thus, at Twin Oaks, 'men are free to choose gayness or bisexuality as a sexual preference. Long hair and skirts are not uncommon. A gentleness and softness characterize male styles of interaction; sarcasm and put-downs are relatively uncommon.'[18] More and more single-gender groups were formed in this way once the feminist wave had swept through Twin Oaks. Some, especially at the beginning, focused primarily on activism, while others concentrated on close sociability (exchanging confidences, mutual support) and conviviality (making friends, having a good time together, celebrating birthdays or someone's return from holiday, and so on).

After the 1970s, the early feminist spirit faded somewhat. Desires and proposals waxed and waned. Several initiatives nonetheless continued to change gender relations and male practices. In the 1980s, for example, it was decided after a long debate that the community would no longer subscribe to magazines such as *Playboy*, considered degrading to the image of women. During the same period, measures were put in place to address male sexual aggressiveness, which was given the name 'wolfing' (Goldenberg, 1993). Female newcomers were warned of the predatory tendencies of certain male Oakers who pursued women like sex-hungry wolves. In 1987, the Twin Oaks visitor's guide stressed the importance of friendship and solidarity among women in the community, regardless of their sexual orientation.[19] Regular events (Saturday tea), women-only spaces, and a specialized library served to maintain this gender-based sociability.

To spread the principles of feminism beyond the strict confines of its territory, Twin Oaks has also hosted a Women's Gathering since the late 1970s, organized under the auspices of the Federation of Egalitarian Communities. The first was held in 1978 with the theme 'Speculum'78 – A look at ourselves'. The aim of the conference, which has been held annually since 1983, is to form an inclusive community of sisters for several days.[20] During this short break, the participants attend workshops on diverse themes (intersectionality, football, politics, sexuality, learning a musical instrument, growing mushrooms, scheduling a meeting with Doodle, meditation, etc.), socialize, and enjoy live music and shared meals.[21]

The 2010s revival: think tank and feminist ecovillage

Men, but also some women, have not always looked favourably on the feminist desire for community within the community. Does it not fundamentally contravene the principle of equality that binds Twin Oaks together? When the first women's conference was held in 1978, several signs indicated an obvious lack of understanding: posts taking a dubious view mushroomed on the Opinions & Ideas board, some men set up a parallel conference, while others, by way of protest, had baked goods delivered to the conference participants assembled at Merion, an abandoned farm. Older women also disapproved of the initiative. Some felt that this type of gathering gave lesbianism more than its due. 'I did not (and still do not) like the feel of women who get up on stage and their breasts are hanging out and they are hanging on to each other, and they are chanting some words to a silly dance,' wrote Kat Kinkade for example. 'I just feel stupid. As a woman I feel I do not belong and that I do not want to belong.' (Cited in Passehl, 2004, p 44). Unlike their elders, the younger women enjoyed being able to get together with other women, escape the male gaze, forget about the beauty stakes, and finally feel free. ... Three years later, tensions were reignited when some women of the younger generation wanted the right to live in a small living group exclusively for women. The Oneida project was born. It did become a reality, but construction work only began after much heated debate.

In the early 2000s, after a long slump, Twin Oaks rediscovered the appeal of separate women's groups and culture through past activities (teas, sports, theatre) and new ones (full moon rituals, monthly potluck dinners, and the celebration of International Women's Day). Interest in feminism was also rekindled. In the terms used by Twin Oaks members, adopting a feminist culture meant undermining the gender hierarchies of mainstream society and promoting full equality between women and men, regardless of their gender identities and sexual preferences. Was this approach sufficient to support the claim that Twin Oaks belonged to the narrow circle of 'the most nonsexist social systems in human history'? (Wagner, 1982, p 38). Those most concerned – Twin Oaks women themselves – would most likely say no, or at least be sceptical. They knew that in this area, as in others, a gap remained between what was said and what was actually done. Sexism had not completely disappeared, and the community was struggling to relegate the gendered division of labour to distant memory.

This explains the launch in 2015 of the Feminist Think Tank (FTT). The FTT meets twice a week and is 'open to anyone of any gender who: 1. Acknowledges the patriarchy exists, 2. Identifies as a feminist or feminist ally, and 3. Recognizes that patriarchy is at play at Twin Oaks and wants to do something about it'.[22] Following in the footsteps of their elders, the members of the FTT hold workshops on harassment, consent,[23] and discrimination, propose festive events, take a collective and public stand on pressing political issues, and publish a 'zine'. One of the issues published by the FTT draws readers' attention to elements of feminist awareness:

> You might be a feminist at Twin Oaks if [...] you've ever asked a male visitor to put his shirt on at a meal-time; you've ever shared a Diva [menstrual] cup; you've ever done a post-structuralist, anti-colonialist, neo-marxist deconstruction of a Disney princess movie ... while singing along with the movie; you've ever been assigned non-traditional work for your gender and realized you enjoyed it; you've ever been assigned non-traditional work for your gender and didn't even notice it was non-traditional.[24]

Clearly, the conviction is stronger than ever that while Twin Oaks is less sexist than mainstream society, there is still a long way to go from the utopian ideal to actual practices.

The entrenchment of feminist culture took yet another turn over the course of the 2010s, a time when the US community movement was being won over by the ideas of permaculture and the ecovillage wave. Twin Oaks decided, along with two other communities (Dancing Rabbit and Earth Haven), to call itself a feminist ecovillage.[25] According to its most committed members, the label makes sense: Twin Oaks perfectly embodies the values of ecofeminism, which denounces the destructive effect of patriarchy on both nature and women (Mies and Shiva, 1998). As one female Oaker put it in a magazine published in 2014:

> The extraction of resources from our natural world mirrors patriarchal society, which extracts resources from women in general. The patriarchal system sees women as a natural resource to be exploited through domestic work, rape, reproduction, and a kind of submission to men. There is a connection between rape and the destruction of natural resources; between the 'secondary' statuses given to women and to animals. We will not get rid of one without refusing the other.[26]

In other words, ecofeminism offers the means to keep H.D. Thoreau's naturalist legacy alive while incorporating gender issues that it did not originally include.

Marriage, sexual freedom, and polyamory

B.F. Skinner's book *Walden Two* proposed a simple solution for satisfying young men's carnal appetites and freeing women as soon as possible from the burden of motherhood: early marriage. When the pioneers of Twin Oaks founded their community, they immediately dismissed this recommendation as being out of step with the customs of their time. In the months prior to the summer of 1968, they nonetheless shared Skinner's certainty that monogamy was the normal pattern for romantic relationships. But the mood quickly changed. The communards who joined Twin Oaks during and after the cultural revolution of the late 1960s imposed a new norm of sexual freedom, the primary consequence of which was the erosion of marriage as a central social institution. In 1972, Kat Kinkade (1973) noted that the community had been home to a total of nine married couples, three of which eventually separated. Community life, she added, had undone as many couples who had come to Twin Oaks as it had fostered lasting unions between lovers.

How was sexual freedom experienced in practice? Quite tamely, in fact. At Twin Oaks, public displays of affection rarely involved more than two people. As for what went on behind closed doors, no one really knows. In the early 1970s, Kinkade seriously doubted that there had ever been an orgy at Twin Oaks:

> Sex is very important to us, but at the same time we don't make a big deal of it. It is a part of our daily lives, but we rarely discuss it. Like eating and working and going for a walk and playing the guitar, it is a part of the good life. (Kinkade, 1973, p 171)

Looking back on the same topic 20 years later, Kinkade (1994) felt that she had even less to say. The upshot was similar: at Twin Oaks, legal marriages, long-term monogamous relationships, and celibacy were still not the dominant norm. Meanwhile, most romantic relationships involved people who both lived at Twin Oaks.[27] Last but not least, the concrete manifestations of sexual freedom bore no resemblance to the stereotypes that associated community life with unrestrained orgiastic outpourings.

In concrete terms, the principle of sexual freedom takes two forms at Twin Oaks. Firstly, it means that a wide variety of sexual orientations, identities, and conditions are welcome. The door is equally open to LGBTIQA (lesbian, gay, bisexual, transgender, intersex, queer, asexual) people and heterosexuals. In a 2014 interview with *Jeanne Magazine*, an online lesbian magazine, two members of Twin Oaks summed up their experiences on the subject as follows. Valerie:

> One of the things I like about this place is that we don't have to label ourselves gay or straight. At Twin Oaks, sexuality is very fluid. Community members can change their sexual orientation, and you don't have to identify with a particular sexuality if you don't want to. Our culture is such that talking about a member's sexuality is out of place, unless obviously you're interested in that person. Then, of course, you'll want to hear more about it. Apart from that, we have a very strong LGBTQ culture.

Brittany:

> I grew up in a place where lesbians were invisible. I really thought that the kids at my high school were all straight, because no one was openly gay, and even at university, being a lesbian didn't seem like a normal thing. Twin Oaks was the first place where I was able to feel free to love and be publicly affectionate with other women. I met my first girlfriend here, and I don't think it would have been possible for me anywhere else, without the support I got here. Here straight women are not afraid of being intimate with other women. It's really nice.[28]

In the 1990s, the community saw a sharp decline in the proportion of female members. So, it decided to stop accepting men for the visitors' programme. The consequences were soon felt. Not only did the gender balance improve, but the number of lesbians also surged (with more than ten becoming members). In the early 2000s, the restrictions on male visitors no longer applied but the shift in favour of gays and lesbians was cemented. The history of recognition of queers, who are prominent at Twin Oaks and even more so at Acorn, is even more recent. Although the term began to gain currency in the 1980s, the written and photographic archives that I was able to consult in and about the two communities do not mention it until the 2000s.[29] The methodological limits of the study probably have something to do with this. In any case, it is certain that the first Queer in Community (QIC), a queer gathering at Twin Oaks modelled on the one for women, was not held until August 2017.[30] Why, when Twin Oaks and especially Acorn are home to many queer people, was this event so long in coming? The most likely hypothesis is that, as in the past with feminism and homosexuality, intentional communities expand and legitimize certain avant-garde moral trends that already exist, rather than being at the cutting edge in this area.

The same is probably true of the other concrete expression of the principle of sexual freedom, namely polyamory. This practice is informed by a philosophy of non-possessiveness, in line with the values of sharing and equality.[31] At both Twin Oaks and Acorn, openly having several romantic relationships at the same time is common practice. Observation of everyday interactions between members soon makes it possible to draw the sociogram of the moment. In this way, I came to the conclusion that the practice tends to concern the younger generations, primarily those in their thirties; that there are rarely more than three people involved; that one person can have romantic relationships with two others, regardless of their gender and sexual orientation, without the latter two necessarily being romantically involved with each other; and that the relationships can sometimes be short-lived, even if some patterns seem to be fairly successful nowadays (for example, young queer men keeping up a relationship with a woman, who may also be the mother of their child, while having intense homosexual affairs).

An expression of tolerance that contrasts with the dominant model of monogamy in straight society, polyamory is not necessarily as easy to live with as it is publicly made out to be. As elsewhere, the history of Twin Oaks is peppered with scenes made by jealous communards who, unable to bear a third person interfering in their relationship, have preferred to break up with their partner and leave the community. To mitigate the risks, the most common polyamorous practice consists of separating one's relationships with different partners and setting aside time to spend alone with each. Intentional communities more generally have understood the importance of taking the tangle of relationships between many of their members seriously. In 2017, a pink leaflet, 'Polyamory for all seasons' is pinned up in Heartwood (Acorn). It proposes two- to six-day training courses for communards who want to meet other polyamorous people, learn how to manage their multiple relationships better, become part of an extensive network, and so on.

5

The Rules of the Community Game

In 2018, the Fellowship for Intentional Community presented the 'Top 17 myths about intentional communities' in an amusing post intended to dispel such common stereotypes. Alongside preconceptions about communities all being rural, practising nudity, offering no privacy, being dominated by hippie culture, and so on, the FIC discusses the organization of these small alternative worlds. Many people seem to think that a community necessarily functions through a hierarchical system or follows a charismatic leader. The clarification offered is unambiguous: 'Few communities are hierarchical; most are structured around the values of cooperation and collaboration, with decision making structures so that everyone is involved. Most use some form of democracy, or other forms like consensus or sociocracy. Some communities do have clear leaders'.[1] This is not a minor point. More than information about organizational morphology, it is a refresher in elementary sociology: even anarchist communities like Acorn have procedures and rules without which collective life would simply not be possible.

The communards are, of course, well aware of this basic fact. Jonathan, who was always sketching daily life at Twin Oaks when he was a member, is the first to point this out and have some fun with it. In one of his cartoons (reprinted in Kinkade, 1994, p 199), he depicts two Oakers and a visitor. The first communard sings the place's praises to the young woman passing through. 'There's so much *freedom* in our community. People can wear whatever they want ...'. Visibly less enthusiastic, the second Oaker mutters, 'Except for suits, ties and make-up.' 'People can believe any religion they want ...' continues the first Oaker impassively. 'Unless it's in the Judeo-Christian tradition', retorts the second. 'And people can keep anything in their rooms they want', continues the first. His adversary's immediate response: 'Except for T.V.s, drugs, microwaves, pornography and air conditioners!' The third person finally speaks up: 'Sounds like a good system. Are there any drawbacks?' 'Yeah!' the first Oaker ends up admitting, 'people can *say* whatever they want'.

Where does community reality sit on the scale between the absence of rules that some (wrongly) attribute to anarchist collectives and the surfeit of social regulation[2] that Jonathan pokes fun at? To answer this question, I will start by describing how things function at Twin Oaks (distribution of roles, communication, decision-making methods, and so on) and, secondarily, at Acorn. We shall see that the form of social regulation applied at Twin Oaks today still owes much to B.F. Skinner and his *Walden Two*. I will also emphasize that community life does not exclude conflict or deviance. On the contrary, they are immanent to it.

Planners

To avoid situations of anomie, which amounts to social death, intentional communities cannot do without a minimum of organizational structure. As we have seen, Twin Oaks was informed by Skinnerian precepts from the outset. Reproduced with a few minor alterations, the model put in place just a few weeks after the community was founded combined three levels of responsibility and commitment: planners, managers, and members. The planners at Twin Oaks worked as a trio; half the number that Skinner advocated in his utopian novel:

> Last July [1967] we elected a three-man board (called 'planners' for lack of a better name) with authority to make policy decisions. The board meets once a week or oftener to discuss problems as they come up. After each meeting a summary of the material discussed is posted for all the membership to see, and any decisions made at the planners' meetings become effective only after any feedback from the group is received and considered.[3]

The basic principles have remained the same since 1967. Today, planners are responsible for the community's long-term policy: planning building works and major purchases, monitoring budget projections, preparing projects for the future, and so on. The planners also deal with day-to-day issues that are beyond the remit of other regulatory bodies. This particularly demanding work is acknowledged with labour credits. On average, and for many years now, planners devote two thirds of their time to their role of steering the community. The remaining third is spent on more ordinary activities. In 1974, as Twin Oaks attracted more and more members, the community set up a planning council to help planners gather the relevant and necessary information before making any decisions ('Eight Years After', 1975).

Planners are elected by the community for 18-month staggered terms, which cannot be renewed until at least six months after leaving office. In reality, few Oakers have agreed to take on such a heavy responsibility more than once. To do the role justice, the planners meet one to three times a week for meetings that last several hours, during which they deal with a wide variety of problems. Meeting dates and times are indicated on the notice boards. They are open to any members who want to attend. Members are free to intervene in the discussions as long as they do not put pressure on the planners to try and influence their decisions.[4] The subjects dealt with may call for quick verdicts or require lengthy reflection, often preceded by an internal debate within the community or a survey by means of a written questionnaire circulated to all members. After their meetings, the planners always inform the other members of any choices that have been made, points that remain unresolved, and issues worth discussing in the future.

Some decisions are all the more difficult to make because they contradict the anti-authoritarian philosophy that the community prides itself on. In 2014, for example, Adder and Sapphire – the two planners in charge at the time – had to sanction a member who had borrowed $300 but never paid it back because he had preferred to buy a dog (Reece, 2016, p 193). That situation was nothing compared to another incident that placed the two planners of the moment in an awkward position. An elderly Oaker who had become tired of living wanted to end it all and refused to eat. The planners quickly sought advice from lawyers, psychologists, and doctors who informed them that, in the absence of objections from family members, the distressed woman's decision was perfectly legal. Adder and Sapphire decided to respect her wishes. But things took a different turn. Part of the community did not accept the decision to support someone towards their death. More importantly, the woman's son suddenly appeared. He contacted the police. The latter immediately picked up his mother at Twin Oaks and took her to the University of Virginia hospital for a psychological assessment. In the end, she was allowed to return to live at Twin Oaks, but only on the condition that she did everything she could to fight her suicidal urges (Reece, 2016, p 193).

Opinions & Ideas

The planners' meetings, as I just mentioned, are open to the public. On the few occasions that I observed them at work, I never saw more than five people present, planners included. In the picture Ingrid Komar (1983) painted of Twin Oaks in the early 1980s, she was less than enthusiastic about these meetings, which members attended slightly more than they do today. She didn't recognize the people with whom she usually worked, had fun, looked after children, and so on once they had donned their planner's hat. In a position of responsibility, they became timid, cold, and puritanical. At meetings, one planner looked perpetually overworked and preoccupied, the second seemed devoid of the slightest emotion, and the last appeared to have given up his usual smiles. But, as Komar herself admitted, the task is not easy: planners have to work a lot, listen to the members and attend countless meetings, gather a multitude of information before making a decision, account for the choices made, regularly take stock of the community's situation, and so on. Yet the pressure is above all psychological, given the need to combine contradictory requests, listen to demands that are impossible to satisfy ... and constantly take everyone's opinion into account.

At Twin Oaks, opinions are expressed primarily in writing, which explains not only the lack of interest in the planners' oral deliberations, but also the small number of plenary meetings involving all the members of the community. One or two really important plenary sessions are held each year. For the rest, most debates take place through the Opinions & Ideas (O&I) Board, a system adopted in 1970 and still in place today. The principle of O&I is simple: everyone has the right to share their ideas, opinions, and recommendations with the community in writing. The system consists of 24 clipboards stocked with sheets of paper. The clipboards are hung on large vertical wooden panels at the entrance to the ZK dining hall, at everyone's disposal. Each new topic, whether it's informative or calls for discussion, is presented on a clipboard, and members are then free to respond in writing on a sheet of paper placed under the introductory page. Everyone can come and read other people's comments and, if need be, reply in turn. These opinions are invaluable for the planners; they frequently consult the O&I board, and they are not the only ones. All these written exchanges inform the thinking behind important decisions. In 2004, for example, after taking note of the opinions expressed on the O&I board, the planners decided on a new rule. Firearms would henceforth be banned at Twin Oaks; 'This policy', they maintained, 'is a clear manifestation of our value of non-violence'.[5] There is just one exception: a gun is kept under lock and key in the cowshed in case an animal has to be put out of its misery.

This kind of decision periodically feeds into the Twin Oaks bylaws, a document of over 300 pages which serves as the community's quasi-constitution.

Managers at work

The planners are not the only ones to make decisions. Managers also take part in regulating and coordinating the community's activities. As in *Walden Two*, those with manager status have to make countless day-to-day micro-decisions to keep the work areas for which they are responsible running smoothly. It is a key role in the community's organization, which Kat Kinkade defined as follows:

Manager. Being a manager means being responsible for a particular area of work. Usually they control budgets, either money or labor or both, deciding how much to spend on what, and which work is the most important to be done. They may choose crews to work with them, or may work alone. The responsibilities of management vary greatly in size. (Bees, for instance, is a much smaller responsibility than products)[6]

Managers are chosen from among volunteers who are willing to take charge of an area that interests them. It is up to the members of the councils – bodies that bring together managers responsible for similar areas – to appoint their new peers. In 1987, Twin Oaks had 12 councils with a total of 75 basic manager roles, plus a further 25 posts, for a total of around 100 positions of responsibility. Exactly 30 years later, I counted 118 allocated manager positions, plus more than a dozen vacancies. At the time, 18 councils oversaw the whole operation.[7]

The organizational work that managers are responsible for makes them real foremen and forewomen, who are largely autonomous in the way they regulate the work of others. As a result, compliance with working hours varies greatly from one manager to another. Some try to be as punctual as possible. When there is a shortage of work or too many people assigned to a given job in a given time slot, others are quick to send some of the unnecessary workers away or, as I experienced on several occasions with the manager of the seed workshop, to set a leisurely work pace interspersed with numerous breaks. Still others are real little entrepreneurs in their work areas and take the opposite approach. Percy, for example, won't hesitate to stretch his team's working hours out to get through the many projects he always has on the go. When I and others spend a morning under his supervision sorting wood, packing it into bundles, and hauling it, he keeps the group an hour and a quarter longer than he should have. No wonder, he tells us as we are finally heading to ZK for lunch, "time went by too quickly, I need more hands, nobody ever wants to help me …".

Managers are not only responsible for production and work organization in their specialist areas. They must also provide accurate accounts of the resources used, unit costs, and output. The archives are full of figures that show just how seriously the communard managers take the responsibilities entrusted to them, and the close attention they pay to rationalizing the use of resources.

An economic democracy? Resource allocation through the Trade-Off Game

The precise information that managers compile and record does not only serve to account for their actions to the community. It is also invaluable for negotiating the budget allocated to them each year. The negotiations take place through the Econ Plan (for economic planning), which started out as an annual exercise and is now twice-yearly. From October to December, the community rallies to set its objectives for the coming year. Community meetings, member surveys, the submission of personal opinions in writing, and a collective resource allocation exercise are organized. Then, halfway through the year, adjustments are proposed and negotiated. At Twin Oaks, this concern for accounting dates back to the early 1970s.

As Philip, the manager responsible for labour issues, explained:

> Each year, a budget is established for labour credits. The resources are the hours of work: you take the number of members, multiply by their labour quota, and you get a total amount. The managers, for their part, submit a substantiated request for the amount of work hours and the monetary budget they consider necessary for the coming year. They are then assigned a total number of hours for the year. If those hours are exceeded, the people who work for the area in question can't be paid. They're doing voluntary work.[8]

The most original aspect of this system is that resource allocation is subject to collective deliberation. To encourage members to take part in what can quickly become a tedious process, Twin Oaks invented the Trade-Off Game.[9] A game, perhaps, but a serious one, in which all members are asked to give an opinion on the budget requests (in labour credits and dollars) that each manager has made for the coming year. Beforehand, the planners centralize the information and make their own proposals, which each member has a chance to modify in the Trade-Off Game.[10]

Before playing (that is, allocating resources to each work area), each communard is informed of the total budget available to the community. Based on projections for the number of members, the volume of production, and the evolution of labour efficiency (condensed into a slack indicator[11]) that can be expected for the coming year, the total volume of resources to be allocated is established simply as follows: (number of members × weekly labour quota × number of weeks worked in the year) + slack. For 1991, for example, this gives a budget of 152,137 labour hours (69.5 members × 47 labour hours per week × 45 work weeks + a slack of 3.5 per cent). The planners also inform the community of the total monetary budget that can be allocated ($263,000 in 1991). During the Trade-Off Game, each communard receives a document containing previous years' figures and their justifications, as well as the rules of the game and some general information on the community's situation and priorities. Two main sections are then distinguished: ongoing activities (ongoings) and exceptional proposals, or OTRAs (One Time Resource Allocation). OTRAs will only be funded if there are labour credits and money left over after priority allocation of resources to core work areas. In the ongoings section, a table provides comparative data for each specialist area. It then remains for each member to make a proposal in the right-hand column.

On examining the various accounting reports in the archives, it would appear, first of all, that most of the time the planners accepted the managers' requests or were content to lower their ambitions only moderately. Second, in proof of a real ability to anticipate, the gap between allocated budgets and actual expenditure was never very large, at least for the years 1986 to 1992 for which the archives provide detailed information. In 1990, the projected budgets were 136,642 hours and $182,409 respectively. As the 1991 report shows, actual expenditure in 1990 was 149,874 hours and $179,537.

When finances permit, each communard is also asked during the Trade-Off Game to vote on OTRA requests to fund one-off projects that are not meant to last more than three years: replacing a window in a bedroom, equipping a building with an emergency exit, building a yurt, setting up a dog food production workshop, paying for a child's tutoring, setting up a reading group, putting on a play, and so on. Like the managers, those making an OTRA request must fill in a form outlining the project and provide upper and lower estimates of their requirements in terms of labour credits and hard cash. In the same way as for ongoings, the members decide by proposing an allocation within the ranges indicated. The planners, on the other hand, do not indicate their preferences. They simply centralize the responses and allocate the OTRA budget to the most popular projects.

To work, the Trade-Off Game requires a great deal of preparation. It also expects members to be familiar with all the community's activities. Few actually are. Some communards, exasperated by this limitation, are not afraid to protest. Leslie, for example, posted an O&I decrying the material impossibility of going into the details of every proposal, the lack of information on working conditions and managers' real needs in their specialist area, and so on. 'There's no dialogue, no opportunity to ask, get information, think, ask something else, work on problems, make suggestions. [...] To me, this stinks.'[12] This criticism sparked a flurry of reactions (14 to be exact), ranging from agreement to suspicion (is Leslie hinting at some unknown political issue?). The majority, however, make do with the system while stressing the need to improve it as much as possible. The process was modernized in the 1990s with computerization. Today, the procedure is largely electronic. Managers submit their annual budget requests and justify them to the community online.[13]

Conflict prevention and dispute management

In his book on North American libertarian communities, Creagh discusses Twin Oaks' organization, the role of the planners, and the means of decision-making. 'All this is relatively easy', he writes, 'because, according to several testimonials, the members trust each other completely. Interpersonal conflicts are rare.' (Creagh, 1983, p 274). This diagnosis is overly optimistic. In one way or another, disputes have always disrupted community life at Twin Oaks, so much so that very early on its members devised rules to prevent them or smooth them over. The concern for cohesion and efficiency has never been purely theoretical and the related questions remain as relevant as ever in the second half of the 2010s: What should be done if someone refuses to work or declares hours that they haven't worked? Or if a manager abuses their authority in the workplace? Or when some people never tidy up the kitchen after they've used it? Or if a member misuses the shared vehicles? What can be done about cases of gender or racial stigmatization? More generally, what should be done if someone does not respect the behavioural codes in place at Twin Oaks?

When the community was still in its infancy, the Oakers adopted an initial rule – the anti-gossip rule – prohibiting anyone from spreading information behind a person's back that that could be damaging to them. This clause is enshrined in the community's first behavioural code. 'We do not speak negatively of other members to a third party. Direct feedback, on the other hand, is encouraged.'[14] Meanwhile, if something needed to be said internally, the whole group needed to be able to hear it. The communards hoped in this way to avoid misunderstandings and defuse potential conflicts. In this spirit, for the first few years of Twin Oaks' existence, the community tried using a Generalized Bastard. The principle was simple. To avoid multiple quarrels, a single person was officially tasked with relaying criticism to the offender, while the names of the complainants remained anonymous. Unfortunately, the first person to take on the role soon realized that being a walking repository for verbal complaints was a particularly unpleasant exercise. So the system switched to written notes. After three years of service, the Generalized Bastard was replaced by the Bitch Box. If a member wanted to air a grievance against someone, they could write a note – worded as sharply as they liked, signed or not – and drop it in the Bitch Box. The notes would subsequently be collected by the bitch manager. The latter would not necessarily pass on the information to the people concerned in the sometimes very blunt terms used by the disgruntled party. He or she would inform those concerned in an urbane manner and encourage them to change their behaviour.

In the 1990s, the tools for managing disagreements were a little different. After all, in the meantime the group had swelled. The community therefore had to devise new rules and adopt new instruments, but without abandoning the use of tried and tested mechanisms (such as confession). Certain situations, such as romantic disputes, admittedly remained difficult for the group to manage and continued to provoke departures.[15] For the rest, the

Oakers weren't short of imagination. Contracts were one useful means of sorting out tricky situations. To help Denis, a psychologically unstable member prone to anti-social behaviour, Twin Oaks proposed that he sign a written contract setting out his rights and obligations. Denis undertook to seek outside treatment, to meet regularly with a community member to discuss the progress of his treatment and his day-to-day problems, to report to a three-person committee on the state of his relations with the community, not to take on any managerial responsibilities, to continue to manage his personal budget on his own, and so on.[16]

In the 1990s, two other methods, O&I and the appeal procedure, were used even more frequently. In fact, they became the main channels through which collective problems were conveyed, grievances expressed, and solutions discussed. These instruments are still in use three decades later. O&I papers are not necessarily intended, it is true, as a vehicle for adversarial debate. Yet it is not uncommon for the comments written in response to an O&I post to reveal divergent opinions, fuel controversy or, on the contrary, attempt to suppress it. In the mid-1980s, after six and a half years living at Twin Oaks, John settled his score with the community in a leaving letter riddled with acerbic remarks.[17] The vitriol was so harsh that someone saw fit to draw a skull and crossbones on the first page, followed by pigs' heads on several other pages. John had indeed levelled copious accusations: the Oakers were all dishonest, arrogant, cold, driven by a pathological desire for poverty. ... They all suffered from a chronic inability to cope in the real world. There were many reasons for this: drug addiction, sexual deviance, pathological laziness, problems with the education system, a bad divorce, extended adolescence, psychological fragility. Was this just a provocation? In any case, after his first volley of insults, John officially asked for a $40,000 loan! In the following pages, he mocked the Oakers once again, calling them 'Oinkies' for living like pigs. Keenan replied quickly and calmly.[18] Among other things, he explained that the conditions and standard of living at Twin Oaks were much better than John had suggested, and that the problem was not fitting into the real world but the real world itself, its values and its practices. Eleven comments of enthusiastic support for Keenan's remarks immediately followed this rebuttal.

In the event of conflict in a work area, appeals are another procedure designed to allow the protagonists to air their differences and delegate to a collective third party (all the managers in the council for the area concerned) the task of settling the dispute and making constructive proposals. When a dispute arises between a member or members and a council, the appeal is lodged with the planners. Finally, if the planners' decision is contested, the appeal takes a different form again. Anyone wishing to challenge the planners' decision has three weeks in which to do so once it has been made public. They have to post an O&I explaining the ins and outs of their appeal.

Those who support the proposal to override the decision sign their name on the document. A simple majority (50 per cent plus one vote, based on the number of full members) is enough to win the appeal.[19] In 2016, for example, Pam appealed against the possibility being offered to members to withdraw $10 a month from a 'vitamin' account in order to buy healthy food. Pam, who was still in charge of the garden at the time, took the initiative very badly, mainly on the grounds that Twin Oaks already offered quality food.[20] She won her appeal.

A fowl dispute: how to raise chickens humanely at Twin Oaks

The evidence is clear: not only are conflicts not unknown to seemingly the most consensual communities but, if the experience at Twin Oaks is anything to go by, these communities were very quick to come up with ways of averting them, easing them, if not resolving them. A concrete illustration will clarify the subject more explicitly and reveal the extent to which conflictual relations are immanent in groups whose members do not necessarily share the same opinions, nor sometimes even the same values. When Jake decided to leave Twin Oaks, he asked Jim to take over as the manager of chickens, for which he had been responsible until then. Jim accepted and quickly enlisted Nina's help. As soon as they took the helm, the new management duo started to innovate. While Jake had let the chickens roam free in a vast fenced enclosure, Jim and Nina adopted a new model – the pastured poultry system – which consisted of keeping the birds together in a small, partly covered, wire-fenced pen which could be easily transported from one place to another. The two managers had given the change a great deal of thought, weighing up the pros and cons of such an innovation. Certain of the benefits of the new approach, they did not feel it necessary to inform the community of their initiative. After all, weren't they the ones responsible for this activity, which, when they took over the reins, was no minor affair? At the time, the chicken coop was home to 70 young chickens destined, once they had reached a reasonable weight, to be slaughtered, frozen, and eaten.

Once the new system was set up, the reaction was swift. On 3 July 1992, Alexis posted an O&I on behalf of himself and three other members (Alder, Inge, and Susan), all of whom were outraged by the treatment of the chickens. The birds, they claimed, were not being treated humanely. They sometimes ran out of water during the day. Worse still, they were piled on top of each other. Shutting them in and depriving them of space was a barbaric practice. Finally, when the sun was shining, the heat was excessive, and the chickens could no longer take refuge in the shade of the trees. Alexis explained that with the support of his three accomplices, he had immediately alerted the managers. The latter had undertaken to rectify the situation, at least in certain areas. But he was not sure that this would be enough. So, concluded Alexis, 'I strongly encourage people to go down and look for yourself. You don't have to believe anything but your own eyes.'[21] The five comments that followed were in a similar vein. For Forest, for example:

> All of the chickens are very dirty from having to sit in their own shit for hours. The cage(s) need to be moved several times a day so that they always have fresh grass – both to sit on and to eat. Also the cage is not well-ventilated on the sides that are covered with tin. This should be changed too. I'm very dissatisfied with the conditions these animals are living in.[22]

Four days later, Jim replied with Nina's support. 'Are Jim and Nina mistreating the chickens? Are we being inhumane or cruel? Are we harming the chickens? Are we treating them worse than last year? Are the chickens overcrowded? Are we mismanaging the chickens? The answers to these six questions are "no", "no", "no", "no" and "no".'[23] To justify their actions and positions, Jim claimed to have expertise that the protesting members clearly did not. If the chickens were mistreated, they would fight amongst themselves and all of them would lose feathers. That was not the case. Jim added that he had looked after the chicken coop at East Wind community for a long time and knew what he was talking about. Next, having checked, the temperature in the cage was much lower than in the sun. Everyone could see all that. Following this corrective O&I, Nina immediately wrote her own.[24] She began didactically by explaining all the advantages of a system that other 'progressive' farmers had tried out before them. Because the shelter is mobile, the hens always have access to fresh grass. In a traditional chicken coop, that is not the case, and the animals soon become lazy and asocial, defecating where they stand. ... With a mobile shelter, you gain in terms of cleanliness but also solve other problems. In the fields where the cage is placed, the chickens feed on plants that the cows won't graze on. Poultry also break up the cow pats to peck at the maggots, which prevents concentrations of flies, and so on. Nina also referred to a scientific publication to prove that the space available to the hens at Twin Oaks more than met their needs. Finally, she concluded with exasperated irony, the night before some people had seen fit to move the chicken coop without consulting the two managers. The result: a bird was killed in the manoeuvre. 'Please,' Nina begged, 'don't just do stuff without talking to us.'[25]

Judging by the written comments that followed Jim's and Nina's contributions, their explanations patently failed to convince. So, two days later, several members decided to appeal to the Agriculture Council. 'We are appealing to the AG council the current farming techniques being used by Jim and Nina. We have witnessed that the chickens being raised by Jim and Nina are living under conditions which are inhumane, disgraceful and not acceptable in this community (in our opinions).'[26] The instigators of the appeal added that they had not sought to gather signatures of a majority of Twin Oaks members to support them, as appellants often do, so as to avoid aggravating the conflict and spreading unnecessary rumours. On the other hand, they insisted that certain improvements had to be made quickly: more space for the chickens; more shade; appropriate ventilation; water as required; better protection against predators; and the construction of a second cage.

After a visit to a 'progressive' local farmer, whose poultry farming technique had inspired Jim and Nina, the agricultural council met to deliberate with the two chicken managers present.[27] Before nine of their fellow managers, all of them similarly specialized in agricultural issues, the pair were given the chance to share their expertise once again, explaining that the chickens were not all of the same breed and that most of those that the community had bought (Cornish Crosses) were better suited to the pastured poultry system than the others. So it was not enough to go and look at the chickens to make an objective judgement. After a lengthy discussion, Jim and Nina confirmed their intention to improve the system in all the areas mentioned above. But the wound did not heal. Some time after the council meeting, the two chicken managers wrote another O&I to report back on the actions they had taken.[28] Susan, who had been one of the managers' most virulent critics, immediately explained her disagreement in writing. She had tried to talk to Jim and Nina, but they had bluntly refused; she couldn't bear to see the hens in cages, and a lot of people supported her …

This reaction twisted the knife in the wound. So Nina wrote back in turn: Jim wasn't refusing to talk to Susan, he just wanted to go through a mediator from now on. It was understandable, given the strong personalities they both had and their ideological differences. Jim was not to be outdone. In an O&I significantly entitled, 'Chix N'Clux. The saga continues', he accused Susan of lying, explained that he was still waiting for the information she had promised to give them about the standards of the American Society for the Prevention of Cruelty to Animals, criticized her for not having apologized for unfairly accusing him and Nina of cruelty to animals, and so on:

> We gave you some knowledge about chickens. We told you our chickens weren't pecking at each other, that the featherless patches were genetic. We measured the temperature of the cages and of the shady trees and found they were essentially the same. […] We also said that even tho [sic] we thought it unnecessary, we would build a second cage and *you said you would be satisfied with that*. […] Do you have a hidden

agenda here? I ask this because it feels like you have a zero tolerance for animal agriculture, and your actions are political harassment, not concern. Am I wrong? I hope so.[29] (Emphasis in original)

All this indicates that while the administrative appeal process may have enabled new proposals to be adopted to improve the welfare of Twin Oaks chickens, it did little to ease the conflict between protagonists with such radically opposed views. The incident confirms the existence of diverse sentiments among the Oakers about important issues, in this case animal welfare.[30] The 'we', in other words, is not always as solidly established as the communards might have us believe. Behind disputes that may at first seem trivial, opposing values sometimes crystallize that are quick to set 'I's' against one another. It is difficult under such conditions – as some Oakers are well aware – to hope one day to hit on the optimal organizational formula that would prevent all conflicts.

Infringements and offences

Along with conflicts, a lack of respect for certain collective rules is another stumbling block that can compromise the running of the community. Since the early days at Twin Oaks, the main deviations from the norm that can be identified are the theft of food, rule-bending, verbal abuse and, more rarely, the deliberate destruction of equipment (Kinkade, 1994, pp 216 ff.). Kat Kinkade recounted the time that the four ice cream bars she had bought with her own money and stored in a refrigerator went missing. Annoyed, she asked the planners to reimburse her for the damages incurred (that is, four times 45 cents). They refused on the grounds that such a precedent would encourage theft. Daily life in Twin Oaks is littered with similar incidents, the disappearance of beer cans being the most common offence. But whether the missing items are beer or other food and drink purchased with members' own money, very few thief hunts have been successful. So, apart from those who fall victim to the thefts, the Oakers have learned not to bother about these petty incivilities.

These days, bending the rules (for example, declaring more hours of work than were actually worked) and verbal abuse (typically in the context of a lover's quarrel) are breaches that elicit a bigger reaction from the group, whether via the planners or appointed intermediaries. When the offences are more serious, the members of Twin Oaks – and the same goes for Acorn – readily turn to the rules and institutions of the wider world. At Twin Oaks, engaging in sexual activity with a girl or boy under the age of 15, even if it is consensual, is punishable by expulsion from the community. The offender must then answer for their actions before the mainstream justice system which, in Virginia, considers age 15 as the boundary between what is lawful and unlawful in this area. The members of Acorn are also conscious of the problem – all the more so given that the degree of promiscuity is higher than at Twin Oaks and that the community's libertarian outlook can lead to misunderstandings. The rules of conduct on the website, on the other hand, are unambiguous:

> It is essential to obtain a person's consent before entering into physical interaction with them. Touching someone without their permission is an offence under Acorn's rules. Entering someone else's room without permission is another. Kissing someone after they've consented to a hug is another. And so on.[31]

In both communities, other forms of deviance call for stringent reprisals, which may also be imposed by outside institutions. If money is appropriated or stolen to the detriment of the community, the Twin Oaks bylaws stipulate that expulsion is inevitable. Kat Kinkade noted that when such a case arose, the planners decided to take matters further. On moral grounds, they contacted a financial organization mandated to recover losses and asked it to deduct the equivalent of the sum stolen from the offender's assets and income. Among the various cases of deviance that Acorn has learned to deal with in practice, one of the most serious was when a member deliberately set fire to a building where other communards were sleeping. The matter was referred to the courts. The Louisa district court sentenced the offender to a hefty prison term and, in 2017, rejected his appeal. It must be said that such cases are exceptional, as are expulsions.[32]

Commitment through confession

In the range of instruments that intentional communities use to increase people's commitment to the collective and thereby temper the risk of division and deviance, the staging of confessions complements all the strategies discussed above. In the language of R.M. Kanter (1972), it is a form of mortification, a technique for detaching the individual from themselves to better place them under the control of the group. Twin Oaks experimented with this early on in its history. The idea formed in 1969 during a series of reading workshops on utopias, when the communards discovered Oneida. Founded in 1848 by John Humphrey Noyes, Oneida was an income- and property-sharing community that practised complex marriage (Klaw, 1993). Members met every evening to discuss individual and collective problems. In addition to these daily meetings, members regularly submitted themselves for criticism before a committee of six to twelve judges or, more rarely, the entire community. The aim was to encourage reflexivity: everyone should become aware of their strengths and weaknesses, hear and understand how they can improve and, ultimately, help to build a good community spirit, the 'we-spirit'.

For a year and a half, Twin Oaks tried its hand at the exercise. Kat Kinkade summarized in her diary how the first meetings went. When it was Jenny's turn, for example, six or seven people gathered in a bedroom:

> Practically everybody said the same thing – that her work was sloppy, and she is careless and inconsiderate about leaving things for other people to do. Also some people said she made sharp comments to people without meaning to hurt as much as she does. Simon said she talks as if she is Miss Twin Oaks and knows all the answers. (Kinkade, 1973, p 155)

As reported in the community newsletter of September 1969, the comments from the first six people to be hauled over the coals were more positive:[33]

> It wasn't as bad as I expected. People said things that might have been rough on me, but they said it so nicely that I didn't feel resentful. I just felt 'I'd better watch that; I didn't realize it annoyed people so much.' And I did find out new things.[34]

Despite the participants' optimism, the pool of volunteers for critical scrutiny dried up and the practice was discontinued.

Other instruments with the aim of cultivating mutual trust – feedback and discussion groups, awareness groups, and the like[35] – also enjoyed a fleeting success in the late 1960s and early 1970s. Twenty years later, a new attempt was launched. In August 1991, 15 or so people set up a group called Belize, in reference to the Central American country of the same name,[36] with access restricted to full members. Belize met for two hours, twice a week. Initially set up to apply the feedback learning model from Ganas (a New York community), the aim was to help everyone better assess their own situation and difficulties by using the group as a mirror. The operation therefore called for frank and direct communication. With Twin Oaks values as its common moral requirements, Belize gradually evolved into a body concerned with fostering its participants' personal development, teaching people how to manage their emotions, and playing an active part in resolving interpersonal differences.

In the mid-2010s, volunteer Oakers still got together for meetings of this type. While the spirit was the same, a few changes had been made. Children, visitors, and guests were now allowed to take part. And the accepted term was now the Transparency Tools group. Paxus, who initiated these new mutual criticism meetings, explained in a presentation document that transparency is a way of getting to know others better, and getting to know ourselves better at the same time.³⁷ The aim of the exercise is to share intimate details in an appropriate environment. It is not a therapeutic technique, although it can have beneficial effects on health. The primary objective is to strengthen the bonds between people and thereby prevent misunderstandings and conflict. Paxus added that generally, three levels of transparent tools were used. On reading the document, I realized that I was familiar with the first, which is often used at Twin Oaks and in the rest of the community world. Group members aiming for transparency learn to introduce themselves with the opening sentence: "If you knew me more, you would know that …". Each person then completes the sentence as they like, describing a character trait, a favourite pastime, a piece of personal history, etc. The second tool, crosstalk, involves describing one's emotional response to what others have said. The important thing is to take great care not to hurt others when presenting and commenting on one's reactions. The last tool is similar to the first, but much more demanding in terms of transparency. Each participant in turn starts a statement with "What is hard for me to say is …". The confession that follows may evoke shame, embarrassment, shyness, and so on.

The policy of confession is not reserved for communards who agree to attend meetings such as those described above. At Twin Oaks, when a person doesn't do enough work (they're said to be in the 'labour hole') or has spent more than they can afford (they're in the 'money hole'), the bylaws stipulate that they must explain themselves publicly to the community. A letter usually serves as a vehicle for the confession. One evening in May 2016, I'm hanging around in ZK. An O&I document catches my eye. Its author has entitled it 'Explanation and plan around my money hole situation'. To understand the meaning and significance of the letter, one first needs to know that each Oaker has three internally managed financial accounts: one for their monthly allowance, one for money earned during their holidays (Vacation Earnings), and one for any monetary gifts they may have received. A communard falls into the money hole when they have spent more than the resources they have, bearing in mind that the accounts are balanced separately: the first account on the one hand, and on the second and third together on the other.³⁸

In the document I have before me, the author explains that the last few months have been difficult for them, they've had to cope with unexpected expenses, they tried to earn a bit of money outside the community but in the end they didn't get the jobs, their parents promised to help them out by paying them for odd jobs but then had $3,000 stolen and couldn't pay, and so on. The communard promised that they would do their utmost to get back on their feet:

> It's been humbling if not humiliating. I work hard every day and want to be busy working out of the hole but it's not an easy thing. […]

I should be able to work my way out by mid summer. [...] If anyone has any leads for work, I'd be eager to follow up on it. I'm deeply sorry and am rectifying as best I can.[39]

As we can see, the policy of confession is not just about building relationships of trust. By requiring a public explanation, it strengthens the community's control over each of its members, particularly in crucial areas such as work and financial resources.

6

Work: The Shadows of the Market

One autumn morning in 1969, five young people came to visit Twin Oaks from High Top Commune, a new community 50 miles away. They were struggling to survive on 50 acres of land that the owner had allowed them to use free of charge. The problem, one of them confided, was labour. Many people in the community did not want to work:

> The five of us do almost all the work. Making the fire and keeping it going, cooking the meals, and trying to get some construction started. The others are so young. They've never had to work before. They can't get it through their heads that there are things that have to be done if we are going to survive on the place over the winter. Last night it just got to be too much. We were having our evening meeting, and I suggested that we all commit ourselves to some task for the following day – just agree to work on something in particular, so that we would all be sure that things were being done. But a lot of people didn't like the idea at all. They said it was like the outside world. They said they didn't want to be 'structured'. But man, I didn't want to structure them. I just wanted them to do something. (Kinkade, 1973, pp 17–18)

The living conditions at High Top Commune were rudimentary to say the least (cooking on wood fires, no toilets, all work done outdoors) and the community had little chance of making it through the winter in such precarity. In effect, the experiment lasted just four months. As this community's experience illustrates, to have a hope of supporting their new elective families in the long term, the American communards had no choice but to work. The groups that did not reconcile themselves to this all disappeared soon after their start-up capital ran out. It's easy to understand how this should happen, though it may have appeared contradictory to them. For a lot of the young people tempted to withdraw into community, work had a bad press. A poem by Kahlil Gibran sums up the ethic espoused by many communards of the time: 'Work is love made visible. And if you cannot work with love but only with distaste, it is better that you should leave your work and sit at the gate of the temple and take alms of those who work with joy.' (Cited in Zablocki, 1980, p 123).¹

The message is alluring. But in concrete terms, how can work become 'love made visible'? To answer this question, two others need to be asked first: what kind of activities should be prioritized and how should they be conducted? In practice, intentional communities have provided a variety of responses. Some refuse to play the game of profit-making through commercial activities and sell their products mainly at a low price to poor groups who share similar values to them (Jerome, 1974, p 114). Others have a more instrumental relationship with the market, their main objective being to make enough money to live on without being completely dependent on customers from outside the community. Twin Oaks, which chose the second option, first tried growing tobacco, but soon specialized in making hammocks and finally tofu. An organization initially called Twin Oaks Industries served as the institutional backbone for the latter two economic activities. As for Acorn, their main source of income is a seed business. In both Virginian collectives, the production of goods and services that has been made a priority to assure the communards of a minimum income is doubly revealing. First, it indicates the gradual shift towards activities more in line with the ecological values that Twin Oaks now includes on its list of preferences (respect for the environment, concern for consumers' health and well-being, and so on). Second, it illustrates a form of permanent pragmatism that has a significant effect on the communards' working conditions.

From tobacco to hammocks

Most of the budding young communards who volunteered their labour at Twin Oaks in the late 1960s and early 1970s wanted to become agricultural workers. Indeed, like the farmer who sold them his land, their aim was to make a living from growing wheat, maize, and tobacco. The latter seemed a particularly smart choice. Not only was tobacco already grown locally, but the government was supporting tobacco prices. Meanwhile, whether through ignorance or disinterest, no one at the time thought of questioning the production and sale of a product that was damaging to people's health. Even before they moved in, the first Oakers made an agreement with the owner for him to come and work on the plantation at weekends. Once the initial wave of enthusiasm had passed, the communards struggled to cope with the unpleasant working conditions: physical fatigue, a scorching sun, sap sticking to their fingers and staining their hands black, and so on. Despite some blunders during the drying process, they were able to sell their first harvest at auction. The community made $500 from its first crop. The results were far from gratifying. A third of the sum was paid to the field's owner. Once the cost of fertilizer had been deducted, the profit was a tiny $300. Each hour's work had netted around 20 cents per person – woefully short of a decent living.

Given its unprofitability, tobacco was soon forgotten. Twin Oaks then tried other farming experiments such as raising chickens and ducks, all of which were disasters. The young city dwellers discovered that they knew nothing about farm work and the rural world. When they arrived at Twin Oaks in the late 1960s, some of them didn't know the difference between straw and hay. But thanks to the skills and drive of one of the young communards, the group persevered. At the cost of great effort, which most people found hard to bear, Twin Oaks produced apples, tomatoes, and an abundance of beans and corn. The venture was finally on track. But in 1969, they again faced collapse. Fatigue, ragweed allergy, floods, incompetence, and the departure of the only person capable of working the land intelligently and efficiently once again weakened the community. Twin Oaks bent but did not break. The other available resources (starting with the small herd of dairy cows) and a regular influx of new blood allowed Twin Oaks to survive the baptism of fire.

To stay afloat, realism compelled the Oakers to look for income outside the community. Many members were dissatisfied with such a constraint – none more so than the outside workers themselves, who had to get up early and come home late, accept unrewarding jobs, endure difficult working conditions, spend all day in the straight society that they had sworn to leave, and deal with the feeling of being marginalized from the community. Furthermore, relations with employers were not always straightforward. Two Oakers were dismissed, one for not wearing underwear, the other for being too open about his homosexuality. At the turn of the 1970s, outside work was not unique to Twin Oaks. Many other communities turned to it for want of having developed sufficiently lucrative activities to ensure their economic independence. As at Twin Oaks, the communards became teachers, nurses, secretaries, painters, bricklayers, and so on.

The Oakers also used their imagination to find new sources of income. In a Skinnerian spirit, Brian invented a toilet that automatically rewarded children who urinated properly by distributing chewing gum. The community spent a little money to publicize the project in the newspapers and attract investors. To no avail. Carrie made decorated Christmas cakes but, despite improvements suggested by Sandy, sales failed to take off. In the end, it was Hal who came up with the winning idea: to produce rope hammocks as they are traditionally made in his native Carolina. The equipment required was hardly elaborate, the technical skills were easy to learn, and the number of steps involved in making the finished product (seven in all) was not too daunting.[2] The venture nonetheless got off to a laborious and chaotic start. The problem was not so much the skill required as the lack of funds to buy the raw materials and a reluctance to sell the finished products. In 1971, four years after the first hammock was made (in August 1967), the problems began to ease with the arrival of a new member who was able to provide the necessary impetus. 1,200 hammocks were sold on the market that year, four times as many as in 1970. In 1972, the community's income was $1,200 a year per person. The sale of the 2,500 hammocks alone accounted for a third of the community's modest earnings.

In 1974, more than 3,000 hammocks were made at Twin Oaks. But careless bookkeeping was getting the community into trouble. A handful of Oakers took hammock production in hand, making the workshop more pleasant to use and teaching members how to be more efficient. Also, for the first time, a communard approached outside shops to help sell the product. The initiative was not in vain. The following year, Pier One, a Californian retail chain specialized in seating, placed a major order with Twin Oaks. It would remain a client for three decades. Also in 1975, the last of the communards who had been working outside to bring in income for the community was finally able to give up their daily exile. The decision to manufacture hammocks had paid off. By the turn of the 1980s, hammock sales accounted for 75 per cent of the community's financial resources.

Early on, however, the Oakers worried about the risks of being too dependent on one large customer, namely Pier One. Experience soon taught them that the chain's appetite for the product could have a major impact on the community's working and living conditions. When Pier One suddenly placed a large order with Twin Oaks, they had to be able to meet it fast and well. Weaving hammocks became a collective priority. During such push events, production could reach almost 500 hammocks a week.[3] Some Oakers worked ten to eleven hours a day, seven days a week. In return, the community did everything possible to make the atmosphere in the workshop productive and relaxed. Depending on the season, coffee, drinks, asparagus with hollandaise sauce, barbecued chicken, cakes, and more were offered to those making the extra effort. 'Sunday was great!' wrote Keenan about one of these periods of productive frenzy:

> The shop was full of the smell of fresh cooked waffles all morning. Lots of folks were sitting around the shop hanging out and talking, lots of folks were working, too. It felt very cozy and homey, as it does most Sunday mornings when Rainbow and Jim make waffles. [...] It was very funny. [...] I have been pleased and impressed and excited and warmed by the amount of cooperation I have felt during this push. The hammock shop has been a really fun place to be this past month.[4]

Another, more original operation – the 'hammock shop auction' – was sometimes proposed to finance the time spent meeting the urgent demand. The principle was as follows: any communard who wished could offer an item or service for auction. Proceeds from sales would then be used to pay for overtime in the hammock shop in the form of labour credits. The archives show that people weren't short of imagination when it came to auctionable items.[5] In the 1990 push, proposals included two cherry cheese cakes; the choice between two hours of being read to aloud or a two-hour speed-reading lesson; a philosophical breakfast; your room cleaned, bed-made, and laundry washed, all done with a smile; a painting; an afternoon of sewing to make the object of your choice; and home-made beer. To entice the communards to make hammocks, yet another scheme was devised – and was still in use in the 2010s – this time taking advantage of the communards' friendly nature. In exchange for non-credited labour hours, a member, guest, or visitor could acquire a hammock (or equivalent item) at below-market cost. This was called PFF, or Production For Friends. During a push, it was enough to announce that the PFF conditions were more advantageous than usual to draw the communards into the shop to weave for free, boosting the efforts of those already working hard to meet demand.[6]

Tying, drilling, sawing, weaving, assembling ...

Hammocks, like the community's other flagship products, are woven, assembled, and packaged at Twin Oaks. The wooden spreaders and the rope (since the mid-1980s) are also made on site, at Emerald City to be precise. The conditions in which these different operations are carried out are not all equally appealing. The wooden stretcher and rope production jobs, for instance, are much less popular than those in the hammock workshop in the central courtyard. In 1990, ten people devoted between three and 20 hours of their working week to rope-making. The machines used were old (dating back to 1929), difficult to handle, and very noisy. It was impossible to work without earplugs or a Walkman. As the work was hard and monotonous, those who agreed to take up a post in those days were entitled to a free Pepsi courtesy of the community.[7] The few forays I made into the workshop convinced me that the work there remains taxing.

In the woodworking shop, because the drilling and sawing equipment is just as old, the movements repetitive, and the demand sometimes pressing, it is no easier to ensure excellent working conditions. In the early 1990s, the manager complained about the high turnover affecting his regular team and publicly appealed for volunteers to come and drill stretchers, in an O&I ending with 'Sign up below!'[8] Two years later, in a bid to solve the persistent problem of the job's lack of appeal, seven communards put forward an original proposal. Why not make an exception to Twin Oaks' basic rule (hourly pay) and offer those who preferred a piece rate?[9] The group behind this small revolution estimated that a fast, efficient worker was one and a half times more productive than someone content to meet the standard average (50 stretchers per hour at the time). To incentivize the best workers to further step up their efforts, once they had reached the 50-stretcher threshold, why not pay them according to productivity, up to 1.7 labour credits, for example? Unfortunately, the archives provide no record of what became of this innovative idea. But is doubtful that it was enthusiastically received or that, if adopted, it had an immediate positive effect; indeed, four months after this proposal, the manager of the woodworking shop was fed up with the constant struggle and announced her resignation.[10]

The stages of hammock making that follow the production of rope and wooden stretchers do not take place at Emerald City. This work is done at Ta Chai on the opposite side of the property. In the workshop overlooking the central courtyard, people weave, tie, assemble, and pack. As a rule, the Oakers enjoy these jobs, the most basic of which don't take long to learn. It took me three hours to learn how to weave the rope passably, and even less time to master the knots that attach the main part of the hammock to the two wooden spreaders that frame either end. Weaving requires a repetitive motion and a modicum of attention to complete the right number of loops. Though done standing up, the work is not exhausting. Other, more technical operations are called for to finish the product, such as making the macramé pieces and knots that hold the different parts of the hammocks and rope chairs together. Only the most experienced members perform this work. They do it using specialized, yet nonetheless fairly rudimentary, machines.

Whatever the task, the communards approach it more positively for the fact that they work when they choose, at their own pace, and for as long as they want. What's more, no one ever monitors their work in real time. They have full autonomy. Another advantage is that there are no penalties for making manufacturing errors, even if it is strictly possible to find those responsible. Faulty hammocks are simply sold at a lower price. The only problem is boredom. To fend it off, many ideas have been and continue to be tried: playing music, giving someone labour credit for singing or reading a book aloud, making food available, holding group discussions on a given theme while working, and so on. Furthermore, as two people can weave facing one another over the wooden jig that supports the woven rope, they can chat to each other and reduce the tedium of repetitive work without losing efficiency.

Once a task (weaving, tying, etc.) is completed, the person who did it writes their name on a piece of paper pinned to the unfinished product. This ensures a degree of traceability, so that it is possible to tell at each of the seven main stages involved in making a hammock who did what. As we have seen, unregulated attendance at the hammock workshop and the interest most communards find in going to work there are not always enough to ensure that production levels match demand. The community must then call for volunteers. It does this at push times, but also during the winter off-season, with a view to replenishing the stocks stored at Emerald City. While incentives of various kinds serve to stimulate the collective drive, the pressure of the market never weighs directly on the shoulders of any one person. Individuals are free to decide whether they wish to contribute to the effort required. If they don't, it won't be held against them.

Outsourcing, integration, and business diversification

Well aware of what it means to work for the market, Twin Oaks began early on discussing the risks of being too dependent on a single customer, but also the drawbacks of specializing in a single product. Their deliberations led to the adoption of a strategy combining outsourcing, diversification, and vertical integration. The outsourcing took two forms. First, East Wind community was brought in to help make the hammocks to supply Pier One. Then, in 1986, Twin Oaks decided to provide work for a 'sheltered workshop' in Charlottesville (Workshop V) where some 60 people with mental disabilities worked in a range of fields (hammock weaving, telephone and alarm assembly, electronic circuit making, etc.) under the supervision of a former communard from Shannon Farm.[11] The workers could choose to be paid by the hour ($4) or by the piece (the fastest could earn up to $8 an hour).[12] As long as the Oakers met their compulsory quota within the community, they were allowed to go to Workshop V to work overtime and earn some personal income. Though useful for dealing with the most urgent pushes, the collaboration soon set teeth on edge. Cristey, for example, deplored the fact that the egalitarian spirit so dear to Twin Oaks had no impact on working practices at Workshop V. In fact, the atmosphere there was no different from that of a traditional company.[13] Kate, for her part, observed that in 1992 Twin Oaks was going to order 2,500 hammocks from the Charlotteville workshop and pay them $80,000 ($50,000 for the labour and $30,000 for new material), even though there was no real need for the extra production. This was 'misplaced altruism', raged the communard.[14] They had to put an end to this policy of charity. After a controversial debate within the community, things moved quickly, though as it happens the Oakers could do little about it. In December 1992, Workshop V changed its name to Worksource Enterprises. At the same time, the company decided to stop making hammocks.

Vertical integration was the second economic strategy adopted by the community and was still in place in 2023. Twin Oaks has been making the wooden components of its hammocks since the very beginning. Until the mid-1980s, however, it bought rope from a company in North Carolina. Realizing that the sale of its hammocks was becoming less and less profitable, mainly because of the remuneration policy imposed by Pier One, the community decided to change the formula. The calculation that convinced them was simple: making their own rope rather than buying it would save $1.13 per pound. Selling rope to East Wind would also generate $0.77 per pound.[15] The conclusion was self-evident: it would be worthwhile equipping the community with a rope-making facility.

Diversification, the third strategy adopted by Twin Oaks to curb any kind of economic domination and dependence, was envisaged even earlier than the previous two. In the 1970s, the communards decided to apply and pay for a patent so that they could commercialize a hanging chair, consisting of a rope seat and a U-shaped wooden frame serving as back support and armrests. The manufacture of this new product – which was still being produced in the mid-2010s – required similar equipment, know-how, and operations to hammocks (making ropes and wooden frames, weaving, assembling). In 1980, the sale of hanging chairs brought in $76,000. In the same period, two managers set up a new division of Twin Oaks Industries: Craft Fairs. Its business was to promote and distribute the products made by Twin Oaks and East Wind to small local retailers. Craft Fairs alone accounted for $127,000 in sales in 1980. When in autumn of that year, Pier One suddenly reduced its orders by 15 per cent, the diversification strategy had already borne fruit. Twin Oaks withstood the blow dealt by its commercial partner. In 1981, Twin Oaks Industries boasted a turnover of half a million dollars.

Throughout the years that followed, demand continued to fluctuate: annual production of hammocks averaged between 10,000 and 20,000 units. The early 2000s marked a real turning point in Twin Oaks' economic history. Orders from Pier One began to fall even more sharply until in 2004, the community's contract with the retail chain came to a definitive end.[16] In the short term, the end of the collaboration had disastrous effects. The loss of income was such that the Twin Oaks budget was slashed by almost a quarter ($50,000 for 2004). But it was not the end of the production of hammocks and related products. A decade on, the community was still making 700 hammocks a year. And it knew how to sell them. At first, it did so by mail order and at craft fairs which the communards regularly attended. Until the fire in March 2024, they could be ordered online. Several sites featured the products, prices, shipping options, and so on.[17] The range had also expanded over the years. The community used coloured ropes, produced fabric hammocks, and had specialized in making accessories (pillows, metal stands to support the hammocks, hooks, etc.).

An economic necessity turned ecological virtue?

The development of agricultural and agri-food activities is the last line of diversification and economic development adopted by Twin Oaks. The community first tried its hand at commercial agriculture in the 1970s. The attempt was a resounding failure, with a deficit of almost $10,000 after the first years of experimentation. Fifty years on, the picture has changed entirely. Twin Oaks works with Southern Exposure Seed Exchange, a company owned by Acorn (as mentioned earlier). The Oakers manage the order forms and build wooden display racks for the seed packets sold by their Acorner peers. The Oakers also grow flowers, herbs, and seeds commercially. A team of eight people, working four separate plots of land, produce about 40 varieties of seed (cucumbers, squash, watermelon, tomatoes, onions, and so on) which are sold to the Southern Exposure Seed Exchange, four other retail seed companies, and private individuals.

The most spectacular innovation, however, was to develop the industrial production of tofu and related vegan products. The opportunity arose in 1991, but Twin Oaks had begun considering a move in this direction a long time before. In 1982, the community carried out an initial market study and sought information on the feasibility of the project from a federation of cooperatives. Nothing serious was envisaged at the time. In the late 1980s, an opportunity arose. It was the result of a story that began with Virginia Soywork, a tofu production company founded in 1978 under the name Redbud Creek Tofu Co. The factory passed into the hands of Robert, a former member of Twin Oaks, in 1987. At the same time, Robert acquired a small tempeh production company. He located the whole operation in Nelson County. Unfortunately, an accident with the delivery lorry and heavy debts brought the entrepreneurial momentum to a halt.

When Robert put his business up for sale, Twin Oaks did not show an interest, as some of its members equated tofu production with mess, exposure to heat, and foul odours. Ken, on the other hand, a psychology graduate who had earned his stripes working at and managing the Twin Oaks dairy for several years, wasn't going to let the opportunity pass him by. With the financial help of his parents, both academics who earned a good living, he bought the business out of his own pocket. But he worked alone and quickly burned himself out. In 1991, Twin Oaks ended up taking over. At the time, the community was buying $1,500 worth of tofu and $700 worth of tempeh each year for its own consumption. After a clear vote (47 in favour, eight against, two abstentions), Twin Oaks purchased the company for $10,000. And promptly changed the name. In 1992, Virginia Soywork became Twin Oaks Community Foods.[18] The purchase of additional equipment and, above all, the construction of a new building – the Tofu Hut – right next to ZK cemented the community's new commercial ambitions.

Since production began, the company has enjoyed growing success. In 2004, turnover for this business alone amounted to $100,000 for the year. In 2015, after steady growth barely interrupted by a sales plateau during the 2008 crisis, the figure stood at $700,000.[19] Meanwhile, the product range has become more varied: plain organic tofu, tofu with herbs, tempeh, plain vegetarian sausages, spicy vegetarian sausages, peanut and ginger tofu, and spicy Thai tofu (with quinoa and amaranth). Together, the build-up of experience and product diversification have paid off. In the mid-2010s, Twin Oaks was producing a tonne of tofu a day (Reece, 2016). In the 2010s, this production has been the leading source of income for the community, ahead of hammocks.

In choosing to exploit a new market niche with tofu as its flagship product, the Oakers were not only compensating for the loss of a long-standing customer (Pier One) that had provided an outlet for their hammocks. They were trying to bring their business activities into line with their values. The dissonance they aimed to reduce in this way already had a long history. After tobacco growing, which the Oakers had accepted without really thinking about the product's harmful effects (but they were hardly equipped to do so at the time), the decision to start making hammocks had already sown discord. For some members, such objects symbolized bourgeois luxury. To be consistent, they argued, the community should have been producing essential goods. A similar criticism was voiced about the use of synthetic (polypropylene) rope to make the hammocks, this time in the name of ecological concerns. The pro-hammock side invariably countered these objections with two arguments (Komar, 1983). Cotton, the natural fibre best suited to the requirements of the products woven at Twin Oaks, is much less hard-wearing than polypropylene. And a hammock is a useful object. It's an excellent way to relax for American families under the constant pressures of straight society. In the early 1990s, a time when environmental awareness was starting to emerge, no choice could have been better suited than tofu to meet the new economic challenges that the market was imposing on the community, without forcing its members to renounce the convictions they shared.

At Acorn, economic necessity similarly harmonized with ecological virtue at the turn of the 1990s to 2000s. The credit goes to one of its members, Cricket, who at the time was working outside the small anarchist community. Cricket was employed by a biologist at the University of Virginia who ran a small seed production and sales business, the Southern Exposure Seed Exchange. Overwhelmed by the success of his company, the academic was looking to refocus on his research rather than spending his time filling seed orders. Through Cricket, Acorn was able to buy the business. By the mid-2010s, it was more successful than ever. The community generates half a million dollars in turnover a year, essentially through online orders.

The fact that such an activity is lucrative is not in itself a problem for members. Their primary concern is not to be contaminated by the productivist, bureaucratic, and anti-environmental logic that undermines the actions of large agri-food companies. The Southern Exposure Seed Exchange produces, buys, stores, and markets over 700 varieties of seed, with a preference for open-pollinated seeds. None of them has been genetically modified. As well as those produced on site, the seeds that Acorn stores and sells come from a number of neighbouring farms and communities (including Twin Oaks) whose members share the same philosophy of nature and life.

Environmental convictions are not just a pretext for choosing a business activity. They also inspire collective action. Along with almost 80 other farms and organizations committed to organic farming and permaculture, the Southern Exposure Seed Exchange joined forces with the Organic Seed Growers and Trade Association (OSGATA) to bring legal action against Monsanto in March 2011. They all accused the industrial giant of contaminating farms with its Genuity® and Roundup Ready® GM oilseed rape, thereby exposing small farmers to the major risk of losing their organic label. A second concern was behind the complaint: Would Monsanto not take their cynicism so far as to sue those who had been unintentionally infected by its products for infringement of intellectual property rights?[20] On 27 February 2012, a federal judge in Manhattan dismissed the case on the grounds that no contamination had been proven and that Monsanto had never taken legal action against farmers whose land had unwittingly been exposed to GM seed. The legal battle continued in 2013. Following that case, OSGATA and its allies could not defend their interests before the Supreme Court. The farmers nonetheless obtained binding assurances that they would not be harassed in the future under the false pretext of having used Monsanto products illegally.[21]

Producing vegan food

While hammock making and the production of vegan food products are both commercial activities, they involve very different production models: the first is a craft process, the second is an industrial operation. So when in each of these areas the pressure of rationalization makes itself felt more acutely than before, what are the implications for activities subject to the dictates of the market? Can work and utopia still be compatible? More specifically, what are the steps involved in producing tofu and other soy products? How is work organized in the Tofu Hut? The first answer to these numerous questions is simple: the work is organized in three shifts that keep production running non-stop from 6 am to 9 pm, Monday to Friday (and sometimes on Saturdays). Five basic functions (starting and monitoring the production line; making the curd; filling the trays and cleaning; packaging; packaging assistance) occupy between three and six people during the day, depending on the job. At 6 am, one person starts the production process. Others arrive at 7.30 am. From 9 am onwards, the workforce (five to six people) is at full strength.

Participant observation is unquestionably the best way to provide more precise answers to the above questions. My first experience in the Tofu Hut was helping to make tempeh. The process is as follows. After being carefully sorted by hand outside the building, the soybeans are placed in a large tank filled with oil and heated. They are then rinsed under running water and packed into a string bag. The full bag is passed through a spin dryer before the contents are mixed with a greyish powder in large aluminium tanks. One person stirs it all by hand for at least ten minutes. The treated beans are then weighed. Each batch is inserted into a plastic bag which has been pierced beforehand with a fakir (two nail boards in the shape of a jaw), then carefully stacked on a trolley to be stored in the refrigerator. Later, the tempeh will be packaged, labelled, and boxed before being sold to local businesses.

An early afternoon in April 2016. It's 12.30 pm when I join a team of six people at the Tofu Hut to take part in the production process described above. Like all the others, I don boots, a large apron, and a hairnet before entering the main room, dominated by stainless steel vats and metal machinery. As soon as I step inside, I'm engulfed in a thick blanket of sound in which the noise of the machines competes with the music of Thao & The Get Down Stay Down.[22] I quickly see that the organization of tasks is rather anomic. Betty, who is in charge of the workshop and the team, and another experienced member take care of the oiling, rinsing, and spin-drying. With little regard for our manager's instructions, we take it in turns to do the other jobs (stirring, weighing, packing, piercing, stacking) according to everyone's liking or availability. We work standing up. The music assaulting our ears makes it hard to talk to each other. I prefer to use gestures to communicate, as any words are drowned out by the hubbub of machines and sugary pop.

We work fast and sometimes a little clumsily. Soon a little competition starts up between us to see who gets to stir the hot paste. Every quarter of an hour or so, Betty fills a large tub with soft beans fresh out of the spin dryer. She then dumps the contents onto a stainless steel worktable. It's time to stir. Plunging your arms into the big lump, becoming one with it, breathing in its aromas, enjoying its warmth, feeling the plant matter stick to your skin so that you become a part of it. ... There's an almost animal pleasure in the operation. It's not surprising that we jump at the chance every time a new tubful is made available. The other operations are less sensual. Bagging is a tedious job, though with a minimum of experience it is easy to place just about the right volume of beans on the small scales to make 300 grams. Piercing the bags and stacking the small packages is not much more interesting. The competition helps to kill time. The winner is whoever most cunningly manoeuvres to get to the stirring table at the right time, or the most skilful at filling a bag to the correct weight at the first attempt.[23]

Tofu production, which I'm also involved in on a number of occasions, demands more physical effort than making tempeh. Usually, five people make up the team. The first fills barrels with a yellowish liquid. Together with a helper, she pours them into a vat where she adds soy powder. The mixture is stirred and then heated. The cooking process produces a white paste that is collected by a third person. The thick curd is cut into blocks using a home-made machine (the blades are domestic kitchen knives that have been welded onto a main shaft). The resulting pieces of tofu are hydrated and then placed in metal trays. Once the operator has placed a cheesecloth and a synthetic board over each of these containers, the trays are placed under a large machine for pressing. The round metal plates that press each batch of tofu wring out every last drop of liquid. The curd is then cut into small slabs ten centimetres long and wide and about half as high. Finally, two people collect these blocks of tofu, examine their quality, feed them into an automatic packaging machine, and place the finished products on trolleys ready for sale.

When I arrive at the Tofu Hut for the first time to help make the precious curd, I'm entrusted with none of these operations. The manager asks me to crumble up any imperfect blocks of tofu. Once they have been broken down as finely as possible, the small pieces are packed into a container and then pressed again by the millipede machine with its circular pressing-plate feet. I spend the next two and a half hours crumbling tofu – with some distaste – while trying to ignore the neo-electronic music blasting from the speakers in the workroom. At the end of my shift, like everyone else, I spend more than half an hour cleaning and putting away the bins, vats, machines, scales, and knives and scrubbing the floor. Everything has to be spotless when the morning shift arrives the next day.

Back in the little food factory three days later, I am offered new tasks. June, who is supervising operations, puts me in front of the automatic tofu packaging machine. Open plastic trays, linked together in sets of six, move past at a regular pace. The first person fills them with portions of tofu. The machine then hermetically seals the package with a tough film of transparent plastic. If the border is blue, the tofu is plain; if it's red, the tofu contains herbs. The film also provides all the health and marketing information required to sell the product. The second operator in charge of packaging – today, that's me – has to manually split apart the six trays that come full and covered out of the back of the machine, like you do with yoghurt pots. By bending the packs slightly to exert pressure on the connecting plastic parts, then breaking the link with a sharp snap, it's easy to perform the operation. But that's not all. The post also requires the operator to check the quality of the final package (to detect air bubbles, spot imperfectly sealed film, and so on) and put any defective packages aside. These will be cut open and the product put back into circulation.

The work may seem straightforward, but you have to move fast if you don't want to be overwhelmed by the flow of packages that emerge from the machine at a fair pace before tumbling into a bin almost a metre deep. After a good 15 minutes of agonizing and hesitation, I find that it's simpler not to separate all the packets one after the other, but to split apart whole bands of three first before they pile up at the bottom of the bin, and then to break off the individual packages. I also learn to quickly judge the quality of the package. At first, I'm aghast at the number of products I'm setting aside – almost every fourth block. June, who regularly comes over to check my work, approves almost all my choices. Fortunately, the defects soon become rarer. My real problem is keeping pace. There's no time to breathe, the rate is hard to maintain, the machine won't wait for me … I'm constantly afraid that the packets of tofu will swamp me and spill out over the sides of the holding bin. In my defence, the conditions aren't optimal: I work standing up, bent forward to grab the blocks coming out of the machine or to fish for those that have already fallen to the bottom of the bin. When, after an hour of torture, I stop to take a break, my back is wracked with pain.

After two one-hour sessions, June puts an end to my ordeal. She suggests I switch to cutting. Here, I collect the large blocks of tofu arranged in batches of ten on metal plates immersed in clear water. I then weigh each piece to make sure it comes within a range of around 450 to 550 grams. If not, the surplus must be removed or the undersized block supplemented with a slice from a previous overweight one. Most often, it's a case of adding, not taking off excess. Like others before me, I quickly realize that the easiest way is to prepare the extra slices with a whole block that you sacrifice from the start. With a few hours practice, I also end up learning to easily anticipate the right size of piece that needs to be added to reach the desired total weight.

Food production as I've just described it is not to all the Oakers' taste, and it's easy to see why. Everyone is obliged to pitch in to some extent, but members are unequally involved. Some really struggle to put up with the work, while others find it satisfying. A handful of communards at Twin Oaks have even become food production specialists. It is clear in any case that although vegan food production satisfies most people's axiological requirements, it is not a prime locus of fulfilment through and at work. Moreover, because the managers don't have the same authority as their counterparts in the wider world, the organization of tasks is doubtless a lot less methodical in the Tofu Hut than in a conventional company. Yet engagement in the work is not completely lacking – far from it – and compliance with hygiene standards is adequate. In the absence of strong controls and possible monetary incentives, the feeling of working for a common cause serves as the main stimulus for productive commitment in the Tofu Hut at Twin Oaks.

Is the same true at Acorn? The question is relevant insofar as commercial work also features prominently in the range of activities performed daily by the members of the small anarchist community. While it is continuous, this work fits into seasonal cycles that require varying levels of effort from one period of the year to the next. As readers will recall, Acorn has a huge stock of seeds and young plants, which it regularly replenishes and keeps in temperature-controlled premises. Orders come in from all over the world. In addition to the work involved in managing distance purchases, the communards have to bag the seeds, make up bundles of plants, prepare the parcels for mailing, and so on. These tasks are particularly labour-intensive during the first four months of the year. From as early as March until August, priority is given to cultivating the fields and gardens. In August and September, the communards harvest, clean, and sort the seeds. In the autumn, many orders are sent out before the catalogue is updated and printed over the winter.

During my stay at Acorn, the fields and gardens were a constant collective concern. But the communards didn't spend all their time in them. Several people took it in turns at the Seeds Office to manage the orders placed by telephone or online. There were two shifts, with the first team working from 9 am to 1 pm, the second from 1 pm to 5 pm. Little seed processing and packaging is done at that time of year. But there are always urgent cases. Preparing young plants to be sent by post to their customers is one such task that is difficult to avoid. One evening in June 2017, I'm walking through the seed building when I bump into Josie and Scattwood. They are sitting at a table in the main room with a young woman I don't know. She is wearing headphones. The three of them are extremely busy. When I offer to help, they gladly accept. The job involves packing sweet potato slips (vine cuttings from sprouted sweet potatoes) in batches of six, 12, 48, or 100. To do so, we use pieces of newspaper that we wet, fold, and fill with soil before gently placing the slips inside. The bottom of the bundle is covered with a small plastic bag and a label stick is inserted indicating the type and number of plants. The whole thing is held together by a rubber band. This evening, we're preparing shipments to Puerto Rico and Georgia. The young woman with the headphones works fast: she makes two packages while I struggle to complete one. Lost in her music, she seems hypnotized, her movements mechanical but steady and precise. But the work is hardly pleasant. We all have dirty hands and arms. Due to the water and rather cool temperature, our fingers go numb. Weary after three hours of intensive work, I give up. I offer to come back tomorrow morning. The young woman in the headphones soon talks me out of it. Because of the urgency of the job, work has to start again as soon as the sun comes up at 6 am. "I'm not sure I'll make it …" I tell her a little sheepishly.

Indexing work

At Twin Oaks, the communards do similar types of work to those just described. This essentially involves the production of seeds and seedlings, but on a far lesser scale than that practised at Acorn. The Oakers also perform more administrative tasks such as bookkeeping, order management, task planning, and reception.[24] In addition to these traditional functions, Twin Oaks indexes books for publishing houses and government authorities such as the State Department, which publishes official books and documents. The community added this string to its bow in 1981. They were offered the opportunity by Bill, who did not live at Twin Oaks but was a fervent supporter. An indexing specialist, he secured a contract in his own name and entrusted the community with the job. He immediately trained the Oakers who were interested. Thanks to their time at college, most were effectively qualified for this type of task.

Indexing quickly became an absorbing occupation for those who took it on. As Do Mi explained:

> In the early days, the work was mostly done by hand. The main indexer, or 'redliner', marked up the page proofs with entries and locators, underlining phrases in the text or writing in headings in the margin in red pen. I usually did this work around the community, in my bedroom, out on the lawn, in the dining room, in a hammock. I always had pages of my current index on a clipboard with me as I walked around. It was nice to be able to work in this relaxed way, although we were indexing 'blind,' unable to see the whole index until later in the process. (cited in Browne, 2017)

The annotated pages were given to another indexer, the 'carder', whose job was to write the suggested entries of names and things on small index cards along with the corresponding page numbers, then to alphabetize the cards. Once this was done, the final index had to be typed up, printed, and sent to the client.

Eight years after this new activity was launched, although profitability had begun to decline over the years, the results were positive: in 1989, 16 people regularly contributed to the business, representing an expenditure of 4,455 work hours that brought in $22,000 for Twin Oaks.[25] And 3,000 publications in a wide range of fields had been indexed. Although the overall picture was satisfactory, the question nonetheless arose of modernizing working conditions, to 'keep up with indexing in the outside world where more and more freelance indexers are using computers and are able to offer faster service than we can provide with our present "manual" approach'.[26] As this case shows, accepting to work for the market means exposure to the risks of competition. Despite the reticence of some of its members towards computer technology, Twin Oaks couldn't help but take the plunge. The community decided to modernize.

In the mid-2010s, a small group, reduced to three women and as many men, still specialized in indexing, which was now done on computer. In

Kaweah, the building where the indexing office is located, they also proofread manuscripts before publication to suggest corrections to the authors. When a new member wants to start indexing, they have to complete a six-month apprenticeship before being operational. For this reason, even if they later discover the drawbacks of the job (fairly solitary work, the need to meet deadlines, etc.), they are advised to make their training worthwhile by staying in the job for at least a year. But there is no formal obligation to do so. As one member of the team put it: 'We're not a cult!'[27]

7

Work: Utopia in Practice

When American journalist Eric Reece landed at Twin Oaks in 2014, he went into raptures. 'It is a place', he wrote, 'where everyone seems busy and productive, where obnoxious foremen don't exist, and where all workers share equally in both the ownership and the profits from their labor' (Reece, 2016, p 171). What's more, everything indicated, on the surface at least, that Twin Oaks community had managed to make work into something other than a sad obligation whose potential for individual and collective development had been spoiled by the capitalist world. Since at least the 19th century, the socialist tradition has been searching for the conditions under which the products of human labour would be, in the words of Karl Marx (1932, p 277), 'as many mirrors from which our natures would shine forth'. In the section of the 'Economic and Philosophic Manuscripts of 1844' from which that excerpt is taken, Marx asserts that to produce as human beings requires a person to experience an individual pleasure in work that expresses their individuality. One must also feel the satisfaction of gratifying a human need, be recognized by others as a complement of their own being, and ultimately realize one's authentic nature, that of a sociable being. Private property, Marx adds, is an insurmountable obstacle to the realization of such a vision. When the means of production are monopolized by the few, 'my labour [...] is the alienation of life', it is 'only a *forced* labour', it is 'my *self-loss*' (Marx, 1932, p 278, emphasis in original).

Like other intentional communities that have opted for equality, Twin Oaks and Acorn have abolished private property within their domains. By setting themselves up as little republics of the commons, they have taken a great step towards a world that is still largely unknown: the world of concrete utopias, where work is not reduced to the level of forced labour but is regarded as an emancipatory practice vis-à-vis the institutions of straight society. As shown in the previous chapter, intentional communities cannot do without some form of composition with the market. But the market's shadow is not so pervasive as to taint all the productive activity conducted outside the mainstream world.

At this point, then, we should investigate what part utopia plays in work within community. This is a vital question for the groups I have chosen to look at. Indeed, as Valerie points out, 'The back bone of Twin Oaks is our labor system. [...] That's our religion. We have these high priestesses and priests who are the labor assigners. We fetishize the labor sheet. People here derive a lot of their identity from their work areas' (cited in Reece, 2016, p 197). In putting work at the heart of its members' lives, Twin Oaks falls in line with a vast tradition which, from Karl Marx to Charles Fourier to Alexander Berkman, sees work as a practice that can become pleasure if we give ourselves the means to make it so. Under anarchism, Berkman (1977, p 337) wrote for example, 'each will have the opportunity for following whatever occupation will appeal to his natural inclinations and aptitude. Work will become a pleasure instead of the deadening drudgery it is today. Laziness will be unknown, and the things created by interest and love will be objects of beauty and joy.'[1]

In the field of work, Twin Oaks also maintains its connection with B.F. Skinner. In 'News from Nowhere, 1984', the psychologist revisits the story that helped make him famous, resurrecting two of his heroes, Frazier and Blair. In the conversation between the two men, Frazier begins by saying that the drive to replace human labour with machine labour should not be taken too far. "But it's human nature to avoid work," Blair immediately retorts. Besides, "You *enjoy* washing dishes?" "Perhaps I don't enjoy it," replies Frazier, "but I get something out of it that I lose when I put dishes in a dishwasher. It's what Carlyle meant when he said that all work is noble, even cotton-spinning." Skinner, 1987, p 40). In this chapter, the aim is to take serious consideration of this type of intellectual heritage – starting with Edward Bellamy's – in order to better appreciate the very real innovations spearheaded by intentional communities in the field of work.

Edward Bellamy's grammar of work

To bring their ideal of equality to life, the members of Twin Oaks drew inspiration from the writings of B.F. Skinner and, through him, from the seminal thinking of journalist and novelist Edward Bellamy (1850–1898), whom the author of *Walden Two* had read and claimed an affinity with. So, to gauge what utopia can do for work in practice, it is worth making a detour via Bellamy's masterwork *Looking Backward* (1888). The novel tells the story of Julian West, a young bourgeois from Boston who is irritated at the inconvenience caused him by the labour unrest of his time. In 1887, he is plunged into a deep sleep and awakens on the threshold of the 21st century, transported 113 years into the future. With the help of Dr Leete and his friends, who become the young man's guides, West discovers the Boston society of the year 2000. It has much improved while he was sleeping: wars have disappeared; so too have political corruption, economic competition, literary censorship, prisons, and child labour. Life has also been modernized and democratized: credit cards are now used to trade and goods are transported by pneumatic tube; streets are covered to spare pedestrians the inconvenience of bad weather; education is accessible to all; women have the same rights as men, and so on.

In his novel, particularly in Chapters 6 and 7, Bellamy pays special attention to the question of labour. Work is no longer a problem. In the socialist society that West discovers, all companies have been merged into a single economic entity. Labour is managed by a national organization: for the benefit of the nation, and therefore of all, each citizen dedicates part of their life to productive activity, in a similar spirit and manner to the compulsory military service that used to exist. While the structure is meritocratic (as in the army, people are differentiated and distinguished from each other by rank), everyone receives the same income. In different trades, the hours of labour:

> differ according to their arduousness. The lighter trades, prosecuted under the most agreeable circumstances, have in this way the longest hours, while an arduous trade, such as mining, has very short hours. [...] The principle is that no man's work ought to be, on the whole, harder for him than any other man's for him, the workers themselves to be the judges. (Bellamy, 1888, p 71)

A workers' career starts after completing their education at the age of 21 and ends 24 years later. Occupations within the national industrial system depend on the 'natural aptitude' and desires of each individual. To ensure that there is something for everyone, a system of bonuses (in the form of reduced working hours and other privileges) helps to attract people to jobs that would otherwise be hard to fill.

Looking Backward provoked strong reactions. One of the first to respond to the model of society that Bellamy had imagined was William Morris, who published *News from Nowhere* in 1890. In this now classic work, the hero arrives in utopia following the typical long sleep. William Guest wakes up in 2012 on the banks of the Thames. He sets off to explore a communist society where the state has abandoned its former privileges and plays only a marginal role. Collective decision-making processes have become democratic and respectful of minorities. Institutions such as money and marriage have been abolished. Laziness has also disappeared. Factories have been replaced by collective workshops where it has become pleasurable to work and collaborate. Guest asks of Hammond, his guide to the world of Nowhere, ' "how you get people to work when there is no reward of labour, and especially how you get them to work strenuously?" "No reward of labour?" said Hammond, gravely. "The reward of labour if *life*. Is that not enough?"' (Morris, 1890, p 77). The secret lies in the glorification of creativity and the requirement that all work be pleasurable, even the most routine. Happiness is gained, in other words, 'by the absence of artificial coercion, and the freedom for every man to do what he can do best, joined to the knowledge of what productions of labour we really want' (Morris, 1890, p 79). Compared to Bellamy, then, Morris proposed a far more radical reform of work. The productive grammar he imagined calls for work and art to be reconciled against a backdrop of pleasure and freedom.

B.F. Skinner made his preference between these two utopias of work clear. While familiar with *News from Nowhere*, the psychologist favoured Bellamy's proposals. In *Walden Two*, the work each person does earns them credits that are exchanged for the collective services they receive (housing, education, meals, clothing, and so on). In the community that Skinner envisioned, one hour's work is worth a certain amount of labour credit. As in Bellamy's Bostonian society, the value of each job varies according to its appeal: an hour's work in the sewers is worth 1.4 credits; an hour spent planting flowers is worth 0.2 credits. Thanks to this weighting system, which reverses the usual symbolic hierarchies, everyone participates equally in the production of wealth. Finally, in the moneyless world of *Walden Two*, again as in Boston, work is compulsory. This does not mean that motivation is lacking, however. There are multiple factors that encourage worker engagement: the jobs that each person does are varied, domestic chores are no longer the sole preserve of women, and a powerful incentive (the feeling of contributing to the common good) motivates each member of Walden Two to work consistently and effectively.[2]

Early trial and error

What did the Oakers do with the Bellamian organizational model that Skinner advocated? They did not, in fact, adopt it immediately. To start with, work was the subject of a great deal of trial and error and experimentation. When they first took possession of their land in June 1967, the pioneers simply gave free rein to individual initiatives. Everyone decided what they wanted to do on a day-to-day basis:

> At Twin Oaks we have come to classify this as the 'anti-structure hippy approach'. Not only hippies have this approach; there are utopian idealists who propose that in utopia the people are so naturally good that everything gets done and no one is exploited. Twin Oaks tried this approach for about a month. At first there was much enthusiasm (it was our first month of existence), and everyone was busy doing something. After a couple of weeks, however, we began to notice

that some jobs were avoided by most members, thus leaving them to those people who felt that 'somebody's got to do it, so I'd better, or it won't get done'.[3]

A second warning was sounded by Carrie, who had specialized in cooking and domestic chores. She asked why Kat's 14-year-old daughter wasn't helping her more. The teenager replied that she was not interested in those kinds of tasks and preferred to work wood and the land, as the men in the community did.

These two factors made the group realize that domestic work was an unevenly shared chore. As a result, they decided to introduce a system for distributing tasks. The communards poured over *Walden Two* for guidance. While they did find a theory of work organization in the book, they were at a loss when it came to the rules and measures that would allow them to bring it to life. Above all, they came up against a problem as significant as it was unexpected. What should qualify as work? What about useful but enjoyable occupations, for example? Was that really work? Failing a conceptual solution to the enigma, the community decided to share what were considered thankless tasks equally and let each member devote themselves to the more creative and fun jobs as they saw fit. Domestic chores were initially the only ones to feature in the catalogue of drudgery. But as the weeks went by, the communards reconsidered where the boundary should lie; hoeing, cutting, and harvesting had quickly lost their appeal. After a month, a new agreement was established. Apart from personal reflection, verbal exchanges, reading, and research of various kinds, all activities deemed useful for the group would henceforth be worth labour credits.

To remain true to its basic principles, the community set itself a dual goal. First, it was important to ensure that all members contributed fairly to the collective production of goods and services; second, everyone should be able to do the work that interested them most. But how could these two requirements be reconciled? The answer that the Oakers came up with was to devise a weekly game.[4] The nature and duration of the work to be done in the coming week was written on small cards: 'Prepare lunch on Tuesday, half an hour', 'Pick blackberries on Wednesday, one hour', and so on. The cards were handed out at random to the communards gathered in a circle. Once all the cards were dealt, each Oaker passed the cards for the tasks they did not want to do to the person on their right. Everyone sorted through the proposals they had just received and again passed on those that didn't suit them, and so on. Once a player was happy with their hand, they withdrew from the game. The cards circulated in this way until all were taken, that is, until everyone had reached their labour quota and was more or less happy with the jobs they had. The optimum level of satisfaction was in fact rarely achieved, but the communards accepted the minor frustrations inherent in this process without grumbling. They were all the happier to do so as they could then work out their schedules as they liked.

The system was original but time-consuming. So, after a few weeks, the rules were changed. The cards were placed in a box. Everyone came to look at them and wrote their initials on the cards for their preferred jobs. One member then allocated the jobs according to those preferences. When too many people coveted the same task, chance (the toss of a coin) would decide who would end up doing it. The same method was used to assign work that no one had initially chosen. To maximize equality, the communards adopted yet another measure, which was supposed to offset the unpleasant effects of a partially random distribution of work. As in *Walden Two* and in Bellamy's Boston society, the idea was to adjust the value of labour credits according to the desirability of the task. The initial equivalence was simple: one credit for one hour's work. If several people applied for the same task, the value of the credit would be reduced by 10 per cent (0.9 credit for one hour's work). Conversely, tasks that went unchosen gained in value (1.1 credits for one hour's work).[5] Once the value of the tasks had been estimated, each member decided what they wanted to do. The only requirement was that they meet their quota, that is, the number of labour credits they owed to the collective each week. When an occupation had no takers, a similar method was used to what was previously in place: the task was assigned arbitrarily by the toss of a coin. The same applied for those requested by too many people at once.

The Oakers were satisfied with the new formula. It worked quite well until it was revised again two years later. The reason for the change was that too much variety in occupations could be counterproductive. The Oakers found that with everyone constantly moving from one task to another, those who had started a job could neither follow it up nor complete it. Consequently, no one necessarily bothered to finish what they'd started. Moreover, they would often leave it to the people taking over to put away the equipment and tools, even if the latter hadn't used them themselves. To fix the problem, and despite the fact that most members appreciated the diversity of tasks, the community decided to give members the right to specialize. For work done in teams (making meals, cleaning, gardening, and administration in particular), one or two people in the small group would occupy the same position for the whole week. That way, the memory and continuity of the job would be preserved. In practical terms, specialization meant committing to between 14 and 21 hours in a single occupation. It immediately became clear that:

> this made the old competition and random assignment system untenable. For if you lost a 21-hour block at the flip of a coin, you would have to be assigned 21 hours of something undesirable to take

its place. Large blocks just did not lend themselves to a signup system at all. Something new had to be devised.[6]

For this reason, a new system was quickly put in place. It worked as follows: on their own sheet of paper, each member ranked the jobs they wanted to do. To express their preferences, they assigned a score from 1 to 40 to each of the available activities. The choice was vast. R. Houriet, a visitor at Twin Oaks in August 1970, hesitated for example between kitchen duties (putting provisions away, preparing menus, cooking meals, and so on), laundry duties (washing, ironing, hanging out, mending), agricultural tasks (looking after the cows, milking, feeding the animals, skimming the milk, tending the garden), craft work (weaving hammocks, making wooden stretchers), administrative tasks (mail handling, letter writing, printing, proofreading), and many other jobs (shopping in the nearest town, looking after visitors, and so on). Once the sheets had been filled in, the communards were no longer free to decide what they were actually going to do in the following week. It was up to two people to spend two days' work centralizing the requests and drawing up a schedule for each person that matched their wishes as closely as possible.

Things were further shaken up by another major change concerning the customization of the number of credits attached to each job. The value of a task no longer depended on the number of people willing to take it on, but on its ranking in the individual's preference list. 'That is, you get 0.9 credits per hour for your first preference, 1.0 for the next few on your list, and so forth. Jobs far down on your preference list may go for 1.5 an hour.'[7] Communards who did the same job for the same amount of time could therefore receive different amounts of credit. It all depended on the initial interest each person showed in the work in question. If there really was no taker for a task, lots were still drawn to decide who would do it. As we can see, the interesting thing about the system was that, in theory at least, those who performed subjectively unattractive tasks were rewarded more than those who enjoyed them. Although the Oakers never mentioned him, Charles Fourier would probably not have disapproved of such experimentation.

The aporias of behaviourism

A little more than a year after the reform, the system seized up again. This time, the sticking point was dishwashing. No one wanted to do it. To attract enough volunteers, it would have to be made worth even more than the 1.5 credits applicable at the time. Two credits per hour of work would probably have done the trick. The trouble with such a strategy was that it meant devaluing other, more attractive activities in return. The more hours involved, the bigger the problem. Dishwashing was a recurrent and particularly time-consuming chore. So what could be done? Devalue credits for jobs such as construction, where there was already a shortage of skilled labour? That was hard to envisage. As Kat Kinkade wrote to Ingrid Komar (1983, p 65) in 1980, the most appropriate solution would be to devalue the work done by managers, who received credits for organizing and attending meetings, updating and presenting data relating to their work areas, and so on. But did it make sense to pay 0.4 credits per hour to managers who would then have had to work 90 hours a week to reach their quota? Obviously not. Consequently, the community changed its system once again: from now on, everyone would take it in turns to wash the dishes. The same principle was applied to that other dirty work,[8] cleaning bathrooms.

Although restrictive, the system had a clear advantage. To solve the problem of the unattractiveness of the most off-putting tasks, it was no longer necessary to spend astronomical amounts of credit to the detriment of other jobs that were just as important to keep the community running smoothly. But the damage had been done. In 1972, after five years of experimenting with variable labour credits, Twin Oaks finally threw in the towel. Whatever the task, one hour's work would count for one labour credit. This move was probably the most spectacular expression of the group's departure from the Skinnerian utopia:

> Skinner's system was based on the idea that different work should be valued differently; the Twin Oaks system is based on the idea that all work should be valued equally. Whereas behavioral engineering was at the root of Skinner's labor-credit system – encouraging the completion of undesirable jobs by giving them a higher labor-credit value – Twin Oaks Community has chosen egalitarianism as the principle guiding its labor-credit system. (Kuhlmann, 2005, p 109)

In 1972, under the new system, the Oakers worked almost 40 hours across seven days a week.

Seen in the light of the founding group's initial convictions, the partial relaxation of the principle of job variety in 1970 was not as dramatic as the abandonment of the behaviourist principles that had underpinned the variable labour-credit system for five years. In reality, and with the benefit of hindsight, this second break is not surprising. By using a single parameter (the hour/labour credits equivalence) to achieve two different objectives at once (allocating the available quantities of labour on an egalitarian basis and taking account of the quality of tasks), the communards set themselves up for difficulties from the outset. As certain economists have shown (Akerloff, 1984), with limited resources, there is no way to achieve two things at once using a single instrument without risking pernicious effects. Indeed, when the variable credit system was in place, some members filled in their weekly preference list in a purely strategic manner. They gave priority to the least desirable tasks so as to receive more credits and, ultimately, work less than the others.

It is easy to understand the behaviourist logic that led the Oakers to reward the less attractive tasks more – to increase the value of waste management to the detriment of educational work, for example. But in seeking to increase equality through this means, they ended up undermining it. It is therefore also understandable that, after experimentation, they had to decide between two options: either a market-type incentive (the hours/labour credits ratio acting as a price to adjust labour supply and demand), with the risk of causing major inequalities in the allocation of hours worked; or the choice of equality, with the risk of frustrating those who felt their work deserved greater recognition. As we have just seen, the collective favoured the second option.

Variety, freedom, equality

After much trial and error to find the best way of sharing tasks and getting work done, the Oakers finally set in stone three principles of concrete utopia that were still in effect in the second half of the 2010s. Under the first principle, each communard must be able to prioritize the tasks that interest them, while also doing a variety of jobs if they so wish. The intention is laudable but not risk-free. Indeed, some jobs never find any takers, as was the case in the early 1990s for preparing breakfasts in the morning, drilling the wooden hammock stretchers, making pillows, producing rope, and certain routine administrative duties.[9] Obligation is then the only way to ensure that work deemed essential for the good of the community is carried out. This is still the case at Twin Oaks with the kitchen (preparing meals, dishwashing, cleaning the premises) and tofu production. Everyone is obliged to contribute to these two work areas every week. Only members with health problems, and from time to time those who do similar work elsewhere (cleaning bathrooms, kitchens, and other communal areas in Llano and Tupelo), are exempt from these tasks.

Subject to these exceptions, then, the communards are able to adjust their schedules fairly easily, both in terms of weekly distribution and content. The labour sheet they fill in each week to indicate their preferences offers plenty of possibilities to set time slots to suit everyone. The workable period for the jobs assigned to each communard runs from 6 am to 10 pm every day from Friday (the start of the week at Twin Oaks) to Thursday, Sunday included. There is also a box on the labour sheet to indicate which team the communard would most like to be assigned to in the Tofu Hut. The content of the work is, admittedly, a little more constrained. Managers, planners, and those specialized in a given work area (such as indexing, certain administrative duties, and so on) must reserve between a quarter and two thirds of their time for their responsibilities and their chosen area. Notwithstanding this limitation, the variety of work is real and unanimously appreciated. I did not meet a single Oaker who wasn't happy with this way of organizing things. A student who spent a month at Twin Oaks in 2013 calculated that in those few weeks, he was given the opportunity to try no fewer than 20 different occupations. This was confirmed to me in 2016, when I examined a notice inviting anyone interested to take on some of the jobs usually done by a member who was going to be away for a long period. Excluding domestic chores, 18 occupations were listed.[10]

The Oakers realized early on that the job rotation system had another advantage besides satisfying the urge to chop and change:

> In areas that really do require some training (printing, teaching, typing, skilled construction), we allow managers to request skilled labor only – that is, to restrict the signup to those who can prove they are capable of doing the work. However, even here we insist that the jobs be open to those who want to learn. The apprenticeship rule (you must explain your work to anyone who wants to learn it) is implemented by giving credits to learners as well as teachers of any skill.[11]

In other words, the variety of occupations is a catalyst for learning and upgrading skills. In turn, the resulting skills gains make it easier to assign as many communards as possible to as many posts as possible.

The freedom to manage one's own time is the second Bellamy-inspired utopian principle underlying the community's organization of work. In theory, the communards can work when they want. No one feels guilty for lounging around in a hammock at 10 o'clock in the morning if the mood so takes them. At Twin Oaks:

> We get up and go to bed when we please, work the hours that suit us, take on responsibility when we feel ready for it, work with other members whom we get along with, and participate in the Community decision-making that controls how we define creditable work. (Kinkade, 1994, p 35)

In practice, flexibility and the freedom to work with whoever one chooses are dependent on the type of activity. As soon as there are imperatives that are difficult to influence (milking times, regular meal times, customer calls), the work cannot be done at any time of the day or night. And when it requires intense cooperation on site and in person (as in the case of tofu production), it is impossible for everyone to come to work as and when they please. On the other hand, when the task can be performed alone or in small groups (weaving hammocks, looking after the animals, indexing, bookkeeping), the Oakers are entirely at liberty to adjust their timetable as they see fit – and they make the most of it. At Acorn, because the organization of work is more informal than at Twin Oaks, there is even greater freedom of action. The Acorners say they particularly appreciate the autonomy they are given. "Here, everyone organises things as they like," explained Thomas the first time I had the chance to visit Acorn. "And that's important to us. It's our anarchist side. If you want to work, you work, when you want, on what you want and for however long you want. [...] You can also do nothing. And nobody's going to bother you."[12] The weeks I later spent in the community allowed me to confirm the truth of this claim, but also to observe that those who push laziness too far always end up being taken to task for it. Eventually, the most indolent are systematically shown the door.

The final principle of the concrete utopia of work, equality, combines two complementary requirements. The first is qualitative. It is to recognize that any task is as good as another as long as it proves socially useful. The egalitarian ethic therefore calls for the expansion of the range of activities that can be defined as work. This means bringing out of the shadows occupations that, in the wider world, are not considered as dignified as traditional professional tasks. As such, at Twin Oaks and at Acorn, domestic, charitable, political, and health-related activities have the same status as other work, including jobs that generate income for the community.[13] The hours spent preparing a meal, washing the dishes, cleaning the kitchen, educating the children, going to the doctor, campaigning, voting, or volunteering for a charity must be counted in exactly the same way as the hours spent gardening, crafting hammocks, making tofu, or indexing books for outside clients. The consequence of such an expansion of the sphere of work is an impressive number of tasks – more than 200 at Acorn and twice that number at Twin Oaks – for which credits are awarded. The second requirement for combining work and equality is quantitative. All members have to contribute the same amount of work to the community. At Twin Oaks, a labour quota is set each year. It has changed little over the long term. The working week has always hovered at or more often above 40 hours, that is, between six and seven hours a day – a far cry from the four hours required in *Walden Two* (see Table 7.1). The only notable exception was in 1973. Due to an influx of new members, the quota was set at 35 hours. But the euphoria was short-lived. As the economic crisis made itself felt within the community, the planners soon revised the quota upwards. Since then, it has never dropped so low again. In 2017, the quota was 42 hours, as it was at Acorn. On the other hand, at East Wind, a sister community to the previous two, it was 35 hours.

There are a few exceptions to the quota rule at Twin Oaks. People who are ill benefit from a special arrangement. The same is true for older members.

Table 7.1: Average weekly labour quota at Twin Oaks (in hours, by decade)

Decade	1970	1980	1990	2000	2010
Quota	40	47	45	42	42

Note: These are estimates based on the isolated information provided by the archives.

Each year over the age of 50 entitles the member to a one-hour reduction in the weekly labour quota.[14] This means members must wait until the age of 92 to be fully retired. Under-18s, who are expected to work, are also exempt from the general rule. Their participation is, in fact, relatively recent. The principle was established in the 2000s:

> To begin with, we didn't want the children to work. It took a while before we suggested it to them. Then we prepared a set of rules and discussed it with the children. They asked us, 'What happens if we don't respect it and don't do our work?' 'Nothing,' we told them. And so the children said: 'Well, thanks very much! We won't work then'. So we rewrote the rules.[15]

Today, children start to lend a hand from the age of seven, a stage in their lives when they are taught to weave hammocks. At the age of ten, they must meet a weekly quota of 14 credits, which they divide between work and educational learning, with a minimum of four hours devoted to the first of these two activities and four hours to the second. At 13, the quota is raised to 20 credits and two eight-hour minimums respectively. Between 16 and 17 years of age, the obligations are 30 credits and two minimums of 12 hours. Of course, children enrolled in an institutional school network cannot meet these objectives. Their obligations are therefore slightly less restrictive: three credits for 10- to 12-year-olds, six for 13- to 15-year-olds and twelve for 16- to 17-year-olds. Whatever the children's school situation, if they fail to meet their quota, the community reduces the amount of pocket money they are entitled to.

From principles to rules

At Twin Oaks, the work assigned to each member is planned on a weekly basis. This is the first rule that Philip, a member of 11 years' standing, teaches us at the first orientation session. This meeting for the six of us visitors is entirely devoted to work issues. Seated comfortably in Aurora's small living room, we're all ears when Philip gets into the details:

> The work week runs from Friday to Friday. You have to work 42 hours. Every Monday evening, you need to fill in a labour sheet where you

indicate what you want to do and what you are unable to do. You'll get your sheet back on Wednesday with a proposed schedule. You can ask for revisions. Then you give us the sheet back and you'll get your final schedule on Thursday evening. You wouldn't think it but it takes three of us three days to do the schedules for the whole community. Once you've finished your week, you have to record what you've done, check that you've reached your quota and, like all the other members, hand in your done labour sheet.[16]

Peter doesn't wait until Philip finishes his sentence before asking him exactly what kind of activities can be included on the sheet. "All the income-generating jobs (gardening, making hammocks, etc.), household chores, and educational tasks count towards the quota," says our instructor:

As a visitor, your CVP (Community Visitor Program) training hours should be recorded. You'll find that some managers suggest holding work meetings during a meal. In that case, half the time is counted. When people are sick and can't work, they are entitled to six sick hours a day. But if they still go to work for part of the day, they can't add the time they worked to their sick hours![17]

It's Ruth's turn to ask a question: "What happens," the young visitor wants to know, "if it starts raining, for example, and we can't work in the garden as planned?" Philip replies:

In that case, it's up to you to find some other work to do so that you can still meet your quota. If that happens to you, have a look at the notice board in the entrance to ZK. There are always proposals posted there, especially for help cleaning up ZK after meals.[18]

Another thing: it's the managers who check whether you come to work or not. If the manager is absent, you have to wait at least 20 minutes at the workplace. After that, you can leave and count a third of the credit even if you haven't worked. Try to keep to the schedule when you have to, say when you have to meet up with others to go to the garden, work in a team at the Tofu Hut, or milk the cows in the morning. Otherwise, there are things like hammocks that you can do whenever you feel like it. Even in the middle of the night. You're free.[19]

Philip continues his presentation for two hours. From one week to the next, he explains, it is possible to make up for missed hours or overtime – but without going overboard. In theory, everyone is entitled to a maximum of 60 'flex hours' per year. Each time a visitor asks a question, the communard adds to the overall picture. This time it's my turn to ask him about holidays. He tells me:

> If you stick to your contract – the quota – then you're entitled to two and a half credits per week, which you convert into three weeks' vacation per year, and you can add to that your hours worked over quota. And you can take your vacations whenever you like! You can also leave for a whole year without credit, but if you still want to be a member when you return, you must have lived in the community for at least three years beforehand.[20]

Philip tells us that there are six or seven public holidays a year (each worth three credits). Every communard is also allowed a day off work on their birthday and the anniversary of their arrival at Twin Oaks.[21] The community grants them six credits as a gift. As a conclusion, Philip introduces us to the OPP (Overquota Projects Program), an original scheme that allows people to dedicate the fruits of their labour to original collective projects approved by the community.[22]

The next day, I give Maria, a young Frenchwoman staying in the community, a quick account of our training session. Because she doesn't have visitor status, she has never been able to attend these orientations. But she knows exactly how the community works. Maria confirms most of the information that Philip gave us. The young woman adds that she quickly realized that not everyone plays by the rules as Philip explained them to us. Often, for example, when for one reason or another they are unable to carry out the tasks assigned to them, the communards still report having done them at the end of the week.

My experience as a visitor convinced me that this was true. On a number of occasions, I also noticed that despite the formal rules, the value of certain tasks could be negotiated by mutual agreement with the manager of a work area. To encourage us to carry out the minor maintenance and repair work that members of the community shy away from, several of them (the safety manager and the forestry manager, for example) regularly offered us visitors more credits than the standard rate if we accepted the job. We were each then free to accept the price on offer, or even to haggle for a better deal. Another example: when we visited communities outside Twin Oaks to meet their members, the return trip invariably ended in negotiations with Cade, the co-manager of the visitor program who accompanied us each time. The challenge was to agree collectively on the number of credits that we would declare on our labour sheet for the time spent out visiting, but also lending a hand to the community that had opened its doors to us. Labour credits, in other words, are not an inviolable rate. They are negotiable.

From rules to practices: work in the fields and gardens

Among the array of non-commercial, labour-credited tasks that the communards ordinarily engage in, agricultural work occupies much of the members' time at both Twin Oaks and Acorn. There is a lot at stake here for the communities, as farming is a key means of gaining greater economic independence from the surrounding world. Both communities raise livestock for consumption: goats and pigs at Acorn, poultry in both communities. Twin Oaks also has a herd of several dozen cows that the communards milk twice a day. As well as drinking the milk, the community makes their own yoghurt and cheese. Growing crops is even more important. Although the gardens do not ensure total self-sufficiency in food, they provide ample produce for the kitchens of both groups. Ingrid Komar estimated that 70 to 80 per cent of the fruit and vegetables that the Oakers eat are grown and processed on site.

When I visited Twin Oaks, responsibility for the gardens had long rested with Pam, a communard in her sixties who would decide to hand over the reins in 2017. Her expertise is beyond doubt. Pam knows everything there is to know about planting, weeding, hoeing, cutting back, mulching, watering, and generally looking after the many varieties of plants that are grown here. Indeed, she is the author of a 450-page tome considered authoritative in the field of permaculture (Dawling, 2013). Most of the time, it is Pam who organizes the work of the six or seven communards who meet in front of the garden shed to earn their credits, taking turns every day of the week, in either the morning or afternoon. Sunday is an exception. On Sunday, the tools stay idle. Under Pam's supervision, the work mainly consists of weeding, digging rows for planting, hoeing, covering and uncovering plants, picking fruit and vegetables, watering, and so on. The work is varied but demanding. In the fields, time often seems to crawl by, and I'm not the only one to think so. Pam sometimes gives us a break, but rarely for longer than ten minutes. She also keeps strictly to the scheduled hours. There's no question of letting us go before the end time marked on the schedules. If need be, she can always find a spot to weed to keep us busy for a few minutes. On the other hand, Pam never holds us back once our official work time is over.

This Thursday, the weather is gloomy. Pam decides to put us to work anyway, but we aren't very enthusiastic. The following scene – which I would see repeated several times – makes that clear. After telling us that we could work today, the head gardener suggests that we stand in a circle and take turns introducing ourselves. There are about ten of us. As soon as the last person to arrive, a tall, skinny girl with long grey hair, joins us a little late, we each give our names. After evaluating the workforce, Pam explains that there won't be enough work for everyone. Those who would like to leave should feel free to do so. Four people, all full members, don't wait to be asked twice and immediately take off. I understand that the surplus workforce is a godsend for them. Clearly, none of them wanted to spend the afternoon in the fields.

The rest of the team gathers all the accessories needed for the work Pam has planned: wheelbarrows, spades, buckets, stakes, ropes, and gardening gloves. The first two hours are spent weeding the spinach, radishes, lettuces, and pumpkins. We work crouched down. We each take on a small patch where we conscientiously pull out the weeds around the crops. We're close enough together to chat and joke. Rebecca is opposite me. She explains that while everyone works every day at Twin Oaks, many members manage to organize themselves a lighter workload at weekends. They reserve Saturday and Sunday for housework and other less strenuous tasks related to their managerial duties. These jobs are all worth labour credits. As we pull out the weeds, we also talk about the difficulties that the younger generation has in finding stable employment after university. It's not unlikely, Rebecca tells me, that the inadequacies of the job market have something to do with the long waiting list to come and live at Twin Oaks. Here, at least, no one is ever out of work. ... The discussion with Rebecca is not only informative but also makes the time spent gardening go faster. The last hour is devoted to planting corn and grape vines. At 4 pm on the dot, Pam signals the end of our horticultural activities.

Nothing like this sort of personnel and time management exists at Acorn. Officially, no one is in charge of agricultural production. In fact, it's no secret that because of her skills and her daily commitment, one person and one person only, Alexa, reigns over the fields and gardens. It took me two days after my arrival to realize this. Unlike at Twin Oaks, working the land is not compulsory. At each Sunday meeting, Alexa calls for volunteers to help with the work she has planned for the week. A small whiteboard on the wall of the Heartwood living room shows who has accepted to sign up. Unfortunately, the team is often a few players short and Alexa has to call for extra hands at the last minute.

Working hours at Acorn are far more flexible than at Twin Oaks, with no fixed norms. One day in June, for example, Alexa arranges for us to meet at 7 am in a field near Heartwood. At that early hour, we will be spared the blazing sun. Five of us begin what will be a four-hour stint by covering the huge square of brown earth with a thick layer of straw. This will prevent weeds from interfering with the growth of the tomatoes we're about to plant. Using gardener's lines and little flags, we mark out the exact spots where we'll dig to plant out 200 seedlings corresponding to 62 different varieties of tomato. We work hard, but in good spirits. Some take advantage of the break to lie down and cuddle in the straw. When work resumes, I have a chat with Gryphon. She confirms that the official working week is 42 hours, but that there are no checks. Some people are anxious about all there is to do and work a lot, while others do much less. Sunday is a day like any other. Some mark a small difference by having a late-morning brunch. As for holidays, everyone takes them when they want, up to about two weeks a year.

Alexa arranges for us to meet at 9 am the next day to continue planting. At the appointed time, I find myself alone. I wait a while, then decide to go for a coffee until the work gets underway. Along the way, I bump into Alexa. The young woman is in tears. The people she asked to come and help her this morning didn't turn up. Sorely vexed, she takes refuge in Heartwood's kitchen. She emerges half an hour later in an emotional state that has clearly not improved. It's an awkward situation for the small group that forms around her. Josie offers her a hug; Alexa accepts and quickly calms down. Out of compassion or guilt, four volunteers immediately rally to continue the work in the tomato patch. This was not an isolated incident. One of my roommates tells me that it's a recurring problem. It is systematically repeated because of the trouble Alexa has in convincing the community's workforce to tend the gardens and work in the fields. In the absence of any control regulation that would allow her to get her peers involved using a degree of constraint, she resorts to a strategy combining persuasion at meetings and a marked emotional display (a depressed expression, crying, sulking) when difficulties arise.

Since its inception, Acorn has managed to adopt a sustainable way of operating that combines the principle of equality and anarchist culture in an original way. Besides the overwork and the emotional costs that a part of the community (the hard core, in fact) is willing to shoulder to this end, yet another tribute has to be paid to keep the anarchist ideal that the Acorners share alive. Paradoxically, at least in terms of the community's stated values, it is a form of laxity in materials management. On another day in June, five of us are working in the gardens next to the seed building. Again under Alexa's guidance, we weed the thyme, the vines, the raspberry bushes, and so on. We are not using tools. But all are aware that this part of the garden serves as a hiding place for snakes, some of which are less than friendly.[23] As I'm working with bare hands, I ask Alexa if it's possible to wear gloves. It will be hard to find any, she tells me, because people use them and then don't put them away. Gloves are left lying around, in buckets or elsewhere; they get hard and become unusable. Why not talk about it in a meeting, I ask her? "It's too minor a topic," she replies. Minor? It's not the only case I observed where, as in the early days of Twin Oaks, once the work is finished, tools and materials are left lying around. This also happens with leftover food or drink which, after a party or event, sits waiting a long time for a generous hand to remove it from the spot where it was abandoned.

The tension between equality and freedom

The differences in ways of working that have just been described precisely reflect the opposition suggested in Chapter 1 between societal communities

(Twin Oaks) and anarchist communities (Acorn). Another way to verify the relevance of this opposition is by looking at domestic work. In the kitchen at Twin Oaks, a schedule carefully specifies who is in charge and when. The managers who take turns cooking meal after meal have a heavy responsibility on their shoulders. Some are better than others at satisfying around 100 people at lunch and dinner. In the kitchen, the tasks are shared. The manager on duty divvies up the work, supervises the kitchen hands, and tests the end result. When it comes to dishwashing, the community is equipped with a high-pressure pre-rinse spray valve like those used in commercial and institutional kitchens, which makes the job much easier. Even with this equipment, the dishwashing and cleaning tasks have a way of putting everyone off. It is one of the reasons for people adopting micro-strategies of refusal and resistance. As in any conventional company, the communards are capable of defying constraints. Absenteeism and lateness are two particularly popular ways of doing so. No doubt the situation would be much worse without a minimum of pressure and control. Dirty plates and saucepans would pile up on top of each other, just like in the community's early days.

At Acorn, formal obligations are much more limited than at Twin Oaks. In theory, everyone has to fill in a labour sheet to record what they have done during the week. In practice, nobody does. I was concerned about this as soon as I arrived in the community. "I suppose I have to fill in a labour sheet?" I asked the few communards gathered in the Heartwood living room on the first day. Malcolm laughed and replied: "Labour sheets are only for people we don't like!" As a result, communal meals are prepared as and when people feel like it. At the Sunday meeting, all the communards are asked to indicate the domestic tasks they are willing to take on in the coming week. But the information is only indicative. Nobody knows what people will actually end up doing ...

Despite such uncertainty, the community manages to function. If no one makes up their mind to cook for the whole group, the communards each fend for themselves. And even when meals are shared, individualism predominates. When the handful of volunteers who have made lunch or dinner have finished their task, one of them rings the bell. The buffet is usually laid out in Heartwood's main dining room. Once people have been served, they sit where they like – not necessarily together at the same table as at Twin Oaks. Meals are special, paradoxical moments when the communards are almost always 'alone together': some read in a corner, some chat in small groups, others sun themselves on the deck. Dishwashing also reflects the spirit of the place. Again unlike Twin Oaks, the level of commitment of those who do it is more than unequal. Some simply wash the essentials (plates, cutlery, glasses) and leave the mixing bowls, pots, and pans lying around with food stuck to the bottom for days on end. It's up to the conscientious souls who follow to scrub the dishes abandoned in a dark corner of the dishwashing area.

These accounts of agricultural and domestic work show the extent to which the general principles of variety, freedom, and equality are put into practice differently from one community to another. Although the variety of tasks is a little more administered at Twin Oaks than at Acorn, it is not a problem in either community. The relationship between the principles of freedom and of equality, on the other hand, is less straightforward. In any case, it is embedded in organizational configurations with distinct profiles. For reasons that have to do both with its Skinnerian past and the large number of members, Twin Oaks operates much more than Acorn on the basis of formal rules that may hinder individual freedom but offer more guarantees to fulfil the promise of equality. In short, the main norms are as follows: an explicit obligation for all members to carry out certain tasks considered unpleasant; formalized weekly and daily schedules; transparent accounting of the labour credits contributed by each member; recognition of the particular responsibility granted to managers for the organization and orchestration of tasks.

At Acorn, on the other hand, the anarchist spirit precludes any such formalization. The collective operates horizontally, on the face of it at least: schedules are totally flexible, depending only on the wishes of each individual; work is voluntary, including the least attractive tasks; despite the existence of a labour quota, the hours each member works are not recorded; and no one is formally assigned responsibility for the 221 basic tasks that the community has identified to keep it running smoothly. This system of regulation generates and maintains an even clearer division than that seen at Twin Oaks: on the one hand, those who are intensively and extensively committed to work; on the other, those who remain more on the sidelines. As the fruits of all labour are shared in their entirety, the situation can hardly be described as egalitarian, at least if the relevant criterion for fairness is that everyone participates equally, in quantity and quality, in the collective productive effort.

The comparison between Twin Oaks and Acorn ultimately leads to the same conclusion that Alexis de Tocqueville arrived at, in a completely different way, during his stay in the US. In his writings, the French aristocrat noted his contemporaries' passion for equality. At the same time, he urged his readers to make a careful distinction between the taste for freedom and the glorification of equality. 'It is possible to imagine', he added, a model of society in which 'freedom and equality would meet and be confounded together'; moreover, it is 'to this ideal state [that] democratic nations tend' (Tocqueville, 1840, p 194). But they were not there yet. Worse still, when hierarchies collapse and intermediary bodies vanish, exposing people to the risks of political tyranny, equality becomes the enemy of freedom:

> At such times [...] the passion for equality penetrates on every side into men's hearts, expands there, and fills them entirely. Tell them

not that by this blind surrender of themselves to an exclusive passion, they risk their dearest interests: they are deaf. Show them not freedom escaping from their grasp, whilst they are looking another way: they are blind – or rather, they can discern but one sole object to be desired in the universe. (Tocqueville, 1840, p 199)

Admittedly, Tocqueville's reasoning is macrosocial in nature. Yet transposed to the community level, it is still worth considering. The tension between equality and freedom is immanent in the communities that I focused on, for the simple reason that the societal label and the anarchist label represent two poles with opposing requirements: on the one hand, an equality of condition guaranteed by a set of formal rules, at the risk of limiting individual freedoms; on the other, priority given to individual discretion, this time at the risk of not being able to meet egalitarian requirements. Work, as the communards shape it in order to comply with the grammar developed by E. Bellamy, constantly bears the mark of this major tension, with varying forms and consequences depending on whether the scales tip towards the societal side (Twin Oaks) or the anarchist side (Acorn).

8

The Flip Sides of Community Work

Far from being unanimously rejected, as some discourses in vogue in the 1960s and 1970s might have urged, work plays a central role in intentional communities. Work fulfils traditional functions: as well as providing for the community, it is a major vehicle for everyday social interaction and a source of personal development. Communities have found various strategies, such as developing specialty niches or opting out of the conventional salary system, to compromise effectively with the competitive demands of the economic world around them. In the case of collectives for which equality is a core concern, work has also often been dealt with in an original manner, whose principles owe as much to a particular history – that of the utopias that arose with industrial society – as to the lessons learned from the ingenious experiments undertaken in the 1960s. In intentional communities such as Twin Oaks, the work on offer is varied, free from oppressive controls, more flexible in terms of time constraints than in traditional companies, respectful of member's values, and inclusive of unconventional areas of activity (domestic tasks, activism, and so on). So much for the pleasant side.

But community work also has its less attractive sides. In addition to sometimes trying working conditions and lax, inefficient cooperation, communities have to contend with overwork, unequal participation, some communards having trouble meeting their work quota, and so on. Despite these risks, the communards spend a great deal of their time working. They are all well aware that without such commitment, the community would not survive long. However, as Mancur Olson (1965) showed, the existence of a common interest (the production of wealth) is not enough to explain collective action. When a gain that can be achieved through concerted action benefits everyone, individuals may be tempted to free ride. It is rational to let others spend time, energy, and money while profiting at no personal cost from the product of other people's efforts. To reduce the risk of free riding, organizations usually use selective incentives: they reserve advantages for those who contribute to the collective good, and place constraints on the slackers.

As this chapter will illustrate, on the advantages side, the intrinsic rewards of community work and the possibilities for freedom in effectuating it are not always enough to mobilize the required labour. Extrinsic non-monetary rewards – the positive flip side of work – complete the range of expected benefits. On the constraint side, peer pressure and threats are effective ways of limiting insufficient commitment to work, even when the job is not to a person's liking. At Twin Oaks, communards who fail to meet their quotas fall into the 'labour hole'. They then risk a severe penalty: expulsion.

Incentives and delegation

A lasting commitment to work from all members, while a necessary condition for the community to run smoothly, is not so straightforward. The members of Twin Oaks found this out fairly quickly. When they first began making hammocks, the production of wooden stretchers was a necessary but singularly unappealing task. The work took place outdoors, at times in the blazing sun, and involved drilling and sanding using noisy machines. The movements were repetitive and boring. Kat Kinkade (1973, p 56) recounted that one summer, the community noticed a limit to their organization: the communards were avoiding this job like the plague. Fewer than half the scheduled hours were actually worked. The rest of the time, the Oakers went swimming or attended to other things instead. Yet with hammocks proving so popular, there was a pressing need for stretchers. What could be done? The first solution was to increase the value of credits allocated to this unrewarding task. But the measure had no effect. So the hammock manager decided to task one person with making sure that those who had been assigned to this job on the schedule actually showed up. As nobody wanted to take on the role of foreman, they all drew lots. The position fell to a 17-year-old girl. She tried to call the slackers to order but their hostile reactions brought her to tears and she soon gave up. The community finally solved the problem by deciding to improve working conditions: it invested in more efficient machinery and moved the workstation indoors.

In the late 1970s, Twin Oaks also employed classic work incentive strategies. Material and monetary rewards were promised to those who exceeded minimum requirements. $1 would be paid into a common fund for every hour worked over quota. At the end of each week, the kitty was divided equally between the Oakers, giving everyone a little extra pocket money. Those who had directly contributed to the performance were also rewarded with $2 for each hour over quota. The financial difficulties that the community faced in the early 1980s put a stop to such largesse. A new system was proposed instead to prevent the community's financial reserves from shrinking too quickly. For four weeks, every hour of overtime would continue to earn all members of Twin Oaks $1. For the next four weeks, the personal incentive would take over.

As one might expect, the response was two-tiered. The first month attracted little interest. From the first day of the second month, as McEwan bitterly observed, the volunteers were falling over each other. In the O&I he posted on the subject, his anger was palpable:

> Why are 'they' so self-centered? Why did I work so hard? Why are my motivations so different? Why do some of those same folks mock behaviorism while they're in there pecking away for one dollar pellets? [...] I *have* been working too hard. Martyr syndrome? Too attached? Working hard feels great to me when we're really doing it together. Being part of non-participation and petty divisiveness at this time does *not* feel great.[1] (Emphasis in original)

The debates and discord that followed this type of observation spelled the end of these incentive policies. In 1981, Twin Oaks took a different approach to encouraging productivity by serving snacks to the Oakers who put in their hours in the hammock shop. But such expedients were nothing like as effective as the dollars promised in the previous experiments.

Incentive measures were once again envisaged in the early 1990s, when managers Jim and Rob noticed a major problem with the three 'K-shifts' that worked in turns in the kitchens throughout the day. As mentioned above, the job (preparing the meal, washing the dishes, cleaning up) was compulsory but unpopular. Resistance translated into systematic lateness, which disrupted the work, meant a heavier workload for the punctual communards, and made keeping to the schedule stressful. The consequence was low morale. After doing a quick poll, one of the managers estimated that only 10 per cent of communards were satisfied with their working conditions in the kitchen.[2] What should be done? Jim and Rob noted somewhat helplessly that they could tell the latecomers that their behaviour was unacceptable and explain why, but that it was unlikely to change people's habits. So the two managers suggested that once a month, those who were really put off by the kitchen shift could be exempt and instead do a 'Products' job (hammocks for example). It would be a way of encouraging punctuality. The proposal was deemed inegalitarian and immediately rejected by the community.

Another solution that has frequently been adopted and is still used today is to entrust the nastiest jobs to visitors. This practice is mentioned by most of the observers who have had the chance to take part in community life since Twin Oaks was founded. Their remarks have sometimes been harsh. After a visit in August 1970, Robert Houriet reported the words of some visitors who decided not to become members after their experience because they felt they had been instrumentalized. Not only did the Oakers use the visitors,

Stephanie complained, 'They use themselves. If you were handicapped or mentally ill they wouldn't let you join, because you wouldn't be useful to them.' (Houriet, 1973, p 322). Ten years later, Ingrid Komar (1983, p 62) came to a similar but slightly more nuanced conclusion: 'As a rule visitors were assigned unskilled jobs. These invariably included housekeeping shifts.' For the Oakers with whom I had the opportunity to discuss the problem, palming off part of the dirty work to visitors while the members monopolize the tasks that are considered more noble (because they are more complex) is justified by the fact that it is objectively difficult, not to say impossible, to quickly train people who will only live and work at Twin Oaks for the duration of their visit. Consequently, visitors sometimes find certain rules and practices hard to swallow. In 2014, Eric Reece (2016) was surprised to witness a scene in which an aspiring communard was flatly turned down when he offered to help harvest watermelons. Only full members, he was told, are allowed to tend to the melons.

During my stay at Twin Oaks in 2016, I too quickly realized that passing on the dirty work to visitors was a recurrent temptation for at least part of the community. When there was an uninspiring task to be done, I often heard communards asking out loud if there were any visitors available. Maria, who was also visiting Twin Oaks, told me that she had often been sent to clean the toilets – dirty work *par excellence*. Even if the official argument (that of specializing to the detriment of those who, more than likely, will not remain living in the community for long) is perfectly rational, the hypothesis that work organization is also informed by relations of domination cannot be ruled out. As can be seen in many other social spheres, unequal status often incites those at the top to delegate the less noble tasks to those at the bottom (Hughes, 1958). At the turn of the 1960s to 1970s, visitors were responsible for half the hours spent dishwashing. The same was true of gardening work and, to a slightly lesser extent, certain physically demanding tasks (digging trenches, hauling hay, and the like). In Twin Oaks' defence, other communities succumbed to the same temptations,[3] but in the mid-2010s the phenomenon was much less pronounced than it used to be.

The risks of overcommitment to work

The fact that delegating the dirty work is a recurrent temptation does not mean that the communards do little or no work. Indeed, the opposite is true. The collective encourages a strong commitment to productivity when economic necessity appears to justify it. The risk of burnout is also – perhaps more fundamentally even – the product of engagement motivated by adherence to community values. 'I enjoy that working in tofu production meets my desire for efficiency. [...] I work in tofu because the community needs me to.'[4] As a result of such axiological commitment, some communards pay no mind to boundaries, blithely exceed their quota, and are constantly concerned with keeping the activities for which they are responsible running smoothly. Continually overstepping the limits in this way comes with multiple risks, starting with declining health: chronic fatigue combined with difficulty sleeping properly, multiple aches and pains, colitis, and so on.[5]

In 2016, having sensed dissatisfaction among those who regularly worked in the little food factory, the tofu manager asked them to assess their working conditions. The testimonial written by Cody, a regular fixture in the Tofu Hut for eight and a half years, reflected the general mood fairly well:

> Likes: Good music; Good company; I still marvel at how fast and nifty the packager is, and how nice the packaging looks compared to older versions; When things are going smoothly, a tofu shift is still a decent way to daydream my way through 4 hours of labor credits; It's cool that everywhere I go, I find someone who <u>loves</u> Twin Oaks tofu. Dislikes: For the past 2.5 years my body gets sore (ironically because of an injury while doing Tofu Bod); Everywhere I look in the Tofu Hut, I see problems that I wish I had fixed by now; Hot summer, cold winter; People not covering their jobs, or at least letting someone know. The most absurd thing is when they post an open job card on the Today Board right at the exact time that the shift is supposed to start.[6] (Emphasis in original)

The other comments confirmed that it is because some people are overcommitted, and thus make up for others' laxity, that it is possible to produce more or less properly and overcome recurrent problems.

The second risk associated with overcommitment to work is that when the link between effort and reward is stretched too thin, it all becomes meaningless. Koala, a prominent figure at Twin Oaks in the late 1970s and early 1980s, found this out through bitter experience. Koala was heavily involved in the development of the hammock business. In 1981 he lost his grandfather. Usually, when a member of a communard's family died or was seriously ill, the community would pay for their trip to join their family. Yet in that period, Twin Oaks was facing major economic problems and had consequently initiated a plan to restrict spending. As the travel allowance was part of the budget cuts, Koala was told that he would have to do without. This refusal was incomprehensible to the young communard:

> I have worked willingly too long and too hard to have the door constantly slapped in my face on the most petty bullshit – like when my grandfather died. I had to ask five times if I could draw out the money for a bus ticket to go to his funeral. FIVE TIMES! Sorry, no

money in the budget. Walk there. Vermont is only 600 miles away. (Koala, O&I, cited in Komar, 1983, p 336).

The conflict escalated in a verbal discussion with one of the planners. 'Koala: The economic austerity plan is passe. All I need is $70. I've just produced $200,000 plus worth of sales. *Planner:* That has nothing to do with it. Koala (in tears): Good God, man! That has *EVERYTHING* to do with it!' (Komar, 1983, p 336, emphasis in original). Just a few months after the incident, Koala decided to leave Twin Oaks. His leaving letter hinted at his disappointment at not having been given greater recognition in return for all the 'energy' he had devoted to Twin Oaks.[7] But the tone was calm and the goodbyes friendly.

The third risk associated with overcommitment to work is deepening inequality and the onset of tensions between those who work hard, often the managers, and those who do not. In her second book, Kat Kinkade recounted her disillusionment in this regard. Such was her disappointment that in 1973 she left Twin Oaks for several years (she did not return until 1982 after living at East Wind, a community she had co-founded):

> I saw a larger and larger part of the community sitting around on the front steps of the dining hall smoking cigarettes and drinking their wake-up coffee at 11 in the morning, and heard them ridicule as 'workaholics' the people who made the money and kept the organization together. It looked possible, even probable, that this once-promising community would be undermined and destroyed by its own people. Our communism wasn't working. There was gross exploitation, but in reverse. The proletariat was exploiting the managers. (Kinkade, 1994, p 88)

The situation was very different 40 years on. The divide had since narrowed considerably. On the other hand, Kinkade's description more closely resembles what I witnessed at Acorn.

The final risk of overcommitment to work is a loss of direction. In some cases, the game ends up mattering more than the stakes. By investing their time and energy in commercial success, as two young communards who were leaving bitterly pointed out,[8] some people here were turning Twin Oaks into a kind of suburban economic unit, isolated from its immediate surroundings and unconcerned about the social issues facing the world (such as poverty and war). This confusion between ends and means can also jeopardize the labour-credit system. There is always a strong temptation to argue for expanding the scope of work to include meetings, music rehearsals, time spent preparing one's own meals,[9] and why not even discussions with one's children. This tendency is expressed on a daily basis, particularly when a manager and a worker negotiate whether or not a task is worth credit and how much. It's easy to see why Twin Oaks is sometimes made fun of within the North American intentional community movement for its 'labour-credit mentality'.

Community work and gender inequality

The unequal division of labour between men and women is another hitch in the model promoted by Twin Oaks – a symptom of the limits of both value-based recruitment and of the selective incentive mechanisms designed to give rise to perfect equality. This sore point was a source of debate early on. It's no coincidence. In his study of North American intentional communities in the early 1970s, Zablocki (1980) found that the main explanatory factor for specialization in community work roles was the communards' gender. The distribution of domestic chores was rarely egalitarian. In its early days, Twin Oaks was no exception. Cooking, cleaning the kitchen, and dishwashing were unequally distributed tasks. In 1967, Kinkade reported that:

> Generally speaking, the kitchen at Twin Oaks is handled by women, the tractor by men. The girls have repeatedly been offered tractor work, been urged to learn ('But I tell you, it's easier to drive that the Volkswagen!'), and the men have been encouraged to try their hand at the cooking ('You can *too* cook; you can *read*, can't you?'. But the change is slow.[10] (Emphasis in original)

Moreover, as we have seen, most people were reluctant to wash the dishes. For months, the task fell to the men and more often women who, like it or not, accepted to do it. The communards gradually realized that this situation – a result of the socialization they had undergone in the outside world – was not only iniquitous (and therefore contrary to the values they espoused) but also not conducive to maximum commitment to work from all members.

In 1968, when the community decided to solve the problem by making everyone take turns washing the dishes,[11] two men resisted, arguing that they really did not want to put up with that kind of drudgery, that the promise of Twin Oaks was to allow everyone to work as they pleased. Rather than complying with the new rule, one of them accepted to help clean the bathrooms, another task for which volunteers were in short supply. The second didn't give in to pressure. He never once did the dishes the whole time he lived at Twin Oaks. Apart from these two exceptions, since the new rule was adopted, the norm has been one of strict gender equality for all the collective tasks to be done within the community, with dishwashing remaining compulsory for all members regardless of their identity, seniority, or preferences.

The demand for equality does not just concern domestic chores. In the late 1960s and early 1970s, the women of Twin Oaks voiced loud and clear their desire to have access to all jobs, including those typically seen as men's work. This began with the maintenance and repair of the community's cars (Higgins, 1979). At the time, Twin Oaks had a small fleet of three cars that needed constant attention. To this end, several women trained as mechanics and, like their male peers, quickly became mainstays of the garage. When Robert Houriet visited Twin Oaks in 1970, he further observed that 'unlike many communes, Twin Oaks' women do much of the heavy farm labor, drive tractors, and shovel manure. They hold many of the managerships and have decision-making power' (Houriet, 1973, p 279). Yet practices and representations evolved more slowly than such one-off observations might suggest. In the early 1980s, Ingrid Komar noted that at Twin Oaks there was still a strong tendency for men to take on traditional male roles such as business, carpentry, and planning. At times, women complained not only about this state of affairs, but also that they were viewed solely as sexual objects.

In the same decade, the information leaflet offered to visitors acknowledged these ongoing difficulties:

> All work is valued equally – accountants and childcare workers enjoy the same standard of living as architects and hammock weavers. Our economic system is cooperative and collective. We encourage women and men to learn nontraditional work; women are auto mechanics and woodworkers, men are cooks and childcare workers. Statistically we haven't yet reversed our patterns of sexism. Often we make progress – our level of consciousness as a whole is far greater than that in the nation at large. But even after we have changed our systems to allow for greater choices, we struggle with the ingrained sexism that we bring with us to community.[12]

In 2016, the issue was still very much alive. In one discussion, Cassie told me that cooking and cleaning duties were still associated with women. Many members feel that this type of work does not require any specific skills, so there is no training to prepare members to take it on. In the small living groups (SLGs), the reality of the division of domestic work varies considerably. The most democratic SLG is Oneida, a house reserved for women with a few men nonetheless living upstairs. Elsewhere, it is often a handful of people, mostly women, who take care of the everyday housekeeping.

Sociology and anthropology student Julia Griffin spent 24 weeks at Twin Oaks in 2016 and 2017. During her stay, she was able to access a database which records the allocation of labour credits by gender over a nine-month period (April 2016–January 2017) (see Table 8.1) (Griffin, 2017). Total labour credits spent over the period amounted to 147,331 hours, broken down as follows: income-generating labour (32 per cent), non-income-generating labour (42 per cent), and solidarity (26 per cent).[13] In 2016–2017, the breakdown of members by gender was as follows: 45 per cent women, 52 per cent men, and 3 per cent gender non-conforming or non-binary. As the number of people included in the latter category is too small, the results used in the table below are based on the classic male/female split (46.5 per cent/53.5 per cent). If we consider that an egalitarian division of labour should reproduce the same proportion of labour credits allocated to both sexes in all work areas as the proportion of female and male members, we can immediately see that the egalitarian ideal has not been achieved. For instance, women perform 35 per cent of all income-generating work, a far cry from the theoretical 46.5 per cent. On the other hand, women dominate the non-income sector (55 per cent). Looking in more detail at the most important activities, it becomes clear that hammock making and tofu production are the most male-dominated income-generating activities. Of the 17,016 hours worked on hammock production over the period, 27.5 per cent were worked by women and 72.5 per cent by men. In addition,

Table 8.1: Division of labour credits by gender and activity at Twin Oaks (April 2016–January 2017)

	Labour credits	Women (%)	Men (%)
Income-generating work including	47,450	35.0	65.0
Hammocks	17,000	27.5	72.5
Tofu	18,300	35.0	65.0
Sales	7,700	41.5	58.5
Indexing	1,300	38.5	61.5
Seeds	2,000	50.0	50.0
Non-income work including	61,400	55.0	45.0
Educating children	15,000	60.0	40.0
Cooking	8,120	49.0	51.0
Cleaning	6,650	59.0	41.0
Shopping	2,290	83.0	17.0
Care	940	69.0	31.0
Solidarity labour credits (sickness, birthdays, holidays, pensions, etc.)	38,450	Unavailable	Unavailable

Source: Data produced by Griffin (2017)

shopping, care work, and education activities are the most female-dominated in the non-income sector.

What about the responsibilities that women and men take on as managers to run the many different activities that take place on a daily basis at Twin Oaks? To help answer this question, I was able to gather valid data for 1991 and 2016 (see Table 8.2).[14] At the start of the 1990s, the community had 79 members (48 per cent of whom were men) and the community had identified more than 400 work positions. A manager's role could be shared by several people, but in most cases a single person held the post. The managers of each area sat on one of the 12 councils that brought together people working in related fields. Twenty-five years later, the document in ZK listing all the managers showed that there were now only 118 positions, with a further ten or so vacant. Because the same post can be shared by several people, there were in fact 174 positions (with one person being able to hold several at once) held by 91 men and 73 women. In 1991, the figures were 407 positions held by 288 men and 190 women.

The differences in typologies used for the two years and the choices made in constructing these basic statistics preclude any one-to-one comparison between 1991 and 2016. And there is yet another limit to the exercise. Presented in this way, the data does not make it possible to distinguish between the managers who in effect head up the councils and those who do not. In the case of agriculture, for example, in 2016 the council was dominated by men. But it was a woman who had long been overseeing the community's policy in this area. Despite these weaknesses, a conclusion can nevertheless be drawn: there is a medium-term constant in the gendered division of labour. To be more precise, from the point of view of both basic work and management, men continue to specialize in income-generating activities, while women specialize in certain non-income areas (primarily education, health, and care). No more than in the early days of the Twin Oaks adventure have the communards been able to completely shake off the gender habits forged before their arrival in the community. But let's not throw the baby out with the bathwater: although the division of labour remains unequal, at least the value attributed to the activities that are performed more by women is strictly equal to the others, which is not the case in the wider world.

The labour hole

The multiple downsides of community work mentioned above (dirty work, fatigue, loss of meaning, inequality) do not deter the vast majority of Twin Oaks members from devoting much of their time to the production of social utilities recognized and validated by the labour credits system. Most communards meet their weekly quota. Some, however, do not. In local

Table 8.2: Distribution of managerial responsibilities at Twin Oaks by gender (1991 and 2016)

	1991			2016		
	Male-dominated	**Equal**	**Female-dominated**	**Male-dominated**	**Equal**	**Female-dominated**
Councils concerned	Income work (hammocks, tofu, etc.) Construction and maintenance Domestic work Events and communication	Agriculture Culinary Planning Cross-cutting services Transport	Child education Health Office work	Construction and maintenance Office work Events and communication Cross-cutting social services Transport Production (wood) Other income-generating production	Domestic work Planning Production (rope)	Child education Community service Culinary Grounds Health Material support
Relative weight of the councils	38.6%	43.7%	17.7%	61.0%	19.5%	19.5%

Note: In terms of overall gender distribution, in 1991, men were proportionally dominant among managers of income-generating work areas. Positions in male-dominated sectors account for 38.6 per cent of total managerial positions.

parlance, as readers may recall, they are said to be in the 'labour hole'. The history of Twin Oaks abounds with anecdotes on the subject. One of the first episodes takes us back to autumn 1967 (Kinkade, 1973). Twenty-eight-year-old Charlie, a self-proclaimed poet and philosopher, spent most of his time playing guitar. It must be said that the young man had had little experience of working life, having always lived off his successive lovers. He refused to take part in the labour credits system, insisting that a decent utopian community should provide for artists like him. He had the support of Marie, who arrived at Twin Oaks at about the same time as he did and had fallen in love with the rebel. To spare her partner the reproaches that his hostile attitude to any form of productive activity soon provoked, the young woman decided to fill in Charlie's labour sheet, allocating hours to him that were officially done with her (cooking, washing) but were actually done by her.

As the community was still small at the time (12 people), the trick was soon discovered. It was then decided that only people who did a job could receive the corresponding credits. Marie was the first to complain about the new deal. Why shouldn't she work more for free out of love for her partner? 'When someone demands the right to be exploited, the designers of an equalitarian society feel muddled, to say the least', admitted Kinkade (1973, p 47). But the group did not give in. For good measure and to save face, Charlie agreed to get to work. When the mood took him, even at the most unlikely of times, he wove hammocks. But his enthusiasm was minimal. The community was not fooled. Four weeks later, they gave the indolent man an ultimatum: he could either catch up with his 75 missed credits or he could leave Twin Oaks. Without hesitating, Charlie chose the second option.

It would be easy to include endless similar anecdotes. Since 1967, the community has regularly had to negotiate with members who fail to fulfil their work obligations, whether voluntarily or not. In 1990, on leaving Twin Oaks, Emma depicted herself in a short comic strip chronicling her disappointments. In the beginning, everything was perfect:

> All these groovy folks were about, leading groovy lives. Of course I was afraid of not fitting in ... but mostly I just started dancing and singing and laughing ... that was until I started having 'trouble with quota'. TROUBLE WITH QUOTA is a very ugly thing. It makes you scared of falling into <u>HOLES</u>. So you push, push, push yourself ... and I'd never had to do that before; except in things that I liked to do, and then I didn't have to push.[15] (Emphasis in original)

Emma ended up falling ill. She tried as best she could to get back on track. But it was too late. By the time she was back on her feet, frustration, anxiety, and bitterness had outweighed all the rest. She no longer belonged at Twin Oaks.

Whatever the reason, finding oneself stuck in the labour hole is an uncomfortable position to be in – all the more so because the communard concerned must account for their situation to all their peers. An O&I posted by Loki in 2016 perfectly illustrates what I referred to earlier as the policy of confession:

> I messed up with my labor contract Letter. I have had a bad couple months with my health, really it's been about a year, but the last 8 or 9 weeks was really bad. I've now been to the doctor 4 times and trying to get well. I will do my best to get out of this labor hole as soon as I can.[16]

The risk of falling into the labour hole also raises persistent questions about the 'right' forms of recognition for the work done (Komar, 1983). Some of the questions posted at regular intervals on the O&I board speak eloquently to this: 'To each according to his ability …? Isn't equality just an unattainable goal?' 'Are the metas [child carers] really working hard when they're out for a walk with the kids?', 'Is our goal to reinforce the Protestant work ethic?', 'Could the quotas be lower?', 'Isn't the lifestyle we promote by working the way we do too consumerist?', and so on.

Counter-gifts in the community system of gift-exchange

While it may serve as a stimulus to work, the fear of falling into the labour hole alone is not a powerful enough selective incentive to motivate all the communards. The real incentive is positive. It takes the form of various counter-gifts (*contre-dons*) that every member who fulfils their share of obligations receives by right. On joining the community, each new member signs a contract. Initially, communards pledged not only to share all their sources of income, but also to donate their assets. The rule was later revised. Apart from income earned working during holiday periods or small gifts from family and friends, all the financial resources that a communard receives accrue to Twin Oaks (such as rent on a house that the communard owns or interest on a financial investment). Assets acquired before joining the community, on the other hand, remain the private property of the new member.

Although in many respects, the relations that bind each member of Twin Oaks to the community escape the threefold injunction (give, receive, reciprocate) that Marcel Mauss (1925) used to describe the gift dynamic, they are more akin to Mauss's model than to exchanges calibrated by rational calculations. Apart from those linked to the quota policy, there are no constraints or controls weighing on individual Oakers to determine what they are entitled to in return for their qualifications, seniority in a post, productive performance, and so on. The desire for equality that structures community actions and interactions is such that everyone is entitled, at least in principle, to the same counter-gifts. And these counter-gifts are numerous given that, as there is no remuneration for work performed, they must cover each person's needs. The 'Basic Scheme' as set in stone in the bylaws is as follows:

> You don't pay to join. You don't get anything when you leave. The Community supports you while you're here. Twin Oaks provides for its members on the basis of need or equality. Equality is a fundamental community value which informs the property code. We try to avoid displays of wealth which may give rise to envy. With the exceptions described below, we expect members not to use outside income or pre-existing assets during their membership in Twin Oaks.[17]

Under this principle, accommodation, food, medicine, and clothing are free for all members. When a new member arrives, they are guaranteed a room, a bed, a mattress, a desk, shelves, a lamp, and supplies to paint their room.[18]

Clothing is also provided. For this purpose, Twin Oaks has a communal clothing area called 'Commie Clothes'.[19] Almost the entire upper floor of Harmony is devoted to it. Stored here are trousers, dresses, shirts, underwear, shoes,[20] hats, fancy dress, sheets, blankets, towels ... all of which have been donated to the community. There is a vast range of sizes, cuts, and colours to choose from. The Oakers are the kings and queens of this little kingdom of apparel, where everything is clean and sorted. The principle is simple: any member can come and take whatever they like. When, after an hour, a week or a year, the borrowed item is no longer required, the user simply returns it to the laundry area. Every day, teams of workers take it in turns to wash, dry, sort, and put away the communal clothes. As with food (particularly coffee, beer, ice cream, and sweets), members do not rely entirely on this communal supply system. Indeed, there are few who dress exclusively in Commie Clothes. Many supplement that collection with their own personal wardrobe. In this case, it is up to the owner to wash dry, and put away their clothes in their own time. Most living quarters are equipped with the necessary facilities (washing machines, washing powder, tumble dryers, and so on).

The use of means of transport operates on a slightly different basis. The cars are common property. They are placed under the responsibility of the vehicle use manager, who may or may not approve their use. Vehicles are available to all members and can be booked at the main office in Llano.[21] Those who use a vehicle for collective and social purposes (to run errands for the community, for example) can count their transport time towards their labour-credit quota, up to two hours per person per journey. The same rule applies when a communard travels by bus. The cost of travel (primarily petrol for the cars) is borne by the community, with the exception of trips for personal recreation. If a member has to go to a medical appointment in Charlottesville, they are encouraged to travel with one of the people who go into town almost every day to do shopping or manage community business. The costs of health-related travel are covered by the Health Team.

Without going into detail about the many rules governing the precise use of all the other goods and services provided to all Twin Oaks' members (newspaper subscriptions, use of video cassettes, classes and workshops, and so on), it is important to highlight the attention the community pays to everyone's physical, mental, and social well-being. As readers may recall, when someone is ill and unable to work, they automatically receive six credits for each sick day. This sick leave is unconditional:

> If you get sick, you don't have to work. If a doctor sends you to a hospital, you don't worry about the bill. Either we qualify for financial aid because of our low per-capita income, or we will pay the bill, and in either case it's taken care of by the office people. (Kinkade 1994, pp 42–43)

Members are urged to visit the dentist at least once a year and, when necessary, to go to the least expensive healthcare facilities. When their condition requires specialist care, most make an appointment at Charlottesville University Hospital. Time spent in treatment (transport and consultation time) is eligible for labour credits.

In the mid-2010s, members of Twin Oaks benefited from a special healthcare scheme for the region's most disadvantaged (University of Virginia indigent health care). Twin Oaks also insures all its members in a catastrophic health insurance plan called Peach, set up and run by the Federation of Egalitarian Communities. Twin Oaks joined this programme in late 1989. In exchange for a low premium paid by the community ($10 per member it wishes to insure), Peach helps cover very high medical costs. The community practises yet another form of solidarity. From time to time, the 'Weeds and Knots' committee asks members to donate labour credits that would normally go into their holiday accounts.[22] The Weeds and Knots budget is also funded through the annual resource allocation plan. With the funds collected, the Weeds and Knots group helps communards who so request to carry out a project close to their hearts or to pay for a holiday.

These credits cannot, however, be used to cover the negative work balance of a person who has fallen into the labour hole.

Living without money ... or almost

In the very first pages of the book Margaret Grundstein (2015, p 2) wrote about her experience living in a commune in the remote woodlands of Oregon in the 1970s, she recalled with irony the paradoxical relationship that communards and all other manner of rebels had with money:

> What we didn't know was that *utopia*, in its Greek roots, meant nowhere. Money was a problem. We refused to earn any. 'Steal this book,' Abbie Hoffman exhorted in his 1971 work of the same name, a do-it-yourself manual for revolution against the Pig Empire. To his embarrassment, the book sold over a quarter of a million copies, ending up on the bestseller list of the *New York Times*.

Besides, added the former communard, why should they have worried about money when all they had to do to live, at least in theory, was to catch a salmon, pick berries, and gather wild plants? 'We were very naive about money when we started,' Kat Kinkade (1973, p 71) likewise admitted. 'We hoped for a while that it might not be necessary.' Before long, they had to come to terms with reality. The initial financial support ($200 a month that a friend sent to help get the project off the ground) and the rent that two members collected in Washington and donated to the community would not be enough to sustain the project, nor would the initial meagre income from tobacco growing.

We know how things turned out. Twin Oaks accepted to play the game of 'composing' with the wider world and, through business, to draw substantial resources from it. In 2016, the community managed a budget of almost $700,000, with daily costs estimated at around $2.50 per person. Monetary income levels classify the members of Twin Oaks as 'poor' according to the US poverty threshold of 50 per cent of the median income (that is, around $16,500 in annual income for a household of two adults under the age of 65). The difference between income and daily costs, which is almost $16 per person per day, indicates that the community nonetheless has comfortable margins. Twin Oaks is not rich because commercial production is a large source of income, but because its members have opted for asceticism, self-production, virtually total sharing of resources, and the exchange of services.

At Twin Oaks, the communards do not use personal bank accounts. If they have one, it is frozen for as long as they remain in the community. The communards do not pay any bills in their own name. And the community takes care of paying taxes for all its members in accordance with the specific rules set out in section 501(d) of the Internal Revenue Code. But that doesn't mean that money is unheard of. Every month, each member receives a small allowance – $103 in 2016 – to satisfy their particular wants.[23] This allowance is mainly used to buy coffee, beer, fruit juice, cigarettes, cinema tickets, and small items for various uses.

The monthly allowance is not enough to satisfy every desire, let alone what the community defines as the 'real needs' that deserve to be covered. Some of these, such as the need for enough food, are largely uncontroversial. Others, however, are subject to negotiation. Managers are on the front line in deciding day-to-day whether or not certain items of expenditure are appropriate. For example, when a communard asks the clothing manager for the collective to buy a jacket or pair of trousers that he likes, his request may be turned down on the grounds that they are too fancy, or do not correspond to the communal standard of living. If he really wants to wear such an item, then he will have to pay for it out of his own pocket. In 2016, $40 was allocated to each member to help them satisfy such sartorial desires.

Twin Oaks also allows its members to work independently during their holiday time. They are then free to use their Vacation Earnings, or VE in Twin Oaks' terminology, as they see fit. While it may suit some, this provision has never been universally accepted. In 1992, in a sharp O&I comment, Ross flatly condemned the possibility: 'VE is inherently unequal. Let's abolish it.'[24] The reason for such condemnation is simple. The communards do not enjoy the same conditions or the same resources during their holidays. Some have every opportunity to make them pay by working, while others are unable to do so because of family obligations (elderly parents, for example) or because they lack the social capital that would provide them with job opportunities. At the turn of the 2000s, Kat Kinkade estimated that only half the members had the means to work during their holidays and therefore to earn a personal income.

McCune had already inveighed against the Vacation Earnings system back in 1988.[25] He noted the way it could be abused and denounced the increase in inequality caused by the use of money earned during holidays. To curtail the abuses, he suggested increasing the personal allowance to compensate for a reduction in VE. In his view, the solution was all the more apt as it corresponded to the communards' growing desire to have more money of their own and also met the requirement for equality. What was at stake, he concluded, was nothing less than getting the community back on the road to egalitarian socialism. The proposal was not acted upon, but it left no one indifferent. The idea of going to work in the outside world to boost one's personal income revolted Rosemary, for example, who firmly supported McCune. Rollie took the opposite view. 'I feel Twin Oaks already regulates my life enough and what I do on my free time is my business.'[26]

In addition to Vacation Earnings, Twin Oaks allows its members to receive gifts and money from relatives and friends. The regulations specify that gifts of money may be accepted provided that the money is spent outside Louisa County on a trip lasting more than 24 hours and only on consumable items, unless the gift money has been earmarked:

> For example, your family may give you a sweater for your birthday, or they may give you money to buy a sweater. If they give you money, but don't tell you what it's for, you can't use it to buy a sweater. (You can use it on vacation). So if you want to use gift money to buy things to use on the farm, ask your donor to earmark it.[27]

It is true that the differences in income resulting from VEs and gifts from friends and family are relatively small, amounting to a few hundred dollars a year at most. But the very existence of possibilities to find extraordinary funds is enough to make the claim – as some most vehemently have – that there is no real equality of condition.

Personal Service Credits or Personal Codas (PSCs) are another possible source of personal enrichment. These are labour credits that members allocate to their peers in return for goods or services (a haircut, a theatrical performance that was well-liked, etc.). To make such a transaction, a member must have labour credits in advance and, therefore, have exceeded their compulsory quota. When more than three PSCs are exchanged during the week, the communard who did the work has, in theory, to indicate this on their weekly labour sheet. Again in theory, labour credits serve as the sole currency for intra-community transactions. In reality, dollars are also used. The ZK hall is the hub of this micro-market for goods and services, where supply and demand information circulates. Regularly, between 7 pm and 1 pm, Herbert offers to make pizzas and deliver them to the customer's room. On the menu are cheese pizzas (75 cents) and pepperoni pizzas ($1.50). Those who like can add olives, mushrooms, or other toppings. The poster I read about this on one May evening in 2016 specifies somewhat mysteriously: 'Only vegans have to pay with a PSC or a flex hour'.[28]

It's the same day, after dinner. Many of the communards have stayed in the building, talking or reading. In the hall, one table displays an assortment of objects available for free ('grabs' in local parlance): a huge pink bag, a yellow plush banana, hooks, a medieval-looking glass, a checked shirt, a book about China, a drawing, a scout handbook, pencils, a few CDs, and more. It will be several days before the batch finds all its takers. Right next to it, another table displays hand-printed postcards. The creator has specialized her product with a unique floral motif. She has also written a short explanation of the procedure used. A price is displayed: one PSC or $2.50. Anyone interested is asked to write their name on a sheet of paper, along with the desired quantity and payment details. By the end of the evening, 18 cards had been sold for PCS and a further 18 for hard cash. Every year, in the same spirit, Valerie organizes a craft fair in ZK. Oakers sell items they have made themselves, such as figurines, paintings, embroidery, wood carvings, and so on, for dollars or PCS.

The other flip sides of work: leisure, recreation, holidays

Although the Oakers devote a lot of time to work, it is not their only occupation. In addition to the leisure activities afforded by the site and its facilities (aquatic activities, country walks, the sauna, smokers gathering in the Compost Café, and so on), recreational practices are quite varied. The community has a collection of over 15,000 books of all kinds (novels, history essays, science fiction books, documents on everyday life, militant literature, etc.) and subscribes to numerous newspapers and magazines. CDs and videos are also freely available. The most regular moments of sociability outside of work that I observed took place in the evening, just after dinner. Many Oakers meet up in the small rooms adjacent to the kitchen and dining hall in ZK. There, in the mailroom in particular, they talk about anything and everything, joke around, swap information, read the newspapers, and generally hang out. At Acorn, this same type of ceremony almost invariably rounds off the day. Weather permitting, the younger members gather around the fire or in the smoking hut to chat, have a cigarette, and drink beer. In both communities, playing music is also popular. As at Acorn, the Oakers are proud of their musicians, from chamber music specialists to the in-house rock band Flying Tomatoes. On a regular basis, the members of Twin Oaks put on concerts and musicals ... for the benefit of none other than the community itself.

Learning and practising dance, yoga, aikido, tai chi, meditation, and so on (the leaders of these workshops sometimes coming from outside the community) complements the range of sporting activities, such as volleyball, basketball or frisbee, in which various members regularly take part. In 2016 and 2017, cornhole – a game in which small bean bags are tossed at a raised, angled board with a hole at the far end, with the aim of getting the bag through the hole – was a regular favourite. During the day, some people prefer to do DIY: the photo laboratory and the workshops used for more productive purposes (the garage and the wood shop) are well enough equipped for most people to find the materials they need for their hobbies (carpentry, pottery, painting, etc.). Classes and workshops of all kinds (language, poetry, science, religion, etc.) are also run by those with the desire and skills to do so. In the evenings, the Oakers also enjoy getting together for theme-based discussion groups, board games (cards, Scrabble, backgammon, chess, Othello, Dungeons and Dragons ...) and, more especially, partying and singing at the top of their lungs at karaoke nights. Starting with birthdays, there's never a shortage of reasons to get together to listen to music, dress up, dance, drink alcohol, and so on.

The communards don't shy away from outings away from their land either. They do this on their own during the three weeks' holiday they are entitled to each year (more in reality, as their labour credits very often allow for this). Trips away are made for a variety of purposes. They are used either to visit relatives or friends, to discover new horizons, or to take up paid employment. The rest of the time, communards who want to escape from Twin Oaks usually prefer going to town. Charlottesville, Richmond, and Washington DC are the most popular destinations for shopping, seeing friends, going to the cinema or a concert, or attending a political event. More occasionally, some get together in small groups to go hiking in the Blue Ridge Mountains or swimming in the Atlantic Ocean.

Community work on balance

Even if working conditions are not as perfect as most communards would have wished, community work is different in many ways from work in the wider world. Not the least of its original features is the feeling of working for all and for oneself. As Warren, a former Oaker, confided:

> Part of the attraction of being at Twin Oaks, after spending 6 years working in the same factory, was that we worked our own businesses. [...] The few years I was there felt equal to 15 years of living outside the community. At Twin Oaks I got exposure to a variety of people and views, and an opportunity to try all different types of work [...]. I miss the work situation at T.O. Now I'm an employee. I can't regulate my schedule. ('Leaving Twin Oaks', 1977, p 27)

During the group interview from which this extract was taken, another ex-member explained that if he hadn't lived at Twin Oaks, he wouldn't have been able to acquire the professional electrician skills from which he now makes his living. This does not mean that the communards ignore everyday chores. Another remarkable innovation of egalitarian communities is that they have managed to give domestic activities full work status and, in so doing, have promoted the sharing of these often thankless and invisible tasks. One statement, taken from a set of concrete recommendations distributed at Twin Oaks, sums up the prevailing spirit of the place. Here, 'we only live in utopia, not in paradise. Everyone is expected to wash the dishes and clean the bathroom.'[29]

Starting with the many counter-gifts in kind, in sociability, and in cultural capital that communities offer to those who agree to devote their strength and energy to them, there are many other reasons why, all things considered, the balance sheet is deemed positive by the communards themselves. The paradox is that success can lead almost automatically to failure. In a long letter to his peers in 1993, Ross (aged 45) lucidly observed that since the 1960s and 1970s at Twin Oaks, generation after generation of 'hippy' communards had given of their labour, their time, and their intelligence. They had built homes, grown vegetables, launched a lucrative hammock business ... so that the community had slowly grown, despite a high turnover throughout the years. As a result:

> Today, approaching a hundred members, with hundreds of thousands of dollars in the bank, we are playing the stock market, building a luxury swimming pool and clear-cutting new patches of forest for ever more plush new residences. Now thousands of people know we are a RICH community and more new members are joining to partake of our wealth, caring very little for any concept of equal sharing, instead favoring the ideas and habits they learned in the 'real world'.[30]

More than thirty years after Ross put his concerns in writing, is this fear still well-founded? Today, Twin Oaks is, admittedly, a thriving community in financial terms. There are some strategic-minded members who found refuge there, having been unable to fit into the job market in straight society. But, as at Acorn, the vast majority of Oakers live there above all out of conviction – feminist, environmentalist, left-libertarian, and so on. They do not hope for massive personal wealth. In everyday life, whether at work or in other activities not labelled as such, practices remain informed by a powerful desire for equality. It's true that the utopian engine has had a few misfires. But despite persistent imperfections, it continues to run at full speed.

9

Community Destinies

The sun has shown up. It's not the only one. It's 16 June 2017, Twin Oaks' anniversary, and over 100 former members have travelled here to celebrate 50 years of the community's existence with those who keep it alive today. All look forward to two days of catching up with old friends, talking, eating, drinking, singing, and dancing. Tents have been pitched next to the central courtyard. Food is provided for everyone at ZK and near the wood workshop. A marquee serves as the main gathering place. On stage, the house bands (The Flying Tomatoes for Twin Oaks, Gooseband for Acorn) perform before the main event of the evening: a concert given by a group of Oakers who play one hit after another – a song for every year since 1967. In a small room, an exhibition looks back at the milestones of Twin Oaks. Former members are invited to fill in the gaps in the timeline and correct any mistakes in the dates.

The guests have opted for matching regalia. All wear simple, loose, colourful clothes. Beards, long hair, and flowery hats are also de rigueur. In memory of the psychedelic years, some older guests have clearly decided to go overboard. One man with short hair and a carefully trimmed beard sports a fluorescent apple-green fringed outfit that clings to his septuagenarian body and shows off his hairy chest. Another, even older man strolls around the festival decked out in a floral T-shirt, red and black skirt, and dark cape, with a colourful headband holding back his long white hair and a black and white parasol to keep the sun off. While the other invitees have gone for more discreet outfits, each wears a badge indicating their name and the period during which they lived at Twin Oaks.

Not all former members have come. If they had, the central courtyard would probably have been too small to accommodate all the ex-communards. Since Twin Oaks was founded in 1967, many people have chosen to return to straight society after living in the community. In the mid-2010s, the most knowledgeable Oakers I was able to question on the subject estimated that on average, a member stayed at Twin Oaks for between five and nine years. However indicative this statistic may be, it conceals the existence of diverse pathways, ranging from very long-term residency (until death in the community) to much more temporary stays. Whatever the case, one thing is certain. Since its creation, and like most other intentional communities, Twin Oaks has sometimes had to contend with high turnover rates. While this does not necessarily indicate dysfunction, it does prompt questions about the long-term dynamics of the collective in general and of individual destinies in particular. This chapter aims to provide some answers.

Pollination, demographic change, and turnover

When the founders of Twin Oaks set foot on their new land in 1967, as readers will recall, they had in mind a project directly inherited from the writings of B.F. Skinner. In the spirit of Frazier, the American psychologist's fictional hero, one of the little group's ambitions was to expand the community to reach a thousand members, as in *Walden Two*. That target would never be reached. In retrospect, this is hardly surprising. As a former member of Twin Oaks observed:

> Among the various forms of contemporary intentional communities: the religious Hutterites split when they reach 150; most cohousing groups have 40 to 70 adults; and some Israeli kibbutzim had over 1,000 members before they gave up communalism and became collective communities on government land trusts. The kibbutzim estimated that a population of about 350 people is needed in order to maintain a complete age-range from youngest to oldest over the generations. (Butcher, 2017, p 27)

Twin Oaks, for its part, has never been home to more than 100 people at a time. The communards quickly realized that beyond this threshold, material difficulties increase, the egalitarian ethic wanes, and the bureaucratic spirit begins to take over. Like many other communities, when it comes to expanding, Twin Oaks has opted for the strategy of dissemination. Since it was founded, the community has helped spawn one satellite in Missouri (East Wind) and five in Louisa County (Acorn, Merion, Living Energy Farm, Mimosa, and Juniper); in 2017, a sixth was being planned, which might be established on neighbouring land that Twin Oaks wanted to acquire.

Early in its history, Twin Oaks experienced the fragility of an open, loosely structured organization. Between 1968 and 1969, the community lost eight of its most active members. They left for multiple reasons: a feeling that community action was not radical enough to change the world; difficulty putting up with people's unequal participation in day-to-day tasks; rejection of an overly work-oriented life; criticism of the excessive power given to planners; a reluctance to live frugally while sharing all (or almost all) resources; jealousy and interpersonal conflict; an inability to tolerate the close quarters, lack of privacy, and poor hygiene; and so on. But the erosion of those pioneering days was provoked above all by disillusionment linked to the toughness of an alternative organization and lifestyle. During the first few years, new members stayed in the community for an average of three months before moving on to other climes in search of new adventures or different ways of testing their moral and political convictions (Kinkade, 1994). Most of the time, the decision to leave was individual. Mass exoduses were rare. Occasionally, after another experience elsewhere, a person would return to Twin Oaks to settle down.

Before too long, the community managed to limit the damage. In the spring of 1968, when the attrition rate was at its highest, Twin Oaks was losing an average of 1.6 members a month. Then began a downward trend with an average monthly loss of 1 in 1969, 0.7 in 1970, 0.4 in 1971, and 0.2 at the beginning of 1972.[1] As of the latter date, the communards who had lived at Twin Oaks for at least one year boasted an average tenure of 16 months. Throughout the 1970s, Twin Oaks had to say goodbye to a quarter of its members each year. But new arrivals more than made up for the deficit. By 1977, the community had grown to 80 adults and seven children. Over the following five years, the number of members stabilized at around 70. These figures confirm that both inbound and outbound mobility flows were significant. Ingrid Komar's (1983) estimate – that 325 people had been members of Twin Oaks between 1967 and 1983 – is therefore not outlandish.

As the community matured, departures were seen less and less as calamities:

> There was a time when turnover was a cause of great concern to Twin Oakers, when people's leaving was seen as a betrayal of the cause, a defection. These days there are farewell parties and little humorous counter-culture gifts for those who move on rather than hostility or criticism. [...] According to the U.S. Census Bureau, Americans move on the average of every two years. The average Twin Oaks membership lasts four years – considerably longer than the national average. (Komar, 1983, p 79)

In the late 1980s, Twin Oaks was still having to contend with departures: 14 in 1987, 15 in 1988, 23 in 1989, and 16 in 1990 (the latter figure applies to the first seven months of the year). Among all these leavers, those who had lived at Twin Oaks for less than a year numbered one, four, eleven and eight respectively.[2] The figures are still not dramatic in themselves, as new arrivals regularly offset the losses.

'I see one of our major problems – turnover – as the source of our major social relevance,' wrote Taylor on the subject. But turnover also has its negative aspects. 'We transform the cooperation skills of everyone who passes through, and they then take these skills with them into all other situations.'[3] Furthermore, a person's flight often causes despair among the communards with whom he or she had become close. For this reason, it is not uncommon for one departure to lead to another. To try and temper thoughts of escape, in 1985 the planners ran a survey to gather members' opinions on what changes should be made to convince them to stay at Twin Oaks for another five years (Kinkade, 1994). There was no overwhelming result, other than two key complaints. Some no longer wished to share their residence with visitors. So the decision was immediately made to construct a building, Aurora, specifically for visitors. Other members complained that they were given too little personal spending money each month.

In response to this last criticism, successive teams of planners in the late 1980s proposed concrete solutions: bonuses, an increased monthly allowance, financial assistance for travel, and so on. While it is difficult to assess the direct impact of these measures on Oaker morale, what is certain is that the turnover rate declined following these various initiatives. It is not impossible that, in addition to these incentive effects, the ageing of the communard population may have begun to positively influence population stability. The fact is that after age 40 it becomes harder to return to the outside world and find an interesting job. In 1992, 42 members had already lived in the community for five years or more. At the time, the average tenure for all the Oakers was four years. Turnover for the five years to 1992 was 0.25: a quarter of the members left each year, with the exact equivalent, or close to it, replacing them at the same time. Half of those arriving and leaving were in fact the same people. In other words, there was a considerable flow of mobility attributable to people (around ten a year) who only stayed a few months after being accepted as new members. The trend continued in 2001.[4] That year, the average age of the 73 adult members was 44. The average length of stay at Twin Oaks had reached nine years, compared with 14 months in 1970, when the average age was 22.5.[5]

What about in the 2010s? In 2017, the community had 100 members, including 15 children. By working through the photo galleries that the community produced between 2007 and 2015, I was able to estimate that nearly 260 people had lived at Twin Oaks during that period (which corresponds to an average of over 90 members present each year). Over the same period, the proportion of women exceeded 55 per cent and the proportion of white people was still overwhelming at over 97 per cent. Meanwhile, turnover was equivalent to that recorded in the 1990s, at nearly a quarter on average. A third of individuals had been continuously present for at least eight of the nine years surveyed. All in all, by compiling all the figures that can be gleaned here and there, it can be estimated that the number of people living at Twin Oaks at any given time has followed

Figure 9.1: The number of adult members at Twin Oaks per year (1967–2023)

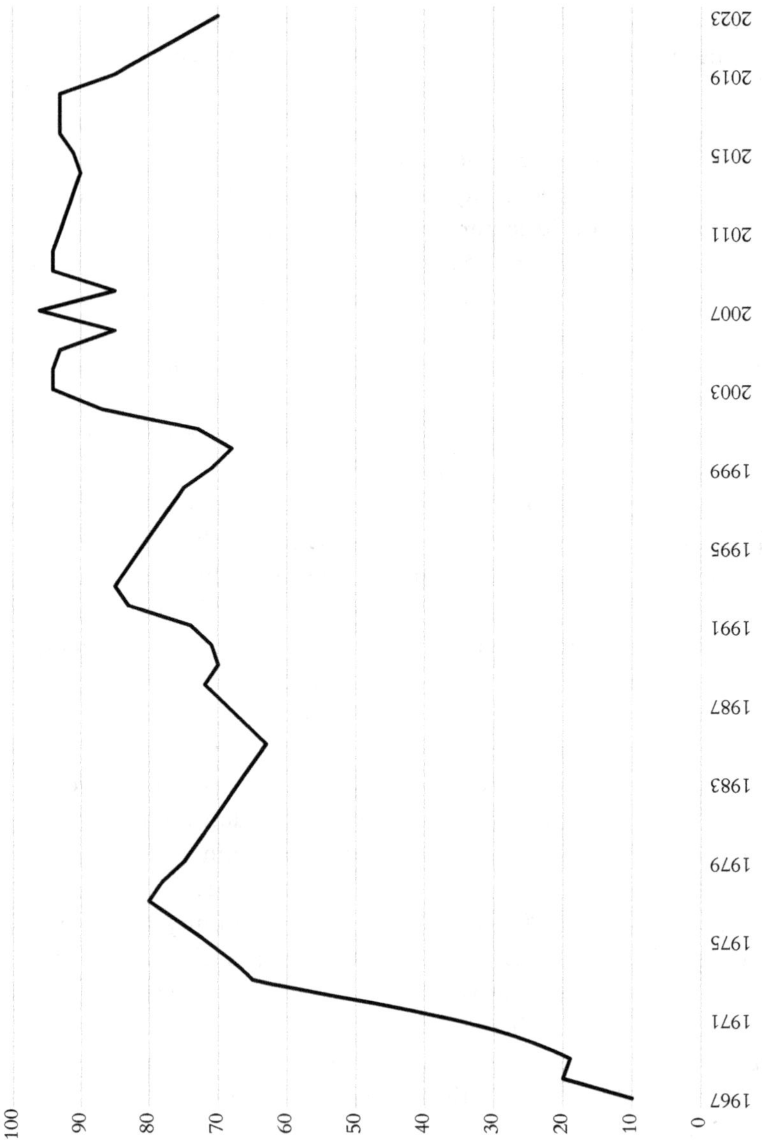

Note: The years 1974 to 1976, 1978 to 1984, 1986 to 1987, 1994 to 1997, 1999, 2010 to 2013 and 2017 to 2023 are estimates.

a rising curve and that more than a thousand people had been members of Twin Oaks during the period 1967–2017.

Since 2017, Twin Oaks has undergone a number of transformations that have affected the size and composition of its membership. The community has had to contend with the COVID-19 crisis, which has forced it, as elsewhere in the world, to withdraw into itself and not welcome visitors for the duration of the pandemic. The profile of the Oakers has also changed somewhat, as have their choices in terms of market production (the community has developed the seed growing and the seed trade). Whatever the nature of the links, direct or otherwise, between these changes and the number of members, there has been a slight decline in the community's population in recent years. In 2023, Twin Oaks had 70 adults and 15 children.

These numbers are a far cry from the original aim of *Walden Two*, which was to have 1,000 people living simultaneously in the same communal space. But experience has shown that this is not necessarily a failure and that, above all, an organization can develop and thrive in the long term with high turnover rates. This observation challenges the view of organizational specialists who see turnover as a sign of dysfunction and a warning that a collective venture is coming to an end. As Zablocki pointed out early on, this is not the case in intentional communities. As long as they manage to maintain a core group of long-standing members who safeguard the community's values and rules, and are able to organize the regular recruitment of new members, they will in fact benefit from the rotation of part of their membership as it not only solves certain problems by way of exit (the departure of members who are least suited to the demands of community life), but also renews enthusiasm, skills, and innovative ideas.[6]

Tired of being poor ... and other good reasons to return to the outside world

Why are some communards tempted to leave the little world in which they had chosen to live? To answer this question, I used a corpus of 182 letters written between 1978 and 1993 by members of Twin Oaks who were about to move on.[7] Writing an O&I to give notice of one's departure is a tacit obligation with which most members comply. But not everyone goes about it in the same way: some write an extremely brief leaving letter, while others fill page after page, telling their story, outlining their plans, saying how happy they are to have been an Oaker and how sorry to be saying goodbye, but also setting out in black and white any grievances and the reasons (positive or negative) why they have decided to end their community adventure. Among the departing members in the corpus, the gender distribution is roughly balanced (56 per cent and 44 per cent respectively), and in any case reflects Twin Oaks' overall morphology. Forty-six people indicated in their letters how long they had lived at Twin Oaks. The average obtained using this information is five and a half years, with a relatively low standard deviation.[8] This figure, which is not incongruous, confirms that for many of the Twin Oaks communards, community involvement is no fleeting fancy of a few months' duration. Understandably, then, leaving is not easy. Most of the time it is an individual decision. However, in one in five cases (at least over the period analysed using the letters), the return to the outside world is undertaken by couples, sometimes with their children, and more rarely by a handful of close friends who decide to make the move together. While there are many different reasons given for leaving, they can nonetheless be categorized and classified.

The first motivation is weariness of community life, an avowed tiredness of living in poverty. Such fatigue is also expressed in terms of desires: a desire for more freedom and privacy, a desire to escape organizational problems, a desire to develop friendships or romantic relationships that don't exist in the community, a desire for less tedious working conditions and a recognized profession. More than a third of the letters (35 per cent to be exact) explicitly use such arguments to justify a forthcoming departure. 'I promised myself years ago', explained Velma for example, 'that when I had had enough of being poor and living within the limitations of our property code, I would not abuse our rules, or try to change Twin Oaks – I would leave and live elsewhere – this is that time.'[9] The desire for a different job with better recognition is another constant. 'I am unable to value my work here highly enough.'[10] 'Making Quota and my needing increased personal vehicle usage don't seem to be congruent to Twin Oaks as it is today, not impossible but not in 1986.':[11]

> I took on being general manager of Twin Oaks hammocks when the business was in severe disarray and crisis, and worked 70 and 80 and 90 hour weeks to improve things […]. I AM leaving, but it might be because this is the kind of a place where people don't feel bound by their commitments and reinforce others for breaking commitments, or because I'm tired of community process, or because I don't know how to stop working so hard while I'm here.[12]

The second reason the Oakers give is family-related: either to be closer to family (14 per cent), whether ageing parents or children, or to get married and/or start a family outside the community (10 per cent).

> First, I want to say, that the bulk of the decision is for positive reasons. […] While in San Diego, we lived a lot with Gramma Myrtle [mother of Dale, the letter writer's partner], and through that experience it

became evident that it was where I (we) needed to be. Dale's Dad (Myrtle's husband), died in September, which is why I wanted to spend the holidays in San Diego. Then, just 3 weeks before we arrived, Myrtle's mother died and Myrtle's father moved in with Myrtle. [...] It became very evident to me that she needs help and support, and is asking for it.[13]

There are many letters of this kind, indicating the need to renew ties weakened by community life with parents who, having now reached their twilight years, are anxious for emotional and material support. Mimi's 1992 leaving letter pinpoints this deep and shared concern:

No policy has yet been developed, but inevitably, one at a time, T.O. people will feel obligated to devote more time & energy to their parents as they get really old, or really feeble. Without a policy, each member will be faced with giving up their membership, as I did a year ago last July.[14]

The first analysts of intentional communities who looked into the causes of people leaving, such as Zablocki, could not perceive this factor at the time. Yet the fact that the communards of the 1980s and 1990s were older on average than those of the previous two decades played a significant role in their decision to return to straight society, not only to be closer to their elders, but also to start a family of their own and be able to provide for it over the long term. Some leave to get married and move into a single-family home. For others, being able to live with or near their children all the time is the main incentive:

Well, folks, I was awake all last night. I've decided I just cannot stay here. Many of you will be surprised and some I am sure expected it, but for me it has been hard. I've been away from Shawn (my 4-year-old boy) for two months now and last night I talked to him on the telephone. The crux of the matter is that he's much, much more important to me than I suspected. Even though he will continue to live with his Dad, I know I could be with him as much as I want and I want.[15]

Still other good reasons are put forward by Oakers who are about to enter the transition phase before leaving the community for good. In addition to those mentioned above, the main arguments given are as follows: health problems (depression, burnout, fatigue, etc.) (17 per cent), tension and conflicts that have become too difficult to cope with (7 per cent), the need to find paid work to pay off debts (5 per cent), the feeling of not finding one's place as a lesbian or gay within the community (4 per cent), romantic break-up

(4 per cent), other (illegal situation, Twin Oaks hygiene considered too dubious, difficulty tolerating the local climate, etc.) (4 per cent).

In weighing up the good and bad points of the community lifestyle at Twin Oaks, Rain places many arguments on the positive side: the dancing, the form of governance, the rural environment, the food, his room at Oneida, his responsibilities taking care of the community's children, the hammock workshop. On the negative side, he notes certain people's attitudes towards the children, the difficulty of being Jewish, the quota to be met, class divisions that permeate work relations, the lack of choice in the educational program offered to Twin Oaks children, an unstructured schedule and, finally, difficulty making friends.[16]

The letters announcing a forthcoming departure from the community don't just give an account of their authors' sadness at parting with Twin Oaks, nor of the reasons behind such a decision. They also present what tomorrow might hold for the future ex-Oakers. Besides building a 'traditional' family unit (marriage, children, a single-family home), the plans announced are, in decreasing order of importance, quickly getting a job (one has already been found in many cases) (20 per cent of letters mention this goal), returning to university to pursue or complete an interrupted course of study (13 per cent), moving to another community (10 per cent), extended travel (6 per cent), and involvement in political organizations that have a voice in the wider world (5 per cent). As not all letters explicitly state their writers' plans, these percentages more than likely underestimate the reality of people's intentions. They nonetheless indicate with little ambiguity that the overwhelming majority of those who leave Twin Oaks choose to return to life in the outside world.

What has become of the former members?

Only a handful of communards have spent the final stage of their existence at Twin Oaks. The first was Seth, a young man who died prematurely of cancer at the age of 22 after joining the community four years earlier. The death occurred in December 1980 and was a real shock for Twin Oaks. The young man now rests in the community's woods, a few minutes' walk from ZK. Ten or so other Oakers have since joined him. Two pioneering women are buried here, Kat (who died in 2008 aged 78) and Piper (who died in 2013 in her ninetieth year). Like all the others, their graves blend into the landscape. The places where the bodies are buried are marked by stones arranged in a circle. A simple stele bears their first and last names and dates of birth and death. *All is well* is engraved on that of Kat Kinkade. A few stone statues (including a Buddha and a cat) discreetly enhance the setting. Apart from those two women, the other Oakers buried in the woods lived surprisingly short lives. The details just visible on the moss-covered stones give an average age of 30 for the six people who passed away between 1983 and 2009.

In 2017, the overwhelming majority of those who at one time chose to make Twin Oaks their home were still alive. The probability that the oldest of them will end their days in situ is high. This is certainly the case with Ira, who was living alternately at Twin Oaks and at Acorn when I met her. Aged 70 in 2018, Ira has spent most of her life in community. The adventure began for her in the early 1970s. After studying education sciences, Ira attended a conference organized by Twin Oaks. Though keen to change lifestyles, she was unable to join the community because Twin Oaks did not accept children at the time, and Ira had a four-year-old daughter. So she joined forces with a small group to found the Aloe community near Chapel Hill (North Carolina). There she tried out rural life, an intensive commitment to hard work, and polyamory (through sleepover dates – nights spent with different partners each time, but with no obligation to have sex). She then went to live on a kibbutz for a year before returning to join Dandelion. In 1984, she became a member of Twin Oaks and helped found Acorn in 1993. Since then, Ira has continued to live in these two communities with the feeling that, in the absence of close family, her destiny is to remain there until the end of her days.

What has become of the others: those who, for the reasons outlined above, have chosen to return to straight society? Did they take up or return to a standard job (computer programming, for example, which Kat Kinkade did during her four-year hiatus from the community)? Did the departure from Twin Oaks mark a complete break with community life? To date, there is insufficient data to provide a definitive answer to this question. To sketch out a few working hypotheses nonetheless, I put together a file containing the names and current occupations of 90 people who have lived at Twin Oaks but are no longer members today. To do so, I used the community's written archives and, especially, any traces found on the internet (social networks, blogs, online press articles, etc.).[17] Given the bias introduced by the data collection method, this sample is not representative of the population of some one thousand current and former Oakers who lived in the Virginian community between 1967 and 2017 and, in some cases, continue to do so. It is not completely unbalanced, however, as the following data indicates. The sample comprises 45 per cent men and 55 per cent women (which roughly corresponds to the gender distribution of Twin Oaks members since its foundation); 60 per cent aged 30 to 49, 10 per cent under 30, and 30 per cent over 50;[18] and, finally 46 per cent, mainly women, living in Virginia (Charlottesville, Louisa, and Richmond for the most part). The average length of stay at Twin Oaks for the ex-Oakers in the sample is just over eight years.

However imperfect, this prosopographical survey confirms first of all that most communards, those of Twin Oaks at any rate, completed some higher education before settling in the community. More than eight out of ten people in the sample have a university degree, while most of the others finished high school. The Oakers surveyed chose to study the following subjects: sciences (9 per cent); humanities (6 per cent); social, health/medicine, education, environment (56 per cent); creative arts (12.5 per cent); law, political science, economics, management (12.5 per cent); other (4 per cent). Women are overwhelmingly represented in social, health/medicine, education, and environmental studies (almost 80 per cent trained in these fields). These rudimentary statistics therefore confirm the predisposition, through the chosen course of study, to a commitment to serving others and the environment, of which community experience is one form among others.

Even more interesting is an examination of the occupations and areas of professional specialization that the Oakers who returned to the wider world adopted after leaving the community. Twenty-five per cent became social workers, teachers, or healthcare professionals; 22 per cent became managers, coaches, or consultants, but always in sectors such as personal services or healthcare; 19 per cent are artists (writers, musicians, or photographers); 10 per cent work in the environment and organic food sector; 6 per cent are publishers or work in communications; 4 per cent are farmers; 4 per cent now live in another community; the remaining 10 per cent have chosen other paths.[19] Even if, as I must stress once again, these figures are indicative at best, the choices reflected in this typology of career paths strongly suggest continuity. After leaving Twin Oaks, the majority of communards remain attached to a number of the community's values and engage in activities in line with them: occupations that involve helping others, that are relatively low-paying yet creative, that promote health, personal development, and respect for the environment, and so on. Gender is not neutral in the choices made in this area. In the sample, nine men became artists after living at Twin Oaks compared with only two women; on the other hand, three men embarked on a social work career compared with eleven women.

An analysis of the trajectories leading from university to mainstream society via Twin Oaks provides further evidence that for many communards, far from being an absolute break, the community episode is part of a trajectory marked by at least some coherence. Admittedly, a methodological bias (focusing only on those who publicly mention their communard episode) precludes access to information about former Oakers who have made a more radical break than the others with the values and practices of egalitarian communities. Even so, as shown by the success of Twin Oaks' 50th anniversary (number of attendees, outpouring of messages of support …), this uncertainty does not make the continuity hypothesis unreasonable. To further refine the assessment, three ideal types can be proposed. The first concerns the handful of Oakers who were born and raised in the community. At Twin Oaks, the name that spontaneously comes up in discussions when this kind of background is mentioned is that of Devon Sproule, a well-known musician in the US and winner of a major award (the ASCAP Foundation Sammy Cahn Award).[20] Born in 1982 at Dandelion, a community inspired at its inception by *Walden Two*, Sproule spent her childhood and teenage years at Twin Oaks before striking out on her own into the wider world. She recorded her first album at the age of 16. In an interview given to mark the release of one of her albums, Sproule explained that her desire for singing and music is directly related to her experience of community life, of a group of people who want to communicate with each other and are willing to be versatile in how they do so:

> Growing up in an income-free environment, the lack of money never bothers me much. I always make rent and can afford to take my husband out to dinner when he gets home from tour! So yes, on the whole, I'm proud of my alternative upbringing. I don't mind a bit that my dad (who still lives at Twin Oaks) couldn't afford to buy me a car when I … er … didn't graduate from high school.[21]

Sky Blue, who also grew up at Twin Oaks (he lived there for 18 years), has a similar profile.[22] The child of hippies, as he says himself, in 2017 he took on the important role of executive director of the Fellowship for Intentional Community.

A second typical path, more common than the first, also bears the stamp of continuity. This pattern concerns young people who, having trained in the mainstream education system before joining the community, put their training to use there, then continue along the same career path after they leave. This is often the case of those responsible for educating the Oaker children in Degania. Many of them trained as teachers and worked in straight society before moving to Twin Oaks, then returning to the wider world to continue teaching. Teachers are not the only ones concerned. Scott, for example, obtained a Bachelor of Science in environmental and technical engineering in 1982. After graduating, he worked for almost a year in a mechanical engineering company, specializing in IT maintenance for the company's machines and various departments. In 1984, he became a member of Twin Oaks. He spent 16 years and nine months of his life there. During that time, Scott embraced his niche: he took over management of the community's computer equipment, built a website to showcase his peers' commercial activities and facilitate the customer interface, managed the email infrastructure, developed applications for weekly task planning, set up a computerized accounting system, and helped out computer novices. In 2000, when he took leave from Twin Oaks, Scott found a job as a computer technician at a West Coast university, where he did similar work to what he had long been doing in Virginia. In 2017, he was still in the same job.

The third ideal-type profile diverges somewhat from the previous two insofar as during their time at Twin Oaks, the person discovers and cultivates new skills, on which they are able to capitalize in the post-community period. Because the communard experience gives people the opportunity to learn and specialize in other lines of work, it can sometimes be a real turning point, a fork in the road that leads them, once they have left the community, towards a different professional destiny from the one they envisaged when they were cramming for college exams. For instance, after graduating with a Bachelor of Science in Maryland in 1982, Matthew lived at Twin Oaks for 13 years. There he discovered what it meant to work in and with nature. He was involved in all the activities combining the great outdoors, building, and working the land. When he left the community, he enrolled at the Conway School of Landscape Design and earned his master's degree. He has since made a career as a landscape designer.

Carolin has a similar profile. She became a member of Twin Oaks in 2005, earned her Bachelor of Arts in French and Literature two years later and stayed in the community for exactly six years and eight months. During that time, she worked in the cowshed, looked after customer relations for hammock sales, and was involved in organizing the annual conferences. But above all, she developed a love of working with young children and joined the team looking after the mental health of Twin Oaks members. Shortly before leaving the community, she enrolled in nursing school in Louisville, from which she graduated in 2013. She soon found a job at Norton Hospital, where she was still working in 2017, specializing in children's care. Like all the other members and ex-members of Twin Oaks, when she was a communard Carolin did not devote all her time to a single occupation. She chopped and changed. But when week after week, it came to setting priorities and making her presence in the community meaningful, the choices she made helped to shape her post-community future. By thus building up a sound professional experience combined with strong moral convictions, she, like others, can now continue to uphold original axiological options, but this time at the heart of the wider world.

Conclusion: Towards a Society of Communities?

Since the Second World War, the social space of American intentional communities has been transformed. Each successive decade brought a series of changes of varying tone and significance. The years of reconstruction that followed Germany's capitulation and the return to peace broke new ground in two ways: first, by paving the way for the cooperative movement, and second, by laying the foundations for international relations between various actors who were convinced of the importance of small communities. In 1953, a dozen groups signed up to the Fellowship of Intentional Communities. Among them, Macedonia and Koinonia, two pacifist communities, played a key role (Oved, 2013). The 1960s in the US were a boom time for communes, for reasons that have been discussed at length above. The mid-1970s saw a downturn. As soon as the hippie craze began to fade, pragmatism took over. Often based in rural areas, communities were not shy to draw on the support offered by the wider world (primarily the social welfare system) to have a hope of survival. At the same time, they were not immune to the wave of individualism that followed the shock of the previous decade's counterculture. Yet with the particularly active support of Twin Oaks, North American intentional communities continued to organize, thanks also to the backing of the brand-new Federation of Egalitarian Communities (FEC) and the active role of *Communities* magazine.

The renewed influence of a liberal-conservative ethos in the 1980s was hardly favourable to community ethics and practice. It severely dampened the desire for social change on a global scale. But the straitjacket of pro-market doctrine that expert bodies and government authorities were beginning to tighten had the paradoxical effect of fuelling the desire for equality more strongly than ever. Thus, in the early 1980s, the internationalization of the community movement took off again, thanks particularly to the foundation of the International Communes Desk, whose main achievement was to consolidate relations between North American intentional communities and Israeli kibbutzim. In the midst of this momentum, a series of conferences held all over the world served as crucibles for global sociability and provided the community world with an unprecedented international base. In the overall picture presented by Yaacov Oved in 2013, the final years of the last century and the first of the new millennium were similarly marked by expansion and diversification, with new experiments such as ecovillages. The global reach of the community phenomenon is no longer in doubt, even if the networks that link so many concrete utopias today are not always equal to the new wave of globalization affecting mainstream society.

An expanding and evolving community space

As the brief overview I've just given makes clear, intentional communities in the US did not die out once the left-libertarian wave of the 1960s and 1970s ran aground at the foot of resurgent conformism. Quite the contrary. Of course, not all stood the test of time and the pioneers such as Twin Oaks which have survived to this day are relatively rare. But other, similar experiments have appeared. All in all, as Figure 10.1 suggests, the population of intentional communities has grown from year to year. Although based on a smaller sample, Figure 10.2 confirms that a fair number of communities founded in the 1970s and even before were still very much alive in 2016. *Communities* counted exactly 87 for the years leading up to and including 1975, a pivotal moment that marked the end of the communal wave of the late 1960s.

Compared to those listed by *Communities* and the Fellowship for Intentional Community in the 1970s, the intentional communities identified today are more diverse. This expansion is the result of a dual trend, the respective

Figure 10.1: Number of US communities listed by the Fellowship for Intentional Community

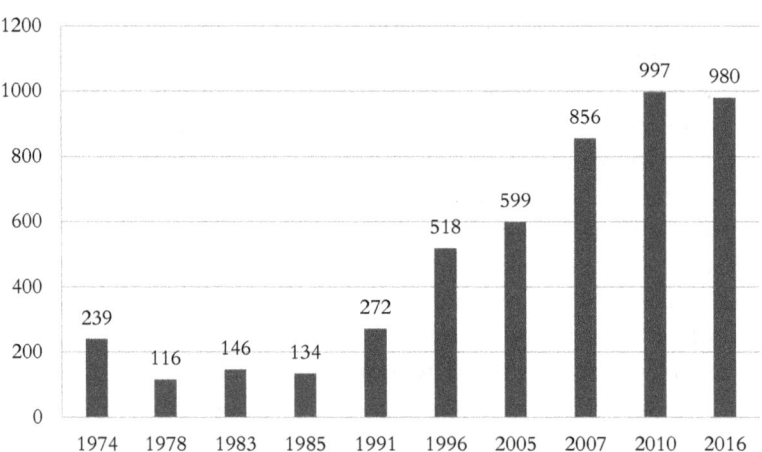

Source: Based on data provided by the Fellowship for Intentional Community

CONCLUSION

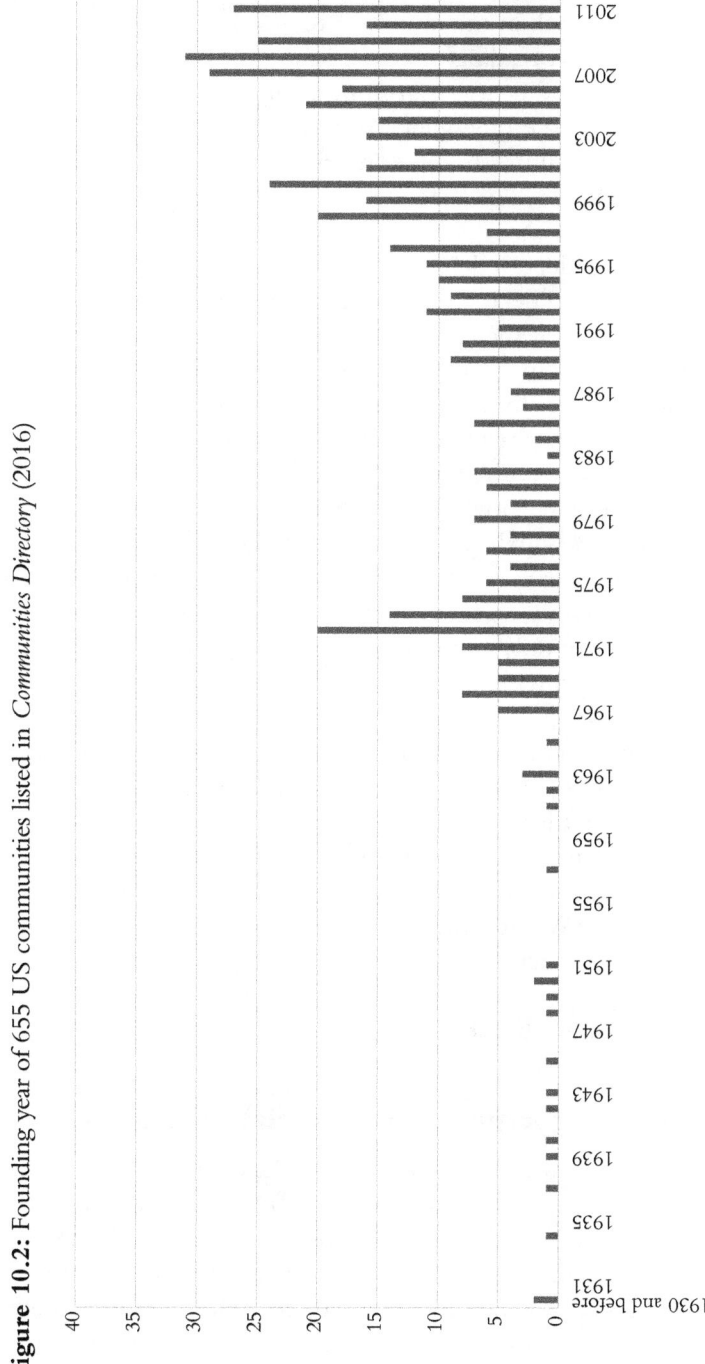

Figure 10.2: Founding year of 655 US communities listed in *Communities Directory* (2016)

Source: Based on data provided by the Fellowship for Intentional Community

contributions of which are difficult to quantify: a more systematic inventory of all forms of community on the one hand (such as student houses, which cropped up at the start of the 20th century), and the emergence of original models (such as the transition towns that appeared in the mid-2000s) on the other. A reading of all the issues of *Communities* nonetheless suggests that the second factor is far from negligible. Indeed, since the late 1990s, we have seen the emergence of new concerns such as sustainable development, permaculture, balanced nutrition, well-being, and so on. As a result, ecovillages have been attracting particular attention from the editors of *Communities*.[1]

We must not be deceived by the differentiation between intentional community models. The oppositions that are impossible to miss when examining the details of their respective structures should not obscure the existence of common interests and values. These cement the rhetoric of community all the more for the fact that, through the work of organizations such as the Foundation for Intentional Community (as the Fellowship for Intentional Community was renamed in 2019) and the FEC, the 'we' is gaining in depth and reach while partially detaching identity markers from the specific place in which one lives. Today, these two organizations are campaigning harder than ever for the values of cooperation, sustainability, and social justice. Using a range of tools (websites, publications, training courses[2]), they act not only to encourage the emergence of new intentional communities, but also with the goal of influencing society as a whole:

> For intentional communities, this means recognizing that creating nice places to live, mini-enclaves where we can shelter away from mainstream society, is not enough. [...] While ICs will always represent opportunities to live our values and benefit from them right now, more and more people recognize that we need global transformation under the same values. We are killing each other and making the planet unlivable for our species. Our lives are at stake.[3]

The message could not be clearer.

Interstitial transformation and social change

Despite the above-mentioned reorientation of the Foundation for Intentional Community, the intentional community world says little about how a community-based society could possibly be organized on a macro scale. In fact, all the work remains to be done. The observations and conclusions set out in this book provide some food for thought. More precisely, they can serve to enrich the model of interstitial transformation that Erik Olin Wright (2010, pp 303, 305) associates in *Envisioning Real Utopias* with all those initiatives that 'seek to build new forms of social empowerment in the niches and margins of capitalist society, often where they do not seem to pose any immediate threat to the dominant classes and elites'. From this point of view, the idea most frequently championed, as Wright himself notes, is that the accumulation of small alternative exceptions could ultimately overturn the dominant social order. To me, this perspective seems a little short-sighted. Applied to the case of utopian communities, it overlooks the plurality of interactions between collectives and straight society and their effects. Yet these take several forms.

The first scenario is the *bubble*. Here, links with the outside world are deliberately reduced. The community is essentially turned in on itself, at the risk of quickly disappearing for lack of sufficient resources and skills. This configuration is the direct counterpart of the passive sect described by Troeltsch. The community can also remain in a bubble despite the desire of some of its members to serve as a model. This was the case, for example, of the Familistère in Guise (France), a working and living community inspired in large part by the precepts of Fourier, which, despite the best efforts of Jean-Baptiste André Godin, its founder and leader from 1859 to 1888, never managed to gain widespread acceptance (Lallement, 2009). One of the most plausible reasons for this difficulty in inspiring emulation was the lack of social predisposition among the captains of industry of the time. In an era when the prevailing economic regulations prioritized extensive accumulation and cost competition, there was very little incentive to adopt strategies such as those practised in the Familisterian community. Indeed, the number of employers in France who decided to embrace an alternative model of work and worker management similar to Godin's can be counted on the fingers of one hand.

A second scenario, quite different from the bubble, is *contamination*. Here, representations and practices experimented within community contexts are adopted by other actors and disseminated throughout society, with or without the consent of those who originally promoted them. The ex-Twin Oaks communards who continue to put some of their principles into practice after returning to the wider world are active participants in such a mechanism. The invention of community gardens in New York City in the 1970s is another interesting example (Baudry, 2011). Collective gardening in urban areas was initially an act of resistance. It later became a tool for sustainable development. But it is no doubt Max Weber (1905) who provided the most spectacular illustration of this form of transformation through contamination. In his famous study *The Protestant Ethic and the Spirit of Capitalism*, the German sociologist showed that 16th-century Puritan communities invented a completely new way of thinking that saw work as an end in itself. This orientation, 'which seems to the pre-capitalistic man so incomprehensible and mysterious, so unworthy and contemptible' (Weber,

1905, p 33), would nonetheless become the norm of Western capitalism a few centuries later. Whether progressive or not, contamination can run counter to the initial intentions of those seeking to promote new ways of thinking, feeling, and acting. Weber was the first to demonstrate this. Luc Boltanski and Ève Chiapello (1999) were only following in his footsteps when they examined the fate of 1960s artist criticism and discovered that its main themes (autonomy, creativity, mobility, and so on) had been appropriated by 1980s management, no longer to oppose capitalism but to breathe new life into it.[4]

Yet another mechanism of interstitial transformation – the third possible relationship between a collective of utopians and the outside world – is the *alliance*. As Isabelle Berrebi-Hoffmann, Marie-Christine Bureau, and I (2018) highlighted in our study of 'makerspaces', the open DIY communities that emerged in the mid-2000s have passed the ten-year mark thanks, among other things, to the invention of hybrid spaces. In such spaces, these 21st-century *bricoleurs* are joined by professionals or informed amateurs specializing in fields such as education, craft production, industrial innovation, and art. The putting together of traditions and expertise serves to trigger innovative practices which, more often than not, easily weave their way into the social fabric.

Multiplying is the last of the scenarios, and the most ambitious in political terms. This mechanism promotes more directly than the others a radical project to transform the dominant system. It draws directly on the momentum that Wright associates with the accumulation of alternative spaces. In the community tradition, multiplying first and foremost demonstrates a refusal to see micro-societies, whose functioning would inevitably be distorted by the coexistence of too many communards, grow beyond what is possible and reasonable. Splitting has long been the preferred strategy for avoiding anomie and the bureaucratic temptation. Even if Fourier's work attracted little interest in the US in the 20th century, the community movement could easily have found out about the spin-off plan that the author of *Le Nouveau monde industriel et sociétaire* had in mind. In addition to urban *maîtrises* (master craftsmen's guilds), Fourier wanted to see the development of numerous rural farms, each comprising at least 40 families – the equivalent of 200 people. That, he thought, was the optimum size for achieving three goals which today's communards would not think beneath them: 'good and economical subsistence, varied and lucrative work, inexpensive management' (Fourier, 1829, p 491). In Fourier's view, such a model would serve as a starting point for the construction of the first age of the social world and provide the impetus needed to reach the ultimate stage of the Phalansterian utopia.

It's not a complete coincidence that this conclusion ends with a nod to the theorist of the Phalanstères, those utopian communities *par excellence*. Fourier helps us, to use a phrase of Michel Foucault's in *The Order of*

Discourse (1971), to 'escape from Hegel'. Viewed from the 2000s, drawing on Fourierist support may seem doubly contradictory. Firstly, unlike Pierre-Joseph Proudhon, Fourier was not an advocate of equality – quite the opposite. It was nevertheless his doctrine that, by infiltrating US territory in the second half of the 19th century, gave new impetus to the utopian collectives of which today's egalitarian intentional communities are in part the heirs. Secondly, Fourier rejected the label of theorist of utopia – chimerical metaphysics that he associated with a 'dream of the good with no means of execution, no effective method' (Fourier, 1967, cited in Mercklé, 2004, p 11). For the philosopher from Besançon, change had to take place in the here and now. But rather than entertain the hope of revolution, Fourier preferred to call for a strategy of leverage: to move the world, all that is needed is a sturdy fulcrum. The lever would do the rest. That is indeed the method favoured by the women and men who have breathed new life into intentional communities since the 1960s, as they strive to make concrete utopias with their sights set on far-reaching social change.

Notes

Introduction

1. http://ahimsazine.com/arch/twinoaks.html. Accessed 22 March 2018. For a photographic presentation of this community, see 'Twin Oaks ('67, VA). Planner/manager government with labor credits', in G. Kozeny, *Visions of Utopia: Experiments in Sustainable Culture*, DVD 1, Rutledge MO, Fellowship for Intentional Community, 2004.
2. Ecovillages are urban or more often rural settlements whose members share the common goal of an economically, environmentally, and socially sustainable lifestyle based on ecological principles (Joseph and Bates, 2003). The term was first used in 1991.
3. The axes are weighted as follows: 15.8 (horizontal axis) and 11.9 (vertical axis).
4. By way of illustration, see A. Laurin-Lamothe, F. Legault and S. Tremblay-Pepin (2023), N. Srnicek and A. Williams (2015), P. Mason (2016), or W. Streeck (2016).
5. In this spirit, see E. Reece (2016) and A. Whitney Sanford (2017).
6. This definition is the one proposed by Monticelli (2021).
7. Utopia derives from the Greek *ou-topos* (no place) but also from *eu-topia* (good place, place of happiness).
8. I borrow the term from Bloch (1954; 1955; 1959).
9. Jenkins' 1979 bestseller *A Walk Across America* has a slightly different status. Only Chapter 20 is concerned with an intentional community, namely The Farm, where the author stayed for six weeks.
10. Twin Oaks Collection, University of Virginia Library, Special Collections, MSS 9840-z, nine boxes.
11. Burrhus Frederic Skinner Archives, Harvard University Archives, HUG(GP) 60.20, box 15.
12. For the purposes of the English edition, the original French text has been edited and abridged. Priority has been given in this edition to the ethnographic part of the book published in French.

Chapter 1

1. With regard to this death certificate, Creagh refers readers to Fairfield (1972).
2. Sky Blue (2017) 'Movement at a Crossroads – 30th Birthday, Day 1', 31 October, www.ic.org/movement-at-a-crossroads-30th-birthday-day-1/. Accessed 4 January 2018.
3. Miller (1990) offers a full and purportedly exhaustive picture of American intentional communities before the 1960s in *American Communes 1860–1960. A Bibliography*.
4. The original article appeared in April 1971 in *The Saturday Review*.
5. This first issue was preceded by two instalments published in July and September 1972 under the name *Communitas. A New Community Journal*.
6. *Communities* devoted special issues to inventories of intentional communities in 1972, 1974, 1975, 1976, 1978, 1981, 1983, and 1985.

NOTES

[7] *Communities Directory* appeared in 1990 (with an update the following year), 1995 (also with an update the following year), 2000, 2005, 2007, 2010, and 2016. Unfortunately, I have never been able to get hold of the volume published in 2000.

[8] The figure rose to 259 in 1975. In 1976, only 81 communities were listed. The reason for the drop in numbers was that the magazine only included communities that agreed to write one or more paragraphs presenting themselves. In 1978, the presentation was different again. *Communities* published a summary table that included 98 US communities, each associated with a series of predetermined characteristics (location, number of members, surface area, diet, etc.). The number reached 117 in 1981, 125 in 1983, and 109 in 1985, in each case with reporting on characteristics comparable to those of 1978 as the criterion for publication. In the *Communities Directories* that was subsequently published, there were 275 communities established or being formed in 1990–1991, 488 in 1995–1996, 517 in 2007, 908 in 2010, and 937 in 2016.

[9] A mental construct that emphasises some of the structural features of a phenomenon under study, the ideal type is nothing like the family in Wittgenstein's sense. One can nonetheless use such a tool to help untangle the intertwining similarities and dissimilarities that intrigued the author of the *Tractacus*. For a precise definition of the ideal type, see Weber (1949, pp. 42 ff.).

[10] The axes are weighted as follows: 18.2 per cent for the horizontal axis; 11.3 per cent for the vertical axis.

[11] Gaskin's speeches were transcribed, edited, and annotated by their author. They are published and sold by The Farm's publishing house (Gaskin, 2005).

[12] Jenkins also reported that, in 1974, Gaskin was a bigamist and the father of several children.

[13] Testimonies from members of The Farm about their backgrounds and life in the community can also be found in Fike (1998).

[14] Discussion with Diana, The Farm, 20 October 2018.

[15] I have developed the Weberian interpretation of the Changeover that is suggested here in a little more detail elsewhere (Lallement, 2019).

[16] Discussion with Phil, The Farm, 18 October 2018.

[17] Douglas (2018) 'Presentation of The Farm', conference at The Farm, 19 October 2018.

[18] All dollars in this book are US dollars.

[19] The terms of this vow of poverty were as follows: 'We are organized on a communal basis according to the Book of Acts of the New Testament, Acts, 2:44,45: "And all that believed were together, and had all things in common; and sold their possessions and goods, and parted them to all men as every man had need." We have a common treasury. All money from whatever source is given to our bank which distributes the money according to need—to further our religious and educational purposes, and to provide everyone in our community with food, clothing, housing, and ordinary medical and dental supplies and services. No individual member of our church owns property. (I, we) give all (my, our) property to the Foundation to be held and used in common. This property includes: … Name(s), Date.' Source: The Farm Museum, The Farm, Summertown, TN.

Chapter 2

[1] B. Skinner's published works include *The Behavior of Organisms* (1938); *Verbal Behaviour* (1957), and *About Behaviourism* (1974).

[2] Participants were invited through the 'Breiling' list, named after Jim Breiling, a behavioural psychologist to whom Skinner referred all those who had approached him expressing an interest in *Walden Two*. In 1965, 250 names were on the list.

[3] An account of the event can be found in the issues of *Walden Pool* and the *Walden House* newsletters published in August, September, and October 1966. Excerpts appear in

Experimenting with Walden Two. The Collected Leaves of Twin Oaks (1972) issues 1–15, Twin Oaks Community, Louisa, Virginia, pp. 6–12.

4 'Walden Three' (1971) *The Leaves of Twin Oaks*, No. 14, April, p. 15.

5 For the description of these founding years, I rely on the writings of Fairfield (1972), Houriet (1973), Kinkade (1973; 1994), and on the information provided in *Walden Pool* and the *Walden House* newsletters.

6 'Walden House', excerpt from the *Walden House* newsletter, December 1965, reproduced in *Experimenting with Walden Two. The Collected Leaves of Twin Oaks*, issues 1–15, p. 1.

7 *Walden Pool*, April 1966, in *Experimenting with Walden Two. The Collected Leaves of Twin Oaks*, p. 4.

8 'We arrive' (1967) *The Leaves of Twin Oaks*, 1, July, p. 1. Numbers 1 to 15 of the *Leaves of Twin Oaks* are collected and published in *Experimenting with Walden Two. The Collected Leaves of Twin Oaks*.

9 Kathleen (1969) 'Twin Oaks Leadership', *The Leaves of Twin Oaks*, 9, May, pp. 5–7.

10 Kathleen (1967) 'General news', *The Leaves of Twin Oaks*, 2, September.

11 'Report on Twin Oaks summer conference' (1971) *The Leaves of Twin Oaks*, 15, August, p. 2.

12 In March 1968, seven members were in this situation. They worked, for instance, as nurses or tree planters. Their working hours outside the community (including travel time) were counted as labour credits. 'We get outside Jobs', *The Leaves of Twin Oaks*, 6, April 1968, pp. 1–2.

13 'We become self-supporting' (1969) *The Leaves of Twin Oaks*, 10, September, pp. 1–2.

14 'Outside work off premises', *The Collected Leaves of Twin Oaks*, vol. 2, Issues 16–30, 1972–1974, p. 7.

15 D. Ruth, 'On B.F. Skinner's first visit to Twin Oaks, turnover, and the meaning of life', typed document, 5 pages, Burrhus Frederic Skinner archives, Harvard University Archives, HUG(GP) 60.20, carton 15.

16 D. Ruth, 'On B.F. Skinner's first visit to Twin Oaks', p. 5.

17 Letter from B. Skinner to D. Ruth, 2 November 1976, Burrhus Frederic Skinner archive, Harvard University Archives, HUG(GP) 60.20, carton 15.

18 Letter from B. Skinner to D. Ruth, 21 January 1977, Burrhus Frederic Skinner archive, Harvard University Archives, HUG(GP) 60.20, carton 15.

19 'A World of Difference: Skinner and the Good Life' (1979), www.youtube.com/watch?v=O_EJ20tbL-s. Viewed 7 August 2017.

20 Letter from B. Skinner to Chip, 24 January 1979, Burrhus Frederic Skinner Archives, Harvard University Archives, HUG(GP) 60.20, box 15.

21 Letter from Chip to B. Skinner, 19 January 1979, Burrhus Frederic Skinner Archives, Harvard University Archives, HUG(GP) 60.20, box 15.

22 Nexus (no date) 'Walden Two's Bastard Child', www.twinoaks.org/culture-government-65/walden-two-community?showall=&start=5. Accessed 10 August 2018.

23 The text originally appeared in *The Behavior Analyst*, 8, Spring 1985, pp. 5–14.

24 The book by M. Spiro that K. Kinkade refers to is *Kibbutz. Venture in Utopia* (Spiro, 1956). It is still prominently displayed in the library at Twin Oaks.

25 Brian (2002) 'Twin Oaks: An American Kibbutz?', *The Leaves of Twin Oaks*, 96.

26 For a critical view of Skinner's work and of the influence of *Walden Two* in particular, see Altus and Morris (2009).

Chapter 3

1 Letter from T.S. Martin Jr. to B. Skinner, Burrhus Frederic Skinner archives, Harvard University Archives, HUG(GP) 60.20, carton 15. The letter is not dated. It was probably received in early 1979, after the Nova program on Skinner was aired. See Chapter 4 on this subject.

NOTES

2. R. Sadiq (2006) 'Why is this place so white?', *The Leaves of Twin Oaks*, 103, fall, pp. 4–5.
3. 'Welcome to Twin Oaks!', August 1987, University of Virginia Library, Special Collections, Twin Oaks collection, box 6, folder 1.
4. This technique makes it possible to show one's level of agreement without speaking and helps lead a group to a consensus decision relatively easily.
5. In reality, some men also live there.
6. Zhankoye is the name of a Jewish farming community established in the Crimea in the 1930s.
7. This 62-acre site was acquired in 1990.
8. 'Members only? An inside Look at the CMT' (2015) *The Leaves of Twin Oaks*, 119, spring, p. 3.
9. Cade, *Viz Oreo* Becoming a member, Twin Oaks, 26 April 2016.
10. Gordon and Kat (1993) 'Acorn. The New Community', *The Leaves of Twin Oaks*, 74, January, p. 7.
11. Interview with Ira, Acorn, 19 June 2017.
12. 'Land Day for Acorn. News from the Paisley Binder' (1993) *The Leaves of Twin Oaks*, 75, April, pp. 6, 18.
13. 'Acorn after a Year' (1994) *The Leaves of Twin Oaks*, 77, summer, p. 7.
14. 'Acorn update' (1995) *The Leaves of Twin Oaks*, 78, winter, pp. 4–6.
15. The building has four bedrooms, a kitchen, two common rooms, a bathroom, and a laundry.
16. These letters are archived in box 7 (folders 14 to 26) of the Twin Oaks collection at the University of Virginia Library. The applicants for membership explain who they are and why they want to become Oakers.
17. The distribution by age group is as follows (n = 63): 25 years and under: 28.5 per cent; 26–35 years: 38 per cent; 36–45 years: 22.5 per cent; 46 years and over: 11 per cent.
18. Application letter from Charlotte, 1993, University of Virginia Library, Special Collections, Twin Oaks collection, box 7, folder 26.
19. Application letter from Cathy, 20 March 1990, University of Virginia Library, Special Collections, Twin Oaks collection, box 7, folder 23.
20. Application letter from Judy, 1989, University of Virginia Library, Special Collections, Twin Oaks collection, box 7, folder 22.
21. Application letter from Karin, 1983, University of Virginia Library, Special Collections, Twin Oaks collection, box 7, folder 18.
22. Application letter from Nancy, 1992, University of Virginia Library, Special Collections, Twin Oaks collection, box 7, folder 25.
23. Informal discussion with Damian, Acorn, 16 June 2017.
24. Jonathan, 'How Twin Oakers see the World …', drawing reprinted in Kinkade (1994, p. 306).
25. Application letter from Pat, 1992, University of Virginia Library, Special Collections, Twin Oaks collection, box 7, folder 25.
26. This article is also published on the page about income-sharing on the Twin Oaks website, www.twinoaks.org/about-income-sharing#why-income-sharing. Accessed 17 December 2017.
27. www.twinoaks.org/about-income-sharing#why-income-sharing. Accessed 17 December 2017.
28. www.twinoaks.org/about-twinoaks-community/welcome. Accessed 23 January 2018.
29. Translator's note: In French, in addition to having similar meanings to the English verb 'compose' (to arrange, compose, form, produce), the verb *composer* (followed by *avec*) also means to compromise, to come to an arrangement, to come to terms with. It is the *combination* of all those meanings that the author brings to bear here. Similarly,

the noun *composition* should be understood in the sense of compromise as well as arrangement, configuration.

30 I am deliberately leaving aside a third form distinguished by E. Troeltsch, namely mysticism. A mystic experiences their passion outside the world of mortals and escapes all the burdens of the latter. In the section of *Economy and Society* devoted to the paths to salvation and their influences, Weber also mentions this case.

31 Gordon (1990) 'Machine-Made Hammocks Bed', 4 November, University of Virginia Library, Special Collections, Twin Oaks Collection, box 1, folder 18.

32 *The Leaves of Twin Oaks* (2011/2012) 111, winter, p. 1.

Chapter 4

1 Kathleen (1967) 'General news', *The Leaves of Twin Oaks*, 3, November.
2 Ted (1993) 'An easy course in Twin Oaksese', excerpted from the Twin Oaks New Member Handbook, *The Leaves of Twin Oaks*, 74, January, p. 7.
3 Keenan (no date) 'Twin Oaks Terms', University of Virginia Library, Special Collections, Twin Oaks Collection, box 6, folder 1.
4 According to Passehl (2004, p. 41), Twin Oaks did not invent the pronoun 'co'. The idea came from a New York feminist group.
5 Goffman uses the opposition between 'human selves' and 'socialized selves' in *The Presentation of Self* (1959, p. 56). The distinction between virtual and actual social identities is put forward in *Stigma* (Goffman, 1963, pp. 2–3).
6 'First Twin Oaks Behavior Code' (2016) O&I, ZK, Twin Oaks.
7 The only exception is in correspondence with the outside world (tax authorities, police and courts, doctors and hospitals, etc.) for which an administrative identity is mandatory.
8 'Names' (1970) *The Leaves of Twin Oaks*, 13, October, p. 12. Following the publication of this article, the practice of changing one's name became commonplace, at the risk of fickleness. 'The girl who started out as Susan, then became Sally, is now Josie. Eve became Shawn and then changed her mind and wants to be Eve again. Even visiting children are changing their names.' 'More name changing' (1971) *The Leaves of Twin Oaks*, 15, August, p. 7.
9 Twin Oaks ran into this problem early on. 'We had three Bills here at one time, and it was a nuisance to refer to them as Bill I, Bill II, and Bill III. [...] But it was rather a surprise when all three of them changed their names and we had no Bills left at all.' 'More name changing' (1971) *The Leaves of Twin Oaks*, 15, August, p. 7.
10 These photos were posted on the Twin Oaks Facebook page.
11 www.twinoaks.org/about-twinoaks-community/more-about-twin-oaks#interpersonal-relations
12 This is what Goffman (1967, p. 71) calls the 'acts through which the individual makes specific attestations to recipients concerning how he regards them and how he will treat them in the on-coming interaction'.
13 Hancock (1998, p. 31) observed that in many intentional communities, 'people from working-class and poor backgrounds for example, often feel incapable or stupid. In meetings, they often remain quiet—fearful that they won't be able to say anything "right." They will often avoid intellectual discussions or planning in favor of "getting on with things." [...] People who come from upper-class families (sometimes called the "owning class") tend to find many ways of isolating and distancing themselves from others.'
14 Twin Oaks has the following SLGs: Appletree, Beechside, Harmony, Kawea, Morning Star, Nashoba, Sunrise, Tai Chai, Oneida and Tupelo.
15 'A Child in Community' (1968) *The Leaves of Twin Oaks*, 4, January, pp. 2–3.
16 Steve (2014) 'Inter-Generational Living at Twin Oaks', *The Leaves of Twin Oaks*, 118, fall, p. 2.

NOTES

17 Editorial Research Reports (1971) 'Communal Farms Become Paradise Lost', *Racine Journal Times*, 26 August. Cited in Passehl (2004, p. 40).
18 Dylan, 'Men's Support Groups', unpublished, cited in Komar (1983, p. 204).
19 'Welcome to Twin Oaks!'.
20 Letter from Joanie Kanter on behalf of the Federation of Egalitarian Communities, April 1979, University of Virginia Library, Special Collections, Twin Oaks collection, box 1, folder 4.
21 See https://womensgathering.org and https://twinoaksqueergathering.org. Accessed 5 January 2018.
22 'Feminist Think Tank: Past and Future' (2017) *The Leaves of Twin Oaks*, Spring, 123.
23 At the Social 'Viz Oreo' (Twin Oaks, 27 April 2016), Billie and Rebecca stressed the importance of understanding that when it comes to sexual interactions, 'no' means 'no'. They ran an exercise for our small group of visitors to teach us to say no when someone makes unwanted advances.
24 *Twin Oaks Feminist Zine 2017*.
25 Not all Oakers were happy with the initiative. Some people contested the claim to the 'eco-village' label for a community that uses nuclear power and where some members eat meat.
26 'Des communautés de femmes aux écovillages, quand les lesbiennes vivent autrement', *Jeanne Magazine*, 13 December 2014. www.jeanne-magazine.com/le-magazine/2014/12/13/des-communautes-de-femmes-aux-ecovillages-quand-les-lesbiennes-vivent-autrement_7094/. Accessed 21 July 2017.
27 At Twin Oaks, I only observed two stable couples of which one partner lived elsewhere, in another community as it happens.
28 'Des communautés de femmes aux écovillages'.
29 See, for example, 'Bi the way … being Bi at Twin Oaks' (2002) *The Leaves of Twin Oaks*, 96, Winter.
30 A gathering for bisexuals had, admittedly, already been held at Acorn in 1995. *The Leaves of Twin Oaks* (1995) 77, Winter.
31 As F. Simpère, a journalist who specialises in the subject, suggests, 'if we situate it politically, polyamory today is feminist. A woman can experience the same thing as a man; the symmetry of desire is accepted. Gender equality is one of its characteristics.' *Le Monde*, 5 October 2018.

Chapter 5

1 www.ic.org/myths-about-intentional-communities/. Accessed 12 August 2018.
2 Here, following Reynaud (1989), I use social regulation to mean the production, use, and transformation of rules that structure collective life.
3 'Decision Making' (1968) *The Leaves of Twin Oaks*, 4, January, p. 7.
4 Kat (1987) 'Government at Twin Oaks', September, University of Virginia Library, Special Collections, Twin Oaks collection, box 6, folder 1.
5 www.twinoakscommunity.org/docmanhidden/systems-and-policies/50-collected-policies-2010/file. Accessed 10 June 2023.
6 Kat, 'Government at Twin Oaks'.
7 Posted in the ZK lobby is a document setting out the overall structure of responsibilities, which distinguishes between Domestic Councils and Income Councils. The first set includes agriculture (which brings together basic managerial units relating to bees, dairy production, construction and maintenance of fences and gates, gardening, mushroom growing, seed production, etc.), children, cross-cutting services (such as support for activism), construction and utilities, cooking, domestic tasks (cleaning, pets, etc.), the natural environment, health,

office work, outreach (events and communication), planning, leisure and, finally, transport. The Income Councils are as follows: business management (marketing, sales, etc.), rope goods production (hammocks, chairs, etc.), woodwork, and other activities.

8   Philip, Labour Viz Oreo, 24 April 2016.
9   'Trade-offs 1986 – Explanations and instructions' (no date) University of Virginia Library, Special Collections, Twin Oaks collection, box 6, folder 5; K. Kinkade (1990) 'The Tradeoff Game Tally – Explained by a planner', 8 January, University of Virginia Library, Special Collections, Twin Oaks collection, box 6, folder 10.
10 The periodicity, sections, breakdown by areas of work, and ways of playing the game have evolved over time. I won't go into the rather tedious details of this history here.
11 In the archives, this parameter does not appear in the accounts until 1990. It was 2.4 per cent at that date, 3.5 per cent the following year, and 5 per cent the year after that. This indicator is a way of quantifying the community's ability to adjust to an unpredictable environment (a sudden increase in orders for hammocks, for example).
12 Leslie (1992) 'Why I hate the trade-off game …', O&I, 31 December, University of Virginia Library, Special Collections, Twin Oaks collection, box 6, folder 20.
13 Stone and Audric (2016) Health Viz Oreo, Twin Oaks, 28 April.
14 'First Twin Oaks Behavior Code' (2016) O&I, ZK, Twin Oaks.
15 In 1983, for example, Zammy wrote a long letter in which he explained his unstable and unpleasant behaviour at other people's expense by tensions with his girlfriend. He apologised and announced his departure. Zammy (1983) 'A few words from Zammy (a few days before he leaves)', 3 February, University of Virginia Library, Special Collections, Twin Oaks collection, box 7, folder 31.
16 'Emotional Health Survey', November 1991, University of Virginia Library, Special Collections, Twin Oaks collection, box 1, folder 8. Twin Oaks has had to deal with 'controversial' members on a regular basis, many of whom, like Denis, have been in very fragile physical and mental health. Between 1989 and 1992, six such cases can be identified (see University of Virginia Library, Special Collections, Twin Oaks collection, box 8, folders 10 to 15). The care and attention that the community devotes to and arranges for these members has not prevented some from being expelled, sometimes after extremely tumultuous interactions.
17 John (1985) 'Goodby to Gandhitown', 30 November, 9 pages, University of Virginia Library, Special Collections, Twin Oaks collection, box 7, folder 33.
18 Keenan (1985) 'Hello to Hermit Heaven', 6 December, University of Virginia Library, Special Collections, Twin Oaks collection, box 7, folder 33.
19 'Appeals and Overrides Policy' (2010) *Digital Twin Oaks Policies*.
20 Pam (2016) 'Appeal of the Health Team Decision to Allow Spending of the Vitamin Allowance on Food', O&I, 24 April.
21 'Chickens at Twin Oaks' (1992) O&I, 3 July, University of Virginia Library, Special Collections, Twin Oaks collection, box 1, folder 1.
22 'Chickens at Twin Oaks'.
23 Jim (1992) 'Are Jim and Nina mistreating the chickens?', O&I, July 7, University of Virginia Library, Special Collections, Twin Oaks collection, box 1, folder 1.
24 Nina (1992) 'Buck Buck Buck: more squawkin' about Chickens or What's up with them birds, anyway?', O&I, 7 July, University of Virginia Library, Special Collections, Twin Oaks collection, box 1, folder 1.
25 Nina, 'Buck Buck Buck'.
26 Sharon, Inge, and Susan (1992) 'Appeal to the agriculture council', 10 July, University of Virginia Library, Special Collections, Twin Oaks collection, box 1, folder 1.
27 'Ag Council. Re: Chickens', 12 July 1992, University of Virginia Library, Special Collections, Twin Oaks collection, box 1, folder 1.

NOTES

28   Jim, Nina, and Shal (no date) 'Chix n'Clux. Our experiment went really well ...', O&I, University of Virginia Library, Special Collections, Twin Oaks collection, box 1, folder 1. Shal, who was part of the nocturnal expedition that proved fatal for one of the chickens, had since joined the poultry management team. In this note, the three Oakers indicated that they had slaughtered 40 hens in the last few days, the equivalent of 91 kilos of meat, at a cost of $75 and 75 hours of labour.
29   Jim (1992) 'Chix N'Clux. The saga continues', O&I, September, University of Virginia Library, Special Collections, Twin Oaks collection, box 1, folder 1.
30   See above.
31   www.acorncommunity.org. Accessed 9 March 2017.
32   According to Creagh (1983), two or three expulsions occurred at Twin Oaks over the 15-year period he studied.
33   'Mutual criticism' (1969) *The Leaves of Twin Oaks*, 10, September, pp. 4–6.
34   'Mutual criticism', p. 5.
35   'Awareness Groups' (1971) *The Leaves of Twin Oaks*, 15, August, pp. 7–9.
36   Valerie (1993) 'Belize', *The Leaves of Twin Oaks*, 74, January, p. 13.
37   Paxus (2016) 'A New Open Transparency Tools Group', notice posted on the 3x5 board, ZK, Twin Oaks.
38   Steve (2016) Rules and internal relations Viz Oreo, Twin Oaks, 6 May.
39   Purl (2016) 'Explanation and plan around my Money hole situation', O&I, ZK, Twin Oaks.

Chapter 6

1   The citation is taken from *The Prophet*, a collection of 26 texts by the Lebanese poet Kahlil Gibran (1923), who was particularly popular in American counterculture circles in the 1960s.
2   www.twinoakshammocks.com/how-to-make-a-hammock.html. Accessed 25 October 2016.
3   G. (1986) 'Exciting Hamock News', O&I, 3 May, University of Virginia Library, Special Collections, Twin Oaks collection, box 1, folder 19.
4   Keenan (1990) 'A Pleasant Push', O&I, 10 November, University of Virginia Library, Special Collections, Twin Oaks collection, box 1, folder 18.
5   Cassie (1990) 'Hx Shop Auction', 12 March, University of Virginia Library, Special Collections, Twin Oaks collection, box 1, folder 18.
6   In normal times, PFF makes it possible, for example – the figures here are purely illustrative – to buy a hammock sold on the market for $130 for the equivalent of 20 labour credits, or 20 hours of work. If we estimate that an hour's work brings in $5 for the community, the communard gains in such a deal without the hammock being sold for less than its production cost. During a push period, the hammock manager may decide to reduce the number of credits required to obtain a hammock. This was the case in 1990, when, with the planners' blessing, the manager reduced the rate by 25 per cent until the urgent order was met. Matthew and planners (1990) 'Special PFF rates as an Hx production incentive', 1 March, University of Virginia Library, Special Collections, Twin Oaks collection, box 1, folder 21.
7   Anne and Vis (1990) 'Rope making at Twin Oaks', O&I, 20 November, University of Virginia Library, Special Collections, Twin Oaks collection, box 1, folder 17.
8   Jon (1990) 'Stretcher Drilling Push', O&I, 29 January, University of Virginia Library, Special Collections, Twin Oaks collection, box 1, folder 17.
9   Cassie, Coyote, McCune, Donna, Ann, Libra, and Philip (1992) 'Stretcher Making and Sawmill OPP', 1 July, University of Virginia Library, Special Collections, Twin Oaks collection, box 1, folder 17.

10. Libra (1992) 'Memorandum', O&I, 21 November, University of Virginia Library, Special Collections, Twin Oaks collection, box 1, folder 17.
11. G. (1986) 'Exciting Hammocks News', O&I, 3 March, University of Virginia Library, Special Collections, Twin Oaks collection, box 1, folder 19.
12. Todd (no date) 'Piece work rate info', O&I, University of Virginia Library, Special Collections, Twin Oaks collection, box 1, folder 19.
13. Cristey (1987) 'Ah … Err … Sorry to interrupt the Party BUT …', 7 November, University of Virginia Library, Special Collections, Twin Oaks collection, box 1, folder 19.
14. Kat (1991) 'Disconnecting from Workshop Five', 2 December, University of Virginia Library, Special Collections, Twin Oaks collection, box 1, folder 19.
15. Velma (1990) O&I, 23 March, University of Virginia Library, Special Collections, Twin Oaks collection, box 1, folder 17.
16. 'Pier 1 and Twin Oaks divorced after 30 years' (2005) *The Leaves of Twin Oaks*, 101, winter, pp. 1, 5.
17. www.twinoakshammocks.com/. Accessed 2 February 2023.
18. 'We're changing our name!' (1992) O&I, February, University of Virginia Library, Special Collections, Twin Oaks collection, box 1, folder 26.
19. Tigger (2015) 'The Tofu Upgrade: Another Perspective', O&I, 6 May, Twin Oaks, ZK.
20. www.pubpat.org/assets/files/seed/OSGATA-v-Monsanto-Complaint.pdf. Accessed 17 November 2016.
21. www.cafc.uscourts.gov/sites/default/files/opinions-orders/12-1298.Opinion.6-6-2013.1.PDF. Accessed 17 November 2016.
22. When Stone measured the noise level in the Tofu Hut, he found that it was the noisiest place in the community. The volume hits 97.7 decibels when the machines are running and music is playing. Without music, the level reaches 92.1, which is still higher than the threshold (90 decibels) above which there is a risk of hearing loss. The kitchen, another particularly noisy area when things are busy and the music is on, scored 78.9 decibels. Stone (2016) 'We're doing a good job protecting our hearing', O&I, Twin Oaks, ZK.
23. This type of behaviour was highlighted in a book that has become a classic in the sociology of work: Burawoy (1979) *Manufacturing Consent. Changing in the Labor Process under Monopoly Capitalism*.
24. The job description for the receptionist who greets visitors at the entrance to the community's administrative offices could be mistaken for that of any similar position in an outside company: answering the telephone, recording orders for Twin Oaks products, receiving and sorting payments and invoices, forwarding emails, and so on. The work is routine. The communards who do it devote between 12 and 15 hours a week to this job, with separate morning and afternoon shifts.
25. 'Planner Forum. The future of indexing' (1989) O&I, 3 November, University of Virginia Library, Special Collections, Twin Oaks collection, box 1, folder 22. An hour's work earned the community $7.80 in 1985, $9.00 in 1986, $6.00 in 1987, and $4.50 in 1988.
26. Cameron (1989) 'Indexing at a crossroads!', O&I, 3 October, University of Virginia Library, Special Collections, Twin Oaks collection, box 1, folder 22.
27. Cameron, 'Indexing at a crossroads!'.

Chapter 7
1. The text is taken from A. Berkman (1929) *What is Anarchist Communism?*
2. This system of labour credits is not unrelated to the practices invented and tried out in the US in the late 20th century, in a non-community context, by the labour exchange movement. See Grant (1981).
3. 'Labor credits – Theory and practice' (1968) *The Leaves of Twin Oaks*, 8, December, p. 5.

4   Kathleen (1967) 'General news', *The Leaves of Twin Oaks*, 2, September.
5   To avoid inflationary or deflationary drift, the slate for each task was wiped clean after two weeks.
6   'New Labor Credit System' (1970) *The Leaves of Twin Oaks*, 13, October, pp. 3–4.
7   'New Labor Credit System' (1970), p. 4.
8   This now classic expression in the sociology of work was coined by Everett C. Hughes (1958) to describe tasks that are unpleasant to perform either for material reasons (toughness, repetition, disgust, etc.) or for social reasons (associated with a loss of dignity, social devaluation, etc.).
9   Keenan (1992) 'With all these members. How come there's no Breakfast Cook?', O&I, 10 March, University of Virginia Library, Special Collections, Twin Oaks collection, box 7, folder 1.
10 'Who is covering Casy's jobs?' (no date) O&I, ZK, Twin Oaks. Accessed 5 May 2016.
11 'Labor credits – Theory and practice' (1968) *The Leaves of Twin Oaks*, 8, p. 6.
12 Thomas, visit to Acorn on 3 May 2016.
13 In 2017, apart from meetings that took place during a meal (see below), the most notable exception that I was able to identify was childcare. When a person looks after one child full-time, then one hour's work earns them half a credit. According to the French couple present at Twin Oaks during my visit in 2016, other tasks received a substantial bonus (one hour equalling two credits). Specifically, they meant work of an ecological nature (such as recycling). I was unable to confirm this information with the Oakers themselves.
14 When Eric Reece visited Twin Oaks in 2014, the seniority threshold for a reduction in working hours was still 60, as it had been since the 1970s. But the idea of lowering it to 50 was already in the air. It was a done deal by the time I was a visitor in 2016.
15 Keenan, Children Viz Oreo, Twin Oaks, 1 May 2016.
16 Philip, Labour Viz Oreo.
17 Philip, Labour Viz Oreo.
18 In ZK, as well as the space for general information where job offers can be posted, an entire section of a noticeboard located near the mail area is reserved for one-off job proposals (for example, eight hours' work requested by the garden manager to repair the stairs down to the cellar), permanent jobs (for example, working six hours a week in the rope workshop), and manager positions (for example, the legal manager, who is responsible for drawing up contracts with new members, among other things).
19 Philip, Labour Viz Oreo.
20 Philip, Labour Viz Oreo. Komar (1983) indicated that the vacation entitlement was already similar (two to three weeks a year) in the late 1970s and early 1980s.
21 Initially, seven labour credits were granted for this singular event. It was possible to receive this benefit provided you had arrived in the community before 1 January 1986. Kat (no date) 'How to take birthday free and anniversary free', O&I, University of Virginia Library, Special Collections, Twin Oaks collection, box 7, folder 1. When the community ran into difficulties in the late 1990s, the planners tried make savings where they could. They decided that answering the communal telephone or washing personal laundry would no longer earn credit. At the same time, the number of labour credits granted for the anniversary of arrival in the community also dropped, by half a point to be exact. Gordon and others (1998) 'The News of the Oaks', *The Leaves of Twin Oaks*, 86, winter.
22 Here are a few examples of projects financed by OPPs in the early 1990s: the purchase of a sound system for the hammock workshop, equipment for the Degania playground, charitable donations, funding for a trip for Twin Oaks children, and purchase of books for the community library. Rb, 'Overquota Projects Program' (1991) O&I, 18 July, University of Virginia Library, Special Collections, Twin Oaks collection, box 1, folder 27.

23 In the last seven years, only one person has been bitten and had to go to hospital. During my stay, Alexa also almost got ambushed when she lifted a tarpaulin under which a copper snake was lounging. She told me that no more than ten centimetres separated her bare hand from the creature's mouth.

Chapter 8

1. McEwan (1981) 'Owing it', O&I, 27 April, cited in Komar (1983, p. 148).
2. Jim and Rob (1990) 'Worker morale, manager morale, and a modest proposal to make a major change in the K-Shift scene', 26 January, University of Virginia Library, Special Collections, Twin Oaks collection, box 1, folder 3.
3. Such is the case at East Wind, as Allen, who had lived there, explained in detail. See Allen from East Wind's letter of application to Twin Oaks, November 1985, University of Virginia Library, Special Collections, Twin Oaks collection, box 7, folder 18.
4. Steve (2016) contribution to Kele 'Tofu Testimonials. The Tofu Crew on making Tofu', O&I, ZK, Twin Oaks, 5 March.
5. Brook (1989) Letter of reapplication, 5 September, University of Virginia Library, Special Collections, Twin Oaks collection, box 7, folder 22.
6. Kele (2016) 'Tofu Testimonials. The Tofu Crew on making Tofu', O&I, ZK, Twin Oaks, 5 March.
7. Koala's leaving letter, 25 December 1981, University of Virginia Library, Special Collections, Twin Oaks collection, box 7, folder 30.
8. Leaving letter from Judy and Rick, 16 October 1989, University of Virginia Library, Special Collections, Twin Oaks collection, box 7, folder 37.
9. In small living groups (SLGs), which are equipped with kitchens, the rule that applied in 2016 was as follows: labour credits are only earned for preparing food for at least seven people.
10. Kathleen, 'General news' (1967) *The Leaves of Twin Oaks*, 3, p. 2.
11. 'Labor credits – Theory and practice' (1968) *The Leaves of Twin Oaks*, 8.
12. 'Welcome to Twin Oaks!', Notebook, October 1987, University of Virginia Library, Special Collections, Twin Oaks collection, box 6, folder 1.
13. This typology is neither in use at Twin Oaks nor proposed by J. Griffin. It is my own construction.
14. 'Who works here' (1991) O&I, 5 May, University of Virginia Library, Special Collections, Twin Oaks collection, box 7, folder 1. I obtained the data for 2016 from a document posted in ZK.
15. Emma (1990) 'Emma's Experiment as a Hippie Communard', 16 November, University of Virginia Library, Special Collections, Twin Oaks collection, box 7, folder 38.
16. Loki (2016) 'I messed up with my labor contract letter', O&I, Twin Oaks, ZK.
17. § 1 Basic Scheme, Explanation of Twin Oaks Property Code (2009), *Digital Twin Oaks Policies*, 2016, p. 26.
18. They may also be given a fan, heater, chest of drawers, mirror, carpet, and other such items. Commie Clothes (see below) supplies sheets and pillows. When a member leaves, the contents of their room revert to the community, not to the next occupant. 'Trusterty' (1991) O&I, August, University of Virginia Library, Special Collections, Twin Oaks collection, box 4, folder 1.
19. 'Community Clothes' (1971) *The Leaves of Twin Oaks*, 14, April, pp. 3–4. Acorn also has a Commie Clothes, but it is more modest in its ambitions. Only some of the linen (sheets, pillowcases, towels, etc.) is shared. This is not the case for clothing.
20. As it is not always easy to find suitable, comfortable footwear at Commie Clothes, the community offers a yearly subsidy to help members who want to buy their own shoes.

The same goes for underwear and even socks, which members are understandably reluctant to share.

[21] Again, the system is similar at Acorn. The car keys are available on the board in the Heartwood dining room. The reservation system is more flexible than at Twin Oaks: anyone planning to use one of the cars in the community's fleet must pin a note saying so to the notice board.

[22] 'Weeds and Knots' is a play on 'needs and wants', which aptly describes the committee's function. The communards deliberately refused to use this overly administrative and stigmatising vocabulary.

[23] By way of comparison, the annual income per person in 2016 was $6,730. For previous years, the figures I have been able to find are, respectively, an $11 allowance (1983) for an income of $3,600 (1982), and $50 ($25 for children) for $3,500 (1992). The allowance was $76 in 2009 and $90 in 2014. At Acorn, the monthly allowance was $75 in 2016.

[24] Comment to Cassie (1992) 'Blast from the past', O&I, January 19, University of Virginia Library, Special Collections, Twin Oaks collection, box 1, folder 31.

[25] McCune (1988) 'Personal Money and V.E. A proposal', O&I, 15 November, University of Virginia Library, Special Collections, Twin Oaks collection, box 1, folder 31.

[26] Rollie (1988) comment on McCune's O&I, 'Personal Money and V.E. A proposal'.

[27] Digital Twin Oaks Policies (2009), section 'Explanation of Twin Oaks' Property Code', par. III 'Income during Membership', p. 28. Available at www.twinoaks.org/policies/property-code#income-during-membership. Accessed 27 July 2023.

[28] 'Thorny's Pizza', ZK hall notice board, Twin Oaks, 12 May 2016.

[29] 'Kitchen Norms' (1990) O&I, 5 June, University of Virginia Library, Special Collections, Twin Oaks collection, box 1, folder 3.

[30] Ross (1993) 'Ross is trying to work out, but deciding to leave or stay may take a while in the meantime. The reasons why', 2 November, University of Virginia Library, Special Collections, Twin Oaks collection, box 7, folder 27, p. 2.

Chapter 9

[1] Joe, 'Population Turnover rate', *The Collected Leaves of Twin Oaks*, vol. 2, issues 16–30, Twin Oaks Community, Louisa, Virginia, p. 13.

[2] Cassie (1990) 'Thinking about new members', O&I document, 10 August, University of Virginia Library, Special Collections, Twin Oaks collection, box 7, folder 13.

[3] Taylor's leaving letter (1987) 'Thoughts on leaving', 14 July, University of Virginia Library, Special Collections, Twin Oaks collection, box 7, folder 35.

[4] *The Leaves of Twin Oaks* (2001) 94, Spring.

[5] 'Statistics' (1970) *The Leaves of Twin Oaks*, 12, May. In 1970, members ranged in age from 17 to 39.

[6] My assessment is thus radically different from that of Kuhlmann (2001), who sees an inseparable link between turnover and ongoing failure.

[7] The archives also contain a smaller corpus of 32 'staying letters', which members write on the anniversary of their entry into the community to explain what makes them want to keep living at Twin Oaks.

[8] It is likely that the average length of stay is slightly lower for two main reasons: over the period 1978–1993, a handful of people, most often long-standing members, wrote a leaving letter and then backed out a while later (because they changed their minds, because they did not get the job they had hoped for, etc.); secondly, a reading of the letters suggests that the propensity to mention the time spent at Twin Oaks increases the longer the stay.

[9] Velma's first leaving letter, 20 March 1989, University of Virginia Library, Special Collections, Twin Oaks collection, box 7, folder 37.

10. Rico's leaving letter, 10 April 1986, University of Virginia Library, Special Collections, Twin Oaks collection, box 7, folder 34.
11. Foxfyer's first leaving letter, 1986, University of Virginia Library, Special Collections, Twin Oaks collection, box 7, folder 34.
12. Velma's third leaving letter, 30 December 1989, University of Virginia Library, Special Collections, Twin Oaks collection, box 7, folder 37.
13. Gini's leaving letter, 24 January 1981, University of Virginia Library, Special Collections, Twin Oaks collection, box 7, folder 28.
14. Mimi's leaving letter, 2 November 1992, University of Virginia Library, Special Collections, Twin Oaks collection, box 7, folder 40.
15. Carol's leaving letter, 30 November 1978, University of Virginia Library, Special Collections, Twin Oaks collection, box 7, folder 28.
16. Rain's leaving letter, 26 February 1983, University of Virginia Library, Special Collections, Twin Oaks collection, box 7, folder 31.
17. Seventy per cent of this information comes from Facebook, LinkedIn and personal blogs.
18. These figures concern the number of people for whom it was possible to obtain the information, that is, two thirds of the sample. This rate of non-information is more or less the same for the other selected variables; it is 25 per cent for the specific case of the occupation held after the period spent at Twin Oaks.
19. The majority of ex-Oakers have changed jobs several times in their post-Twin Oaks careers. Most former members have, however, kept to one occupational sector. When this was not the case, I chose to list the type of occupation that they had spent the longest doing during their career.
20. www.ascap.com/eventsawards/awards/foundation/awards/cahn. Accessed 7 December 2016.
21. Cerand (2006) 'The Lux Notus Interview: Devon Sproule', 27 April, www.luxlotus.com/lux_lotus/2006/04/the_lux_lotus_i_1.html. Accessed 7 December 2016.
22. 'Growing the Movement' (2015) *The Leaves of Twin Oaks*, 120, Summer.

Conclusion

1. Reading *Communities* also shows that gender and feminist issues received regular coverage until the early 1990s, when they were gradually marginalised. Coverage of education issues has proved more enduring over time. The theme of ageing, on the other hand, has gained in importance over the years.
2. Fee-paying training courses were developed intensively in the early 2020s, and have had a positive impact on the federation's budget. In 2020, its income was just under $200,000. This rose to over $300,000 the following year. Generating almost $150,000 in revenue, training courses were the main source of income for the Foundation for Intentional Communities in 2021. Source: www.ic.org/2021report/. Accessed 13 October 2022.
3. Sky Blue, 'Movement at a Crossroad – 30th Birthday, Day 1'.
4. Further research is now available which highlights the conditions for the success of this contamination strategy. See, for example, Seyfang and Longhurst (2016).

References

Abensour, M. (2014) *La Communauté politique des 'tous uns'. Désir de liberté, désir d'utopie*, Paris: Les Belles Lettres.
Akerloff, G. (1984) *An Economic Theorist's Book of Tales*, Cambridge: Cambridge University Press.
Altus, D.E. and Morris, E.K. (2009) 'B.F. Skinner's utopian vision: behind and beyond Walden Two', *The Behavior Analyst*, 32(2): 319–335.
Arndt, K.J. (1997) 'George Rapp's harmony society', in D. Pitzer (ed.), *America's Communal Utopias*, Chapel Hill, NC: University of North Carolina Press, pp 57–87.
Baccolini, R. and Tower Sargent, L. (eds) (2021) *Transgressive Utopianism: Essays in Honor of Lucy Sargisson*, Bern: Peter Lang.
Barkun, M. (1984) 'Communal societies as cyclical phenomena', *Communal Societies*, 4: 35–48.
Baudry, S. (2011) 'Les *community gardens* de New York City: de la désobéissance civile au développement durable', *Revue française d'études américaines*, 129: 73–86.
Bellamy, E. (1888) *Looking Backward*, Cleveland, OH: The World Publishing Company, 1946.
Ben-Rafael, E. (2018) 'Kibboutz: les risques de la survie', *Socio*, 10: 139–167.
Berkman, A. (1977) 'Lazy men and dirty work', in G. Woodcock (ed.), *The Anarchist Reader*, Hassocks: Harvester Press, pp 334–338.
Berrebi-Hoffmann, I., Bureau, M.-C. and Lallement, M. (2018) *Makers. Enquête sur les laboratoires du changement social*, Paris: Seuil.
Bestor, A. (1970) *Backwoods Utopias: The Sectarian Origins and the Owenite Phase of Communitarian Socialism in America, 1663–1829*, Philadelphia, PA: University of Pennsylvania Press.
Bloch, E. (1930) *Traces*, translated by A.A. Nasser, Stanford, CA: Stanford University Press, 2006.
Bloch, E. (1954, 1955, 1959) *The Principle of Hope*, translated by N. Plaice, S. Plaice and P. Knight, Cambridge, MA: The MIT Press.
Blue, S. and Morris, B. (2017) 'Tracking the community movement. 70 years of history and the modern FIC', *Communities*, 176: 15–19.

Boltanski, L. and Chiapello, E. (1999) *Le nouvel Esprit du capitalisme*, Paris: Gallimard.

Borsodi, R. (1958) *A Decentralist Manifesto*, Bombay: Libertarian Institute.

Bourdieu, P. (1980) 'L'identité et la représentation. Éléments pour une réflexion critique sur l'idée de région', *Actes de la recherche en sciences sociales*, 35: 63–72.

Bregman, R. (2014) *Utopia for Realists, and How We Can Get There*, London: Bloomsbury Publishing.

Browne, G. (2017) 'Twin Oaks indexing: past and present Twin Oaks members and friends', *The Indexer*, 35(1): 10–18. Available at https://communelifeblog.wordpress.com/2017/03/10/twin-oaks-indexing-collective-past-and-present-twin-oaks-members-and-friends-1/. Accessed 20 August 2018.

Burawoy, M. (1979) *Manufacturing Consent. Changing in the Labor Process under Monopoly Capitalism*, Chicago, IL: Chicago University Press.

Butcher, A. (1987) 'Foundations of egalitarian community', *Communities*, 73: 48–52.

Butcher, A. (2017) 'Fifty years of utopian intentioneering at Twin Oaks Community', *Communities*, 176: 27–30.

Chomsky, N. (1973) *For Reasons of State*, New York, NY: Random House.

Clarence-Smith, S.A. (2023) *Prefiguring Utopia: The Auroville Experiment*, Bristol: Bristol University Press.

Constantine, L.K. and Constantine, J.M. (1973) *Group Marriage: A Study of Contemporary Multilateral Marriage*, London: Macmillan.

Creagh, R. (1983) *Utopies américaines. Expériences libertaires du XIXe siècle à nos jours*, Marseille: Agone.

Cronon, W. (1995) 'The trouble with wilderness; or, getting back to the wrong nature', in W. Cronon (ed.), *Uncommon Ground: Rethinking the Human Place in Nature*, New York, NY: W. W. Norton & Co., pp 69–90.

Dawling, P. (2013) *Sustainable Market Farming: Intensive Vegetable Production on a Few Acres*, Gabriola Island: New Society Publishers.

Dubar, C. (2000) *La crise des identités. L'interprétation d'une mutation*, Paris: PUF.

'Eight Years After' (1975) *Communities*, 16: 23–27.

Fairfield, R. (1972) *Communes USA. A Personal Tour*, Baltimore, MD: Penguin Books Inc.

Farge, A. (2004) 'Écrire l'histoire', *Hypothèses*, 4(7): 317–320.

Fellowship of Intentional Communities (1959) *The 1959 Yearbook of the Fellowship of Intentional Communities*, Yellow Springs, OH: Fellowship of Intentional Communities.

Fike, R. (ed.) (1998) *Voices from the Farm. Adventures in Community Living*, Summertown, TN: Book Publishing Company.

Firth, R. (2012) *Utopian Politics. Citizenships and Practice*, London: Routledge.

Fisher, M. (2021) *Postcapitalist Desire: The Final Lectures*, London: Repeater.

Fourier, C. (1829) *Le nouveau Monde industriel et sociétaire*, Paris: Flammarion, 1973.
Fourier, C. (1967) *Œuvres complètes 11. Manuscrits publiés par la Phalange, revue de la Science sociale, 1853–1856*, vol. III–IV, Paris: Anthropos.
Frase, P. (2016) *Four Futures: Life after Capitalism*, London and New York, NY: Verso.
Gardner, H. (1978) *The Children of Prosperity. Thirteen Modern American Communes*, New York, NY: St Martin Press.
Gaskin, S. (1972) *The Caravan* (2nd edn), Summertown, TN: Book Publishing Company, 2007.
Gaskin, S. (1974) 'Farm history', in *Hey Beatnik! This is the Farm Book*, Summertown, TN: Book Publishing Company.
Gaskin, S. (2005) *Monday Night Class. Revised and Annotated Edition*, Summertown, TN: Book Publishing Company.
Gibran, K. (1923) *The Prophet*, New York, NY: Alfred A. Knopf.
Gibson, T. and Sillander K. (eds) (2011) *Anarchic Solidarity. Autonomy, equality and fellowship in Southeast Asia*, New Haven: Yale University Southeast Asia Studies.
Gibson-Graham, J.K. (2006) *A Post-Capitalist Politics*, Minneapolis, MN and London: University of Minnesota Press.
Goffman, E. (1959) *The Presentation of Self in Everyday Life*, New York, NY: Anchor Books.
Goffman, E. (1963) *Stigma*, New York, NY: Simon & Schuster.
Goffman, E. (1967) *Interaction Ritual*, Chicago, IL: Aldine Publishing Co.
Goldenberg, Z. (1993) 'The power of feminism at Twin Oaks Community', in W. Chmielewski, L.J. Kern and M. Klee-Hartzell (eds) *Women in Spiritual and Communitarian Societies in the United States*, New York, NY: Syracuse University Press, pp 256–265.
Granger, M. (1994) *Henry David Thoreau: paradoxes d'excentrique*, Paris: Belin.
Grant, H.R. (1981) 'Utopia without colony: the labor exchange movement', *Communal Societies*, 1: 43–54.
Griffin, J. (2017) *Unpacking Cultural Baggage: Gender and Work in an Income-Sharing Commune*, Warren Wilson College, Department of Sociology and Anthropology.
Griffin, M.J. and Moylan T. (eds) (2007) *Exploring the Utopian Impulse. Essays on Utopian Thought and Practice*, Bern: Peter Lang.
Grundstein, M. (2015) *Naked in the Woods. My Unexpected Years in a Hippie Commune*, Corvallis, OR: Oregon State University Press.
Hancock, A. (1998) 'Social class & money in community', *Communities*, 98: 30–32.
Higgins, L.W. (1979) *Not Yet Utopia: A Study of Twin Oaks Community, 1967–1976*, PhD dissertation, University of Virginia.

Hoggart, R. (1958) *The Uses of Literacy. Aspects of Working-Class Life*, London: Penguin, 1957.

Houriet, R. (1973) *Getting Back Together*, London: Abacus.

Hughes, E. (1958) *Men and Their Work*, Glencoe, IL: The Free Press.

Jenkins, P. (1979) *A Walk Across America*, New York, NY: Harper.

Jerome, J. (1974) *Families of Eden. Communes and the New Anarchism*, New York, NY: The Seabury Press.

Joseph, L. and Bates, J. (2003) 'What is an ecovillage?', *Community*, 117: 22–24.

Kanter, R.M. (1972) *Commitment and Community*. Communes and Utopias in Sociological Perspective, Cambridge, MA: Harvard University Press.

Kinkade, K. (1973) *A Walden Two Experiment. The First Five Years of Twin Oaks Community*, New York, NY: Quill.

Kinkade, K. (1994) *Is It Utopia Yet? An Insider View of Twin Oaks Community in its 26th Year* (3rd edn/2nd reprint), Louisa, VA: Twin Oaks Publishing, 2004.

Kinkade, K (1999) 'But can he design community?', *Communities*, 103: 49–52.

Klaw, S. (1993) *Without Sin. The Life and the Death of the Oneida Community*, New York, NY: Penguin Books.

Komar, I. (1983) *Living the Dream. A Documentary Study of Twin Oaks* (2nd edn), Louisa, VA: Twin Oaks Publishing, 1989.

Kremser, C. (2020) *Ein Ende der ökonomischen Geschichte. Utopische Visionen in der Geschichte des ökonomischen Denkens*, Marburg: Metropolis.

Kuhlmann, H. (2001) 'The illusion of permanence: work motivation and membership turnover at Twin Oaks Community', in B. Goodwin (ed.), *The Philosophy of Utopia*, London and New York: Routledge, pp 157–171.

Kuhlmann, H. (2005) *Living Walden Two. B.F. Skinner's Behaviorist Utopia and Experimental Communities*, Urbana and Chicago, IL: University of Illinois Press.

Lallement, M. (2009) *Le Travail de l'utopie. J.-B.A. Godin et le Familistère de Guise*, Paris: Les Belles Lettres.

Lallement, M. (2015) *L'Âge du Faire. Hacking, travail, anarchie*, Paris: Seuil.

Lallement, M. (2019) 'Vivre dans ce monde, non de ce monde? L'expérience communautaire de The Farm', *Nouvelle revue de psychosociologie*, Special issue, 'Faire société autrement?', 28: 15–27.

Lallement, M. (2021) 'Living in utopia in the 19th century. A comparison of France and the United States', *Comparative Sociology*, 20(1): 45–69.

Laurin-Lamothe A., Legault F. and Tremblay-Pepin S. (2023) *Construire l'économie postcapitaliste*, Montréal: Lux.

'Leaving Twin Oaks. A Conversation with Former Members' (1977) *Communities*, 28: 20–28.

Looijesteijn, H. (2011) 'Between sin and salvation: the seventeenth-century Dutch artisan Pieter Plockhoy and his ethics of work', *International Review of Social History*, 56: 69–88.

MacLeod, D. and Bedard, R. (1975) 'Women in community. Come unity', *Communities*, 25: 8–15.

Marx, K. (1932) 'Economic and philosophic manuscripts of 1844', in K. Marx, *Early Writings*, translated by G. Benton, London: Penguin Classics, 1992.

Mason, P. (2016) *Postcapitalism: A Guide to our Future*, London: Penguin Books.

Mauss, M. (1925) 'Essay on the Gift. The form and sense of exchange in archaic societies', in M. Mauss, *The Gift, Expanded Edition*, translated by J.I. Guyer, Chicago, IL: Hau Books, 2016, pp 53–198.

Melville, K. (1972) *Communes in the Counter Culture*, New York, NY: William Morrow.

Mercklé, P. (2004) 'Utopie ou "science sociale"? Réceptions de l'œuvre de Charles Fourier au XIXe siècle', *Archives européennes de sociologie*, 45(1): 45–80.

Mies, M. and Shiva, V. (1998) *Écoféminisme*, Paris: L'Harmattan.

Miller, T. (1990) *American Communes 1860–1960. A Bibliography*, New York, NY & London: Garland Publishing, Inc.

Miller, T. (1999) *The 60s Communes. Hippies and Beyond*, New York, NY: Syracuse University Press.

Monticelli, L. (2021) 'On the necessity of prefigurative politics', *Thesis Eleven*, 167(1): 99–118.

Morris, W. (1890) *News From Nowhere*, London: Routledge & Kegan Paul.

Oaks, M. (1980) 'Community living. One woman's choice', *Communities*, 45: 44–47.

Olson, M. (1965) *The Logic of Collective Action*, Cambridge, MA and London: Harvard University Press.

Otto, H. (2010) 'The communal alternative', in R. Fairfield, *The Modern Utopian. Alternative Communities of the '60s and '70s*, Port Townsend, WA: Process Media, pp 19–25.

Oved, Y. (2013) *Globalization of Communes. 1950–2010*, London and New York, NY, Routledge.

Passehl, E. (2004) 'Twin Oaks Community: women's liberation, generational divide, and the evolution of women's culture', *Archive*, 7: 37–47.

Pfaffenberger, B. (1982) 'A World of Husbands and Mothers: Sex Roles and Their Ideological Context in the Formation of the Farm', in J. Wagner (ed.) *Sex Roles in Contemporary American Communes*, Bloomington, IN: Indiana University Press, pp 172–210.

Plockhoy, P.C. (1662) *Brief and Concise Plan Intended to be a Mutual Agreement for Some Colonists Willing to go to the South River in New Netherland*, Otto Barentus: Smient.

Rancière, J. (2017) *En quel temps vivons-nous? Conversation avec Eric Hazan*, Paris: La Fabrique éditions.

Reece, E. (2016) *Utopia Drive. A Road Trip Through America's Most Radical Idea*, New York, NY: Farrar, Straus and Giroux.

Renwick-Porter, V. (2000), 'Celebration & ceremony at Twin Oaks', *Communities*, 107: 38–39.

Renwick, V. (2014) 'Gender-bending on the commune', *Communities*, 162: 24–25.

Reynaud, J.-D. (1989) *Les règles du jeu. L'action collective et la régulation sociale*, Paris: Colin.

Rimmer, R. (1968) *Proposition 31*, New York, NY: New American Library.

Sargisson, L. (2017) *Utopian Bodies and the Politics of Transgression*, London: Routledge.

Sargisson, L. and Tower Sargent L. (2004), *Living in Utopia. New Zealand's Intentional Communities*, Burlington: Ashgate.

Seyfang G. and Longhurst, N. (2016) 'What influences the diffusion of grassroots innovations for sustainability? Investigating community currency niches', *Technology Analysis & Strategic Management*, 28(1): 1–23. http://dx.doi.org/10.1080/09537325.2015.1063603

Skinner, B. (1938) *The Behavior of Organisms*, New York, NY: Appleton-Century.

Skinner, B. (1948) *Walden Two*, Indianapolis, IN: Hackett, 2005.

Skinner, B. (1957) *Verbal Behaviour*, New York, NY: Appleton-Century.

Skinner, B. (1974) *About Behaviourism*, New York, NY: Knopf.

Skinner, B. (1987) 'News from Nowhere, 1984', in *Upon Further Reflection*, Englewoods Cliffs, NJ: Prentice-Hall, pp 33–50.

Spiro, M. (1956) *Kibbutz. Venture in Utopia*, New York, NY: Schocken Books, 1971.

Srnicek N. and Williams A. (2015) *Inventing the Future: Postcapitalism and a World without Work*, London and New York, NY: Verso.

Stevens, J. (1987) *Storming Heaven: LSD and the American Dream*, New York, NY: Grove Press.

Stevenson, D. (2014a) *The Evolution of The Farm Community*, Summertown, TN: Book Publishing Company.

Stevenson, D. (2014b) *The Farm Then and Now: A Model for Sustainable Living*, Gabriola Island: New Society Publishers.

Streeck, W. (2016) *How will Capitalism End?: Essays on Failing System*, London and New York, NY: Verso.

'Technology: Friend or Foe?' (2014) *Communities*, Special Issue, 165.

Thoreau, H. (1854) *Walden; or, Life in the Woods*, Princeton, NJ: Princeton University Press.

Tocqueville de, A. (1840) *Democracy in America*, vol. 3, London: Saunders and Otley.

Traugot, M. (1994) *A Short History of the Farm*, Summertown, TN: The Farm, self-published.

Troeltsch, E. (1912) *Die Soziallehren der christlichen Kirchen und Gruppen*, Tübingen: J.C.B. Mohr (Paul Siebeck).
'Twin Oaks & Little Folks' (1974), *Communities*, 9: 10–12.
Wagner, J. (1982) 'Sex roles in American utopias: an overview', in J. Wagner (ed.) *Sex Roles in Contemporary American Communes*, Bloomington, IN: Indiana University Press.
Weber, M. (1905) *The Protestant Ethic and the Spirit of Capitalism*, translated by T. Parsons, London and New York: Routledge.
Weber, M. (1949) *On the Methodology of the Social Sciences,* Glencoe, IL: Free Press.
Weber, M. (1978) *Economy and Society*, Berkeley, LA and London: University of California Press.
Whitney Sanford, A. (2017) *Living Sustainably: What Intentional Communities Can Teach Us about Democracy, Simplicity, and Nonviolence*, Lexington: University Press of Kentucky.
Wittgenstein, L. (1921) *Philosophical Investigations* (4th edn), Hoboken, NJ: Wiley-Blackwell.
'Women in Community' (1974) *Communities*, 8: 2–6.
Wright, E.O. (2010) *Envisioning Real Utopias*, London and New York, NY: Verso.
Zablocki, B. (1980) *Alienation and Charisma, A Study of Contemporary American Communes*, London: The Free Press.

Index

References to figures appear in *italic* type; those in **bold** type refer to tables.
References to endnotes show both the page number and the note number (175n7).

A

Abensour, Miguel 7
Acorn community
  agricultural work at 127, 128
  cases of deviance at 92
  commercial work at 109–110
  labour sheets 131
  occupations members had before moving to 42
  organization of work at 123, 130
  procedure for becoming a member 51
  seed business 97
  Seeds Office 110
  visit to 48–51
  working hours at 128–129
active composition 59
  and community opposition **59**, 61
  and societal domination **59**, 60
affection, public displays of 76
agricultural work 127, 128, 131
agricultural workers 97
agriculture, commercial 103
Agriculture Council, Twin Oaks 89–90
alliances 172
Aloe community 163
alternative spaces, accumulation of 172
anarchist communities 10, 20, 130
  procedures and rules 79
  see also Acorn community
anti-gossip rule 86
appeal procedure 87–88
appearance, choice of 66–67
application letters
  for membership at Twin Oaks 51–52
  motivations for joining 53
apprenticeship rule 122
'ask to ask' principle 68–69
attaching, group members to create a community 56–58
Auroville, India 6

B

behavioural code 86
Belize (group) 93
Bellamy, Edward 2, 28, 37, 132
  freedom to manage one's own time inspired by 122
  work arrangements developed by 114–116, 118
Bentov, M. 38
Berrebi-Hoffmann, Isabelle 172
bill paying 148
Bitch Box 86
black people, at Twin Oaks and Acorn 43
Bloch, Ernst 1, 8, 9
Boltanski, Luc 172
Borsodi, Ralph 13
Breiling, Jim 175n2
bubble communities, links with the outside world 171
budgets, for labour credits 84
Bureau, Marie-Christine 172
burnout 136
Butcher, Allen 39

C

Cabet, Étienne 2
capitalism
  urban 55
  Western 172
cars
  maintenance and repair of 140
  use of 185n21
charisma, routinization of 23
charismatic domination, communities under 20–22
Chiapello, Ève 172
childcare 73, 183n13
children
  in Twin Oaks 71
  weekly labour quota 124

INDEX

Chomsky, Noam 40
Christianity, communism of early 14
Church, the, definition of 58
class struggle 15
clothing, for communards 56, 146
cohousing 3
collective action 133
collective experiments 8
collective gardening, in urban areas 171
collectives 2
Commie Clothes 146
'commons' 5, 113
communal living 2
communard collectives, heterogeneity of 71
communards, who chose to return to the outside world 11, 162–166
Communes in the Counter Culture (Melville) 15
communities
  under charismatic domination 20–22
  within the community 70–72
  daily life in 62
  founding year of 169
  identity-based 20
  intent on going back to nature 20
  listed by the Fellowship for Intentional Community 168
  three basic forms of 19–20
  three ideal types of 14
Communities (magazine) 9, 17–18, 167, 168, 170
  issue dedicated to communication technologies 55
  issues covered by 186n1
  on Walden Two communities 40
Communities Directory 3, 17, 56–57, 169, 175n7
community destinies 154–166
community front
  building of 62–64
  dress and physical appearance 66
  first names as resource for building 65
  unique first names for community members 66
community gardens, in New York City, in the 1970s 171
community involvement 41–61
  attaching members of the group and sharing resources 56–58
  attraction and selection of new members 43–45
  candidates for community withdrawal 51–52
  compromise between communities and the outside world 58–60
  detachment from the wider world 54–56
  motivations for 53–54
  profiles of candidates for community membership 42–43
  visit to Twin Oaks 45–48

community life
  survey of members who chose 42–43
  weariness of 160
Community Member Team (CMT) 48
community opposition 59, 60, 61
community revival, of the 1960s and 1970s 16–18
community space, expansion and evolution of 168–170
Community Visitor Program (CVP) 44
  training hours 125
community withdrawal, candidates for 51–52
community work 133–153
  differences between work in the wider world and 152–153
  and gender inequality 139–142
  see also work
composition 58–61
compromise, between communities and the outside world 58–61
concrete utopias
  principles of 121
  sociology of 6–9
confession
  commitment through 92–95
  policy of 145
conflicts, prevention of 85–88
constraint **59**, 60
contamination, transformation through 171–172
contracts
  on joining the community 146
  to sort out tricky situations 87
cotton 105
counter-gifts
  'Basic Scheme' 146
  in the community system of gift-exchange 145–148
COVID-19 crisis 159
craft fairs 103, 151
Creagh, Ronald 13, 85–86
criticism, before a committee of six to 12 judges 92–93
Cronon, William 25
culture, among the working classes 54

D

Dandelion community, Ontario, Canada 30, 165
A Decentralist Manifesto (Borsodi) 13
democracy 29
detachment, from the wider world 54–56
dishwashing 119–120, 139
  at Acorn 130
  in Twin Oaks 130
dispute management 85–88
disputes, romantic 86
diversification, at Twin Oaks 103
domestic chores, distribution of 139
Domestic Councils 179n7

domestic work 117, 131
  division of 140
  in Twin Oaks 130
dress codes 67
Dubar, Claude 62
Dutch Mennonites 2

E

early marriage 76
East Wind community 54, 102, 123
ecofeminism 76
economic democracy 83–85
economic necessity, and ecological virtue 103–106
economic security 54
ecovillages 3, 170, 174n2
  feminist 75
egalitarian communities 7
Emerson, Ralph Waldo 26
environment, communion with 57
Envisioning Real Utopias (Olin Wright) 6, 170
epigones 7
equality of work 123
ethnic origins, of members of Twin Oaks and Acorn 43
expulsion
  for communards who fail to meet labour quotas 134
  for engaging in sexual activity with under 15 years old 91
  for stealing money 92
eye contact 68

F

Fairfield, Richard 31
Familistère community, Guise (France) 171
Farge, Arlette 8
The Farm, Tennessee 10, 20–24
Federation of Egalitarian Communities (FEC) 39, 147, 167, 170
Federation of Israeli Kibbutzim 39
feedback
  direct 86
  learning model 93
Fellowship for Intentional Community 9, 16, 17, 79, 168, 170
Fellowship of Intentional Communities 3, 167
feminism, and women-only groups 72–74
feminist culture 75
feminist ecovillage 75
Feminist Think Tank (FTT) 75
financial security 54
firearms, ban of, at Twin Oaks 82
first names 64–66
Fisher, Mark 4
Food not Bombs 61
forced labour 113
former members, destiny of 11, 162–166

Foucault, Michel 172
Foundation for Intentional Community 3, 170
Fourier, Charles 6, 119, 171, 172, 173
Frase, Peter 4
free suffrage 29
freedom
  to manage one's own time 122
  tension between equality and 129–132
Freeland, Maryland 13
freeriding, reducing the risk of 133
fruit and vegetable growing 127

G

gardens 25, 127
  Acorn community 128–129
  Twin Oaks 127–128
Gardner, Hugh 17
Gaskin, Stephen 20–22, 23
gender 72
gender boundaries 66–67
gender distribution, of departing members 159
gender equality 73
gender identities 64–65
gender relations 18–19, 72
Generalized Bastard 86
Gibran, Kahlil 96–97, 181n1
Gibson-Graham, J.K. 4
gifts, from relatives and friends 150
Godin, Jean-Baptiste André 171
Goffman, Erving 62–63, 66, 68
Griffin, Julia 140
Grundstein, Margaret 148

H

Halloween 70
hammock production 98–102, 105
hanging chairs 103
Harrison, Jim 27
healthcare 60
healthcare facilities 147
healthcare scheme 147
High Top Commune 96
higher education, completed by Twin Oak members 164
hippie movement 16, 167
Hoffman, Abbie 148
Hoggart, Richard 54
holidays 126, 152
Houriet, Robert 135, 140
Hughes, Everett C. 183n8
human labour
  possible effects of automation on 4
  products of 113
hybrid spaces 172

I

income, per person 185n23
Income Councils 179n7

INDEX

income sharing 57
indexing work 111–112
industrialization 14
information and orientation meetings 44
infringements, and offences 91–92
intentional communities
  in the 1960s and 1970s 18–19
  analysis of 3–4
  coining of the term 16
  organizational structure of 80
  presentation of self and everyday interactions 63
  publications on 9
  social science research into 4–6
  social space of 167
  strategies used to retain members 11
intentional community models 170
interactions, and rules of conduct 67–69
Internal Revenue Code 149
Internal Revenue Service 24
International Communes Desk 38, 167
internet, and how intentional communities relate to the media universe 55
interpersonal relations 53
interstitial transformation 170, 172
involvement, form of composition 60
Is It Utopia Yet? (Kinkade) 43
Israel, link between US and 38
Israeli kibbutzim 38–39, 155, 167
  Federation of 39

J

Jeanne Magazine 77
Jerome, Judson 17

K

Kanter, Rosabeth Moss 14, 15, 55, 58, 92
Kawea SLG 71
Kerista community (San Francisco) 19
Kerouac, Jack 27
Ketura Kibbutz 39
kibbutz 38–39, 155, 167
Kinkade, Kat 43, 74, 76–77, 92, 138
  article in *Communities* 40
  on debt Twin Oaks owed to *Walden Two* 37
  definition of managers 82–83
  grave of 162
  on hammock production 134
  on members having the means to work during their holidays 149
  on money 148
  observations on kibbutz 38–39
  and problem of over-representation of white people 43
  recount of missing food at Twin Oaks 91
  report on distribution of domestic chores 139
  on submission to criticism judges 93
  A Walden Two Experiment 35, 42
  on work organization 120

kitchen work 135
Koinonia (community) 167
Komar, Ingrid 42, 55, 81–82, 120, 127, 136
  estimation of number of members of Twin Oaks 156
  on tendency for men to take on traditional male roles 140

L

labour credits 28, 117, 120, 150, 183n21
  allocation of, by gender 140–141
  negotiation of 126
labour hole 94, 134, 142–145
labour problem 96
labour quota 123, 124
labour sheets 121, 124–125, 130
The Leaves of Twin Oaks (newsletter) 36
Lee, Robert E., removal of statue of 61
leisure activities 151
lesbian communities 19
lesbians 77
Looking Backward (Bellamy) 114–115
Los Horcones community, Mexico 30–31

M

Macedonia (community) 167
Maclure, William 25
maintenance and repair, of the community's cars 140
male sexual aggressiveness 74
managers 82–83
  gender and 142
  Walden Two 29
market competition 60
marriage 76
Marx, Karl 113
Mauss, Marcel 146
meal preparation, at Acorn 130
mealtimes 69
Melville, Keith 15
men, self-presentation of 67
Mennonite families 18
Miller, Timothy 16, 19
The Modern Utopian (magazine) 9
money
  appropriation or theft of 92
  living without 148–151
  from relatives and friends 150
money hole 94
monogamy 76
Monsanto, contamination of farms by products from 106
monthly allowances 149
moral experiments 8
More, Thomas 2, 54
Morgan, Arthur 16
Morris, Betsy 3
Morris, William 54, 115–116
Movement for a New Society (Philadelphia) 18

multiplying mechanism 172
music playing 151
mysticism 38, 178n30

N

names, practice of changing one's name 65–66, 178n8
National Institute of Health 17
'natural' practices, return to 18
'negative idealization' 66
New Harmony 25
'new social movements' 15
New York Anarchist Federation 13
New York Times 17
News from Nowhere (Morris) 115–116
Newsweek 17
Not on Our Fault Line group 61
Noyes, John Humphrey 92
nudism 18

O

obligation, to ensure work is carried out 121
occupations
  of applicants to Twin Oaks 52
  of former Twin Oak members 164
'Occupy' movement 61
older members 71, 123–124
Olson, Mancur 133
Oneida project 46, 71, 74, 92, 140
Opinions & Ideas (O&I) Board 82, 87, 145
Organic Seed Growers and Trade Association (OSGATA) 106
OTRAs (One Time Resource Allocation) 84–85
Otto, Herbert 19
outside workers 35, 98
outside world
  compromise between communities and the 58
  links with 171
  return to the 157, 159–162
Oved, Yaacov 6, 168
Overquota Projects Program (OPP) 126, 183n22
Owen, Robert 25

P

passive composition 59, 60
peer groups 71
permaculture 127
personal bank accounts 148
Personal Codas 150
Personal Service Credits 150
Phalanstères 6, 172
physical violence 56
Pier One 98–99, 103
planners, at Twin Oaks 80–82
planning council 80
plenary sessions 82
Plockhoy, Pieter Corneliszoon 2–3
politico-economic communities 14

polyamory 78
'polyfidelity' model 19
post-capitalist desire 4
poverty
  living in 22, 160
  vow of 24, 175n19
pragmatism 167
The Presentation of Self in Everyday Life (Goffman) 63
Principle of Hope (Bloch) 9
Production For Friends (PFF) 100, 181n6
profit-making 97
promiscuity 92
proofreading 112
prosopographical survey 163
Protestant sects 14
protests 61
Proudhon, Pierre-Joseph 173
'psychosocial' communities 15
public holidays 126

Q

queer people 77–78

R

Rancière, Jacques 5
Rapp, George 25
real experiments 8
recreational practices 151
Redbud Creek Tofu Co 104
Reece, Eric 113, 136, 183n14
Reformation 14
relationships
  romantic 19–20, 76, 77, 78
  sexual 19–20
religious communities 3
religious groups 14
religious institutions 59
resources
  allocation of 83–85
  socialization of 57
'reverse idealization' 66
rituals 68, 69–70
romantic disputes 86
rope-making 100, 103
rules 11, 79–95
  anti-gossip rule 86
  bending the 91
  lack of respect for 91
  of self-presentation 64
  of small living groups 71
  for visitors who want to become Oakers 48
rules of conduct 67–69, 92
rural environment 53
rural farms 172

S

San Francisco Chronicle 17
Sand Hill community 54

INDEX

Sargisson, Lucy 5, 6
School of Living 13
sects 58, 59, 60, 61
self-presentation 63, 64–66
senior citizens
see older members
sexism 72, 75
sexual activity, with under 15 year olds 91–92
sexual freedom 76, 77
shared housing 3
sharing, of goods and resources 56–58
'sheltered workshop' 102
sick leave 147
single-gender groups 73
situated experiments 8
skills, discovering and cultivating new 166
Skinner, Burrhus Frederic 11, 29, 31, 80, 116, 155
  ambition for *Walden Two* 27–28
  contact with Twin Oaks 35–38, 114
  early marriage recommendation 76
Sky Blue 3, 165
small living groups (SLGs) 47, 71, 140
social change, interstitial transformation and 170–173
social front 62
social regulation 80, 179n7
social transformation 6
social welfare 18
societal communities 20, 129
societal domination 59, 60
Southern Exposure Seed Exchange 104, 105–106
spiritual communities 3
Sproule, Devon 165
student co-ops 3
students, growth in population of 15
support and activity groups 73
Swanendael community 3

T

taxes 60, 149
teachers 165
tempeh 104, 107
Thoreau, Henry David 11, 25–26, 40
  ecocentrism 26–27
tobacco growing 97–98, 105
Tocqueville, Alexis de 131–132
tofu
  production of 104–109
  working conditions 137
Tofu Hut 104, 106–107, 108, 109, 121, 182n22
Tower Sargent, Lyman 6
traces, historical analysis of 8
Trade-Off Game 84–85
training courses, fee-paying 186n2
'transgressive utopianism' 5
transition towns 3
Transparency Tools group 93–94

transport, use of means of 146–147
travel, cost of 147
Troeltsch, Ernst 58–61
Tupelo SLG 71
Twin Oaks
  50th anniversary of 10, 154, 164
  age of members 42
  agricultural work at 127
  as an American kibbutz 38–39
  'anti-structure hippy approach' 116–117
  attempt to apply blueprint devised by Skinner 26
  attraction and selection of new members 43–45
  average age of members 157
  average length of stay at 157, 185n8
  book indexing at 111–112
  buildings 46
  catastrophic health insurance plan 147
  connection with Skinner 114
  deaths of members at 162–163
  dedication of each month to a value 58
  description of 1–2
  distribution of managerial responsibilities by gender 143
  division of labour credits by gender and activity at 141
  economic activities 97
  family-related reasons to leave 160–161
  farming experiments 98
  foundation and early achievements 32–34
  history of 31
  internally managed financial accounts 94
  job description for the receptionist at 182n24
  letters of application to 51–52
  loss of most active members 155–156
  middle class domination of 52
  number of members at 155, 156, 158
  occupations members had before moving to 42
  planners 34
  positive points of community lifestyle 162
  principles of freedom and equality 130
  production of seeds and seedlings at 110
  profiles of members of 42
  raising chickens at 88–91
  relationship between Skinner and 35–38
  small living groups (SLGs) 47, 71, 140
  social regulation applied at 80
  specific vocabulary and way of speaking 63–64
  striving for Utopia at 7
  struggle for economic independence 34–35
  transformations since 2017 159
  turnover rates of members 155, 156–157
  visit to 10
  visitors at 45–48
  work incentive strategies 134–135
  work trial and error experimentation 116
  writing an O&I to give notice of one's departure 159–160

199

Twin Oaks Community Foods 104
Twin Oaks Industries 97

U

unemployment 60
United States (US)
  in 1966 13
  founding year of communities in 169
  link between Israel and 38
  number of intentional communities in 17–18, 168
  poverty threshold 148
  publications on intentional communities in 9
  wilderness in 26
urban capitalism 55
urban life, critique of 53
urbanization 14
utopia
  and action 6
  part played in work within community 114
  see also concrete utopias
Utopia (More) 2

V

Vacation Earnings 149
vacation entitlements 183n20
Validation Day 70
values
  engagement through 57–58
  fundamental 53
vegan food, production of 104, 106–110
verbal abuse 91
vertical integration, economic strategy 102
Virginia Soywork (company) 104
visitors
  application to communities 44–45
  at Twin Oaks 45–48, 135–136

W

Walden, or Life in the Woods (Thoreau) 11, 25, 27, 40
Walden House experiment 31–32
Walden House (newsletter) 175n3
Walden Pool (newsletter) 32, 175n3
Walden Three (collective) 30
Walden tradition, current 39–40

A Walden Two Experiment (Kinkade) 26, 35, 42
Walden Two (Skinner) 11, 26, 27–28, 40, 76, 80
  bringing to life of 29–31
  debt Twin Oaks owed to 37
  labour credits in 118
  letter from a reader to Skinner 41
  managers in 82
  social organization in 28–29
  target for number of members of 155, 159
  work organization in 28–29, 34, 116, 117
  working hours required in 123
Waldenwoods Conference 32
Weber, Max 23, 171, 172
'Weeds and Knots' committee 147
white people, at Twin Oaks and Acorn 43
Wittgenstein, Ludwig 19
'wolfing' 74
WomanShare (lesbian community) 19
women, self-presentation of 67
Women's Gathering 67, 74
women's rights 73
woodworking shop 100–101
work 11, 114–116
  in the fields and gardens 127–129
  importance in the analysis of concrete utopias 8–9
  importance to Twin Oaks applicants 53
  link between effort and reward 137–138
  organization of 60, 96–112, 117–118
  risks of overcommitment to 136–139
  value assigned to different kinds of 28
  see also community work
work tasks, continuity of 118
working classes 15
  culture among the 54–55
working week 123, 124
Wright, Erik Olin 6, 170, 171, 172

Y

Young Zionist Movement 39

Z

Zablocki, Benjamin 17, 139, 159
Zager, Vince 38
Zhankoye 177n6

www.ingramcontent.com/pod-product-compliance
Lightning Source LLC
Chambersburg PA
CBHW051544020426
42333CB00016B/2094